LOVE

ILLINOIS

Your Family Travel Guide to Exploring "Kid-Friendly" Illinois

500 Fun Stops & Unique Spots

Michele Darrall Zavatsky

Dedicated to the Families of Illinois

In a Hundred Years...It will not matter, The size of my bank account...The kind of house that I lived in, the kind of car that I drove...But what will matter is...That the world may be different Because I was important in the life of a child.

- author unknown

For the latest major updates corresponding to the pages in this book visit our website:

www.KidsLoveTravel.com

- **REMEMBER:** *Museum exhibits change frequently. Check the site's website before you visit to note any changes. Also, HOURS and ADMISSIONS are subject to change at the owner's discretion. Note: FAMILY ADMISSION RATES generally have restrictions. If you are tight on time or money, check the attraction's website or call before you visit.*

- **INTERNET PRECAUTION:** *All websites mentioned in KIDS LOVE ILLINOIS have been checked for appropriate content. However, due to the fast-changing nature of the Internet, we strongly urge parents to preview any recommended sites and to always supervise their children when on-line.*

- **EDUCATORS:** *There are suggestions for finding FREE lessons plans embedded in many listings as helpful notes for educators.*

ISBN-13: 978-0-6923545-7-5

KIDS ♥ ILLINOIS ™   Kids Love Publications, LLC

TABLE OF CONTENTS

★ **State Capitals**
◦ County Seat
● **Cities 500,000+**
● **Cities 100,000-499,999**
• Cities 50,000-99,999
• Cities 10,000-49,999
· Cities 0-9,999

---- State Boundaries
---- County Boundaries
—— Toll Roads and Bridges
—— Interstate Highways
—— U.S. Highways
—— State Roads

—— Major Rivers
—— Intermediate Rivers
◦ Lakes

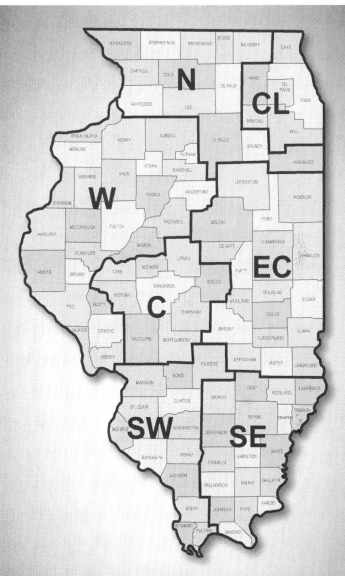

Chapter Area Map

(Chapters arranged alphabetically by chapter name)

HOW TO USE THIS BOOK

(a few hints to make your adventures run smoothly:)

BEFORE YOU LEAVE:

- ☐ Each chapter represents a two hour radius area of the state or a Day Trip. The listings are by City and then alphabetical by name, numeric by zip code. Each listing has tons of important details (pricing, hours, website, etc.) and a review noting the most engaging aspects of the place. Our popular Activity Index in back is helpful if you want to focus on a particular type of attraction (i.e. History, Tours, Outdoor Exploring, Animals & Farms, etc.).

- ☐ Begin by assigning each family member a different colored highlighter (for example: Daniel gets blue, Jenny gets pink, Mommy gets yellow and Daddy gets green). At your leisure, begin to read each review and put a highlighter "check" mark next to the sites that most interest each family member or highlight the features you most want to see. Now, when you go to plan a quick trip - or a long van ride - you can easily choose different stops in one day to please everyone.

- ☐ Know directions and parking. Use a GPS system or print off directions from websites.

- ☐ Most attractions are closed major holidays unless noted.

- ☐ When children are in tow, it is better to make your lodging reservations ahead of time. Every time we've tried to "wing it", we've always ended up at a place that was overpriced, in a unsafe area, or not super clean. We've never been satisfied when we didn't make a reservation ahead of time.

- ☐ If you have a large family, or are traveling with extended family or friends, most places offer group discounts. Check out the company's website for details.

- ☐ For the latest critical updates corresponding to the pages in this book, visit our website: www.kidslovetravel.com. Click on *Updates*.

ON THE ROAD:

- ☐ Consider the child's age before you stop at an exit. Some attractions and restaurants, even hotels, are too formal for young ones or not enough adventure for teens.

- ☐ Estimate the duration of the trip and how many stops you can afford to make. From our experience, it is best to stop every two hours to stretch your legs or eat/snack or maybe visit an inexpensive attraction.

- ☐ Bring along travel books and games for "quiet time" in the van. (see tested travel products on www.kidslovetravel.com) As an added bonus, these "enriching" games also stimulate conversation - you may get to know your family better and create memorable life lessons.

ON THE ROAD: (cont.)

■ In between meals, we offer the family snacks like: pretzels, whole grain chips, nuts, water bottles, bite-size (dark) chocolates, grapes and apples. None of these are messy and all are healthy.

■ Plan picnics along the way. Many Historical sites and State Parks are scattered along the highway. Allow time for a rest stop or a scenic byway to take advantage of these free picnic facilities.

WHEN YOU GET HOME:

■ Make a family "treasure chest". Decorate a big box or use an old popcorn tin. Store memorabilia from a fun outing, journals, pictures, brochures and souvenirs. Once a year, look through the "treasure chest" and reminisce. "Kids Love Travel Memories!" is an excellent travel journal and scrapbook template that your family can create (available on www.kidslovetravel.com).

WAYS TO SAVE MONEY:

■ Memberships - many children's museums, science centers, zoos and aquariums are members of associations that provide FREE or Discounted reciprocity to other such museums across the country. AAA Auto Club cards offer discounts to many of the activities and hotels in this book. If grandparents are along for the ride, they can use their AARP card and get discounts. Be sure to carry your member cards with you as proof to receive the discounts.

■ Supermarket Customer Cards - national and local supermarkets often offer good discounted tickets to major attractions in the area.

■ Internet Hotel Reservations - if you're traveling with kids, don't take the risk of being spontaneous with lodging. Make reservations ahead of time. We don't use non-refundable, deep discount hotel "scouting" websites (ex. Hotwire) unless we're traveling on business - just adults. You can't cancel your reservation, or change them, and you can't be guaranteed the type of room you want (ex. non-smoking, two beds). Instead, stick with a national hotel chain you trust and join their rewards program (ex. Choice Privileges) to accumulate points towards FREE night stays.

■ State Travel Centers - as you enter a new state, their welcome centers offer many current promotions.

■ Hotel Lobbies - often have a display of discount coupons to area shops and restaurants. When you check in, ask the clerk for discount pizza coupons they may have at the front desk.

■ Attraction Online Coupons - check the websites listed with each review for possible printable coupons or discounted online tickets good towards the attraction.

MISSION STATEMENT

At first glance, you may think that this is a book that just lists hundreds of places to travel. While it is true that we've invested thousands of hours of exhaustive research (and drove over 3000 miles in Illinois) to prepare this travel resource...just listing places to travel is not the mission statement of these projects.

As a child, I was able to travel extensively throughout the United States. I consider these family times some of the greatest memories I cherish today. I felt most children had this opportunity to travel with their family. However, as I became an adult and started my own family, I found that this wasn't necessarily the case. Many friends expressed several concerns when deciding how to spend "quality" and "quantity" family time. 1) What to do? 2) Where to do it? 3) How much will it cost? 4) How do I know that my kids will enjoy it?

Interestingly enough, as I compare experiences with my family when I was a kid, many of the fondest memories were not made at an expensive attraction, but rather when it was least expected.

It is my belief and mission statement that if you as a family will study and use the contained information to create family memories, these memories will grow a well-rounded child. My hope is that your children will develop a love and a passion for quality family experiences that they can pass to another generation of family travelers.

We thank you for purchasing this book, and we hope to see you on the road (*and hear your travel stories!*) God bless your journeys and Happy Exploring!

Happy Exploring,   *Michele*

NATIONAL ROAD FESTIVAL - Begin in Marshall on the East, E. St. Louis on the West or some point in between. The National Road – mostly US Rte 40, today parallels I-70 across most of the state. There will be bluegrass music, car & motorcycle shows, museum tours, bocce ball tournaments, historic reenactments, and food. www.nationalroad.org/festivals.htm. (Father's Day weekend)

FIRST NIGHT CELEBRATIONS - A non-alcoholic, family-oriented, New Year's Eve celebration of the arts. Revelers ring in the new year with music, dancing, visual art, drama and fireworks. Admission.

C – Springfield, www.springfieldartsco.org.
CL – Aurora, (800) 477-4369.
CL – Evanston. (847) 328-5864.

EC – Pontiac. (815) 844-6692.
SE – Centralia, Recreation Complex. (888) 533-2600.

General State Agency & Recreational Information

Call *(or visit websites)* for the services of interest. Request to be added to their mailing lists.

LOOKING FOR LINCOLN - Historic Sites and participating communities - (217) 782-6817. www.lookingforlincoln.com.

ILLINOIS TOURIST INFORMATION - www.enjoyillinois.com

ILLINOIS HISTORIC PRESERVATION AGENCY - (217) 782-4836. www.state.il.us/hpa

ILLINOIS DEPARTMENT OF AGRICULTURE -County Fairs. www.agr.state.il.us/fair/countyfairssched.php

ILLINOIS DEPARTMENT OF NATURAL RESOURCES - (217) 782-6302. www.dnr.illinois.gov

NORTHWESTERN UNIVERSITY BIG TEN ATHLETICS - (847) 491-3741. www.nusports.com (Evanston, Ryan Field/Welsh Ryan Arena)

UNIVERSITY OF ILLINOIS GENERAL INFORMATION & SPORTS - Champaign. (217) 333-1000 or www.uiuc.edu. Sports: (866) ILLINI-1. www.fightingillini.com. Campus resources include the world's largest public university library, the National Center for Supercomputing Applications & Memorial Stadium (home of the Fighting Illini football team).

CHICAGO - City Of Chicago Tourism - (877) CHICAGO or www.choosechicago.com

C - Springfield Area CVB - www.visit-springfieldillinois.com or (800) 545-7300

CL - Aurora Area CVB - www.enjoyaurora.com or (800) 477-4369

CL - Greater Woodfield CVB - www.chicagonorthwest.com or (800) VISIT-GW

CL - Heritage Corridor CVB - www.heritagecorridorcvb.com (Starved Rock, Rte 66, Joliet areas)

CL - Lake County (North Chicago) CVB - (800) 525-3669 or www.lakecounty.org

EC - Champaign County - www.visitchampaigncounty.org or (800) 369-6151

N - Galena/Jo Daviess County CVB - www.galena.org or (877) GO GALENA

N - Rockford Area CVB - www.gorockford.com or (800) 691-7035

SW - Southwestern Illinois Tourism - www.thetourismbureau.org

W - Peoria Area CVB - www.peoria.org or (800) 747-0302

W - Quad Cities - www.visitquadcities.com or (800) 747-7800

AIRPORTS - All children love to visit the airport! Why not take a tour and understand all the jobs it takes to run an airport? Tour the terminal, baggage claim, gates and security / currency exchange. Maybe you'll even get to board a plane.

ANIMAL SHELTERS - Great for the would-be pet owner. Not only will you see many cats and dogs available for adoption, but a guide will show you the clinic and explain the needs of a pet. Be prepared to have the children "fall in love" with one of the animals while they are there!

BANKS - Take a "behind the scenes" look at automated teller machines, bank vaults and drive-thru window chutes. You may want to take this tour and then open a savings account for your child.

CITY HALLS - Halls of Fame, City Council Chambers & Meeting Room, Mayor's Office and famous statues.

ELECTRIC COMPANY / POWER PLANTS - Modern science has created many ways to generate electricity today, but what really goes on with the "flip of a switch". Because coal can be dirty, wear old, comfortable clothes. Coal furnaces heat water, which produces steam, that propels turbines, that drives generators, that make electricity.

FIRE STATIONS - Many Open Houses in October, Fire Prevention Month. Take a look into the life of the firefighters servicing your area and try on their gear. See where they hang out, sleep and eat. Hop aboard a real-life fire engine truck and learn fire safety too.

HOSPITALS - Some Children's Hospitals offer pre-surgery and general tours.

NEWSPAPERS - You'll be amazed at all the new technology. See monster printers and robotics. See samples in the layout department and maybe try to put together your own page. After seeing a newspaper made, most companies give you a free copy (dated that day) as your souvenir. National Newspaper Week is in October.

PETCO - Various stores. Contact each store manager to see if they participate. The Fur, Feathers & Fins™ program allows children to learn about the characteristics and habitats of fish, reptiles, birds, and small animals. At your local Petco, lessons in science, math and geography come to life through this hands-on field trip. As students develop a respect for animals, they will also develop a greater sense of responsibility.

PIZZA HUT & PAPA JOHN'S - Participating locations. Telephone the store manager. Best days are Monday, Tuesday and Wednesday mid-afternoon. Minimum of 10 people. Small charge per person. All children love pizza – especially when they can create their own! As the children tour the kitchen, they learn how to make a pizza, bake it, and then eat it. The admission charge generally includes lots of creatively made pizzas, beverage and coloring book.

KRISPY KREME DONUTS - Participating locations. Get an "inside look" and learn the techniques that make these donuts some of our favorites! Watch the dough being made in "giant" mixers, being formed into donuts and taking a "trip" through the fryer. Seeing them being iced and topped with colorful sprinkles is always a favorite with the kids. Contact your local store manager. They prefer Monday or Tuesday. Free.

SUPERMARKETS - Kids are fascinated to go behind the scenes of the same store where Mom and Dad shop. Usually you will see them grind meat, walk into large freezer rooms, watch cakes and bread bake and receive free samples along the way. Maybe you'll even get to pet a live lobster!

TV / RADIO STATIONS - Studios, newsrooms, Fox kids clubs. Why do weathermen never wear blue/green clothes on TV? What makes a "DJ's" voice sound so deep and smooth?

WATER TREATMENT PLANTS - A giant science experiment! You can watch seven stages of water treatment. The favorite is usually the wall of bright buttons flashing as workers monitor the different processes.

U.S. MAIN POST OFFICES - Did you know Ben Franklin was the first Postmaster General (over 200 years ago)? Most interesting is the high-speed automated mail processing equipment. Learn how to address envelopes so they will be sent quicker (there are secrets). To make your tour more interesting, have your children write a letter to themselves and address it with colorful markers. Mail it earlier that day and they will stay interested trying to locate their letter in all the high-speed machinery.

GEOCACHING AND LETTERBOXING

Geocaching and Letterboxing are the ultimate treasure hunt and can add excitement and fun to your driving, camping and hiking experiences. Geocaching employs the use of a GPS device (global positioning device) to find the cache.

Letterboxing uses clues from one location to the next to find the letterbox; sometimes a compass is needed. Both methods use the Internet advertising the cache, providing basic maps and creating a forum for cache hunters.

GEOCACHING

The object of Geocaching is to find the hidden container filled with a logbook, pencil and sometimes prizes! Where are Caches? Everywhere! But to be safe, be sure you're treading on Public Property. When you find the cache, write your name and the date you found it in the logbook. Larger caches might contain maps, books, toys, even money! When you take something from the cache you are honor-bound to leave something else in its place. Usually cache hunters will report their individual cache experiences on the Internet. (www.geocaching.com)

- ## GPS RECEIVER

    You'll need a GPS receiver that will determine your position on the planet in relation to the cache's "waypoint," its longitude/latitude coordinates. You can buy a decent GPS receiver for around $100. More expensive ones have built-in electronic compasses and topographical maps, but you don't need all the extras to have fun geocaching.

LETTERBOXING

The object is similar to geocaching — find the Letterbox — but instead of just signing and dating the logbook, use a personalized rubber stamp. Most letterboxes include another rubber stamp for your own logbook. The creator of the letterbox provides clues to its location. Finding solutions to clues might require a compass, map and solving puzzles and riddles! This activity is great fun for the entire family! (www.letterboxing.org)

Chapter 1
Central (C)

FAVORITES...

Macon County Historical Museum

Lincoln's New Salem

Abraham Lincoln Presidential Museum

Lincoln Home

Knights Action Park

Athens
- Lincoln Long Nine Museum

Carlinville
- Christmas Market

Decatur
- Children's Museum Of Illinois
- Macon County Historical Society Museum Complex
- Mueller Museum, Hieronymus
- Rock Springs Center For Environmental Discovery
- Scovill Zoo

Lincoln
- Postville Courthouse State Historic Site
- Railsplitter, The

Lincoln (Mt. Pulaski)
- Mt. Pulaski Courthouse State Historic Site

McLean
- Dixie Travel Plaza

Paris
- Pumpkin Works

Petersburg
- Lincoln's New Salem State Historic Site

Plainview
- Beaver Dam State Park

Ramsey
- Ramsey Lake State Park

Rochester
- Sangchris Lake State Park

Springfield
- Air Combat Museum
- Abraham Lincoln Presidential Museum & Library
- Lake Springfield
- Lincoln Depot
- Lincoln Home National Historic Site
- Lincoln Tomb State Historic Site
- Lincoln-Herndon Law Offices State Historic Site
- Old State Capitol State Historic Site
- Springfield Theatre Centre
- Illinois State Military Museum
- Comfort Suites - Springfield
- Cozy Dog Drive-In
- Dana-Thomas House
- Illinois State Museum
- Henson Robinson Zoo
- Knight's Action Park/ Caribbean Water Adventure/ Route 66 Drive In
- Lincoln Memorial Garden
- Highland Games & Celtic Festival
- Illinois State Fair
- International Route 66 Mother Road Festival

Springfield (Rochester)
- Prairie's Edge Farm

Taylorville
- Potawatomi Trail Pow Wow

A Visit With the Lincolns

Sites and attractions are listed in order by City, Zip Code, and Name. Symbols indicated represent: 🍽 Restaurants   🛏 Lodging

---

LINCOLN LONG NINE MUSEUM

200 South Main Street **Athens** 62613

Phone: (217) 636-8755 **www.abrahamlincolnlongninemuseum.com**
Hours: Tuesday-Saturday 1:00-5:00pm (June-August).

Located on the way to Lincoln's New Salem Site, Lincoln visited it many times. It now houses audio-dioramas about Lincoln's connection to this town. In 1837, Abraham Lincoln and his dedicated cadre of eight other Illinois legislators had won the General Assembly's approval to move the state capital from Vandalia to Springfield. The nine men were called the "long nine" because they averaged over 6 feet in height, uncommon in that day and age. In August, 1837, the "long nine" members were honored at a banquet. This banquet was held upstairs in this same building.

LONG NINE HERITAGE FEST

Athens - *Long Nine Museum. Parade, presentation by costumed living village reenactors representing pioneer days with demos including blacksmithing and milling. Historical Vignettes depict the life of Abraham Lincoln as a student, postmaster, surveyor and a re-creation of banquet held in honor of the opening of the Museum. Cruise in the carriages and horse-drawn wagons. Voices from the Past tour of cemetery and town with 1st person demonstration. (fourth Saturday in September)*

CHRISTMAS MARKET

Carlinville - *Anderson Mansion. The Mansion's "Destination Christmas" display alone is a touch of seasonal charm that is worth the visit, but guests also can walk the grounds to see an operating blacksmith shop, the print shop, the antiques barn, and the old General Store. In the famous "red barn," hungry visitors will find food, snacks, and drinks, including beef stew, BBQ sandwiches, hot dogs, fresh biscuits, home-made pies, as well as coffee, tea, and spiced apple-cinnamon drinks. Each room decorated with this years theme. Take the trolley to or from the Christmas market. www.carlinvillechristmasmarket.com (first weekend in December)*

CHILDREN'S MUSEUM OF ILLINOIS

55 South Country Club Road (Scovill Park, US 36 east across Lake Decatur. Turn right at first light) **Decatur** 62521

- Phone: (217) 423-KIDS **www.cmofil.org**
- Hours: Tuesday-Friday 9:30am-4:30pm; Saturday 10:00am-5:00pm; and Sunday 1:00-5:00pm. The museum is closed on Mondays (except early June - mid-August) and also major holidays. The museum is open on most Decatur school district holidays.
- Admission: $5.00 (age 2+).

Explore two floors of hands-on exhibits focusing on people and cultures, the arts, physics, humanities, the ecosystem, and even health. Children mail pretend letters, make money withdrawals, and shop in the Johnston Supermarket / Service Ctr / Emergency Dept exhibit. Making giant bubbles, painting on Plexiglas, and maneuvering toys through a water maze are favorites. Upstairs play stations include following the energy trail from coal mine to household appliances, piloting an airplane, and building with giant blocks. The museum's centerpiece: "Luckey's Climber," where children climb a two-story spiral of platforms, encased in safety net. Is it art or is it science? Climb in and decide.

MACON COUNTY HISTORICAL SOCIETY MUSEUM

5580 N. Fork Road (US 36 west to right on Airport Road to right on N. Fork)
Decatur 62521

- | | Phone: (217) 422-4919 **www.mchsdecatur.org**
- | | Hours: Tuesday-Saturday 1:00-4:00pm and every 4th Sunday afternoon.
- | | Admission: $1.00-$2.00.
- | | Note: Prairie Life Days held each May.

The prairie years and the Victorian era come to life in various exhibits and buildings set up in a village. Indoor exhibits cover the Lincoln connection and video "Looking for Lincoln"; Victorian years and the Prairie. Located behind the museum, the two-story Lincoln Log Courthouse structure was new when Thomas Lincoln's family trudged into Decatur in 1830. A tall man like Lincoln would have had to be careful not to bump his head on the second floor supports when he later tried three legal cases there. The Prairie Village also features a one-room schoolhouse, log cabin, replica of Mueller's (the famous inventor) gun shop, a train depot, a blacksmith shop, and a print shop. During busy days, you'll find costumed interpreters. The site director is very focused on keeping the exhibits fresh and interesting to kids. For instance, in the print house, you can observe and take home a fresh old-fashioned print.

MUELLER MUSEUM, HIERONYMUS

420 West Eldorado **Decatur** 62521

- | | Phone: (217) 423-6161 **http://muellermuseum.org/index.php**
- | | Hours: Thursday-Saturday 1:00-4:00pm. Closed major holidays.
- | | Admission: $1.50-$2.00.

Experience the life of Decatur's unsung genius, the man whose inventions revolutionized our everyday lives. Exhibits reflect the story of Hieronymus Mueller's immigration to this country in the mid-nineteenth century, through his brilliant mechanical inventions, the growth of his family and company. Mueller began his business as a gunsmith and repairman of various mechanical devices. In 1872 he patented his first major invention, the Mueller Water Tapper, one still used today. It is difficult to turn on a faucet, roller skate, use a water fountain, or watch firemen use a fire hydrant without using a product made at Mr. Mueller's waterworks factory. Beyond waterworks, Mueller indulged in autoworks. A replica of the original Mueller-Benz, winner of the first unofficial car race in the U.S. in 1895 is on display.

ROCK SPRINGS CENTER FOR ENVIRONMENTAL DISCOVERY

3939 Nearing Lane (US 48 south from downtown to west on Rock Springs Rd) **Decatur** 62521

- Phone: (217) 423-7708 **www.maconcountyconservation.com**
- Hours: Trails: Daily 7:00am-dusk. Visitors Center: Weekdays 8:00am-5:00pm, Saturday 9:00am-4:30pm, Sunday 1:00-4:30pm. Homestead Prairie Farm open Weekends 1:00-4:00pm (June-October). Closed New Years Day, Easter, Thanksgiving and Christmas.
- Admission: Donations accepted, with fees for some events.
- Educators: They have extensive themed programs for all ages available on the web page, For Educators.

The 1,343-acre center is devoted to getting to know our environment first hand including 8.5 miles of hiking trails, 2.2 miles of the Bicycle trail, two picnic pavilions, and the Homestead Prairie Farm historic site. The Visitor's Center features historic and environmental displays, live animals, and movies. Living History programs are offered in a restored 19th-Century farmstead. Today the house is furnished to reflect the lifestyle of the Trobaughs, their boarders, and neighbors in 1860, whose lives were being affected by the important changes sweeping the nation in the last years before the Civil War. A good combination of history and nature. Try to visit during their numerous special events and programs for the best experience.

PRAIRIE CELEBRATION

Decatur - *Rock Springs Center. Music, food, wagon rides, historic tours, trappers and traders, star planetarium, reptiles and prairie hikes. (second weekend in September)*

SCOVILL ZOO

71 South Country Club Road (Scovill Park, US 36 east across Lake Decatur. Turn right at first light) **Decatur** 62521

- Phone: (217) 421-7435 **www.decatur-parks.org/scovill-zoo/**
- Hours: (April - mid-October) Summers Open Daily 9:30am-6:00pm. Spring and Fall weekdays: 10:00am-5:00pm.
- Admission: $3.75-$6.25 (age 2+).
- Note: Pajama Party with Santa and animals held each mid-December.

The zoo covers 10 acres and is home to more than 500 animals. Visitors can enjoy a train ride through the zoo and catch a glimpse of timber wolves, spider monkeys or kangaroos. Children may also enjoy the zoo's petting area or a trip to the herpaquarium with reptiles, amphibians, invertebrates and fish. Be sure to meet the cheetahs Runako and Jafari. Allow time to ride the new "Endangered Species" carousel (extra fee) or romp around Project Playground. Howl with the wolves in a Wolf Howl, feed pygmy goats or have lunch in the Zoopermarket.

POSTVILLE COURTHOUSE STATE HISTORIC SITE

9145 S 5th Street (I-55, take Lincoln Exit 126 (State Route 10)
Lincoln 62656

Phone: (217) 732-8930 **www.illinois.gov/ihpa/Experience/Sites/Central/Pages/Postville-Courthouse.aspx**
Hours: Tuesday-Saturday Noon-4:00pm. Open until 5:00pm (March-October).
Admission: Suggested donation: $2.00 adult, $1.00 child.

Visit the historic downtown Lincoln, where you'll see the 1905 Logan County Courthouse. The present Postville Courthouse, a reproduction of the original 1840 Courthouse, was visited by Lincoln while he traveled the 8th Judicial Circuit. Abraham Lincoln, like most lawyers of his day, traveled the circuit to make a living. Most communities were too small to support resident lawyers. Lincoln and his contemporaries handled simple, low-paying cases. A statue of Abraham Lincoln is nearby. The Lincoln College and Museum (300 Keokuk Street - 217-732-3333) houses a major collection of Lincoln artifacts as well as the Hall of Presidents Museum, honoring the nation's Chief Executives from George Washington through the present.

<u>DID YOU KNOW</u>? Watermelon Christening Site: As the first lots were sold in the town of Lincoln, residents asked Abraham Lincoln to come from Springfield to christen the first town to be named for him. He did so using the <u>juice of a watermelon</u>.

ABRAHAM LINCOLN'S BIRTHDAY BASH

Lincoln - *Postville Courthouse State Historic site. Take a tour through the historic courthouse. Historians will be present and will speak in Abe's historic courtroom. Enjoy period music and exhibits while eating birthday cake. Admission. (second Saturday in February)*

GOOD OLE' NATIONAL RAILSPLITTING CONTEST

Lincoln - *Held around town and fairgrounds. Admission. www.railsplitting.com (third weekend in September)*

RAILSPLITTER, THE

Best Western Lincoln Inn, 1750 5th Street (corner of 5th street & route 66) **Lincoln 62656.** Phone: (217) 628-3338

Located on historic Route 66, this is reportedly the world's largest covered wagon. FREE to look around.

MT. PULASKI COURTHOUSE STATE HISTORIC SITE

113 S Washington St (SR 54 exit SR 121. Turn left at Dekalb St., left on Vine, left on Jefferson, turn right and travel two blocks to the City Square) **Lincoln (Mt. Pulaski) 62656**

Phone: (217) 792-3919 www.illinoishistory.gov/hs/mount_pulaski.htm
Hours: Tuesday-Saturday Noon-4:00pm Closed winter holidays.
Admission: Donations accepted.

Mt. Pulaski Courthouse State Historic Site on the city square in Mt. Pulaski is one of only two surviving Eighth Judicial Circuit courthouses in Illinois where Abraham Lincoln practiced law. When Lincoln first came to Mt. Pulaski Courthouse in 1848 he was senior partner to associate William Herndon in their Springfield law firm. Lincoln's growing ability and reputation helped fuel his political career. After one term (1847-1849) in Congress, Lincoln returned to his law practice with renewed vigor.

DIXIE TRAVEL PLAZA

501 Main Street (junction I-55 and US 136) **McLean** 61754. (309) 874-2323

Heading north from Springfield to the Windy City you can travel all but 11 miles of the original Route 66. Travelers will want to be sure and stop at the famous Dixie Truck Stop, where you'll find homemade biscuits and gravy, and a big slice of apple pie. The Dixie also boasts an extensive Route 66 Hall of Fame collection from its heyday as America's crossroads. Many people say Route 66 is the most famous highway in the world. Most would also agree it was an important passageway that helped shape our country's history and culture. Today, Route 66 still offers an exciting experience, a chance for people around the world to discover America.

PUMPKIN WORKS

Paris - *21788 Lower Terre Haute Road (I-70 exit 154). www.pumpkinworks.com. Offer family entertainment, 9 mazes – 2 for children and 7 for adults, hayrides, bonfires, arts, crafts, snacks. Admission. (weekends in September, daily in October)*

LINCOLN'S NEW SALEM STATE HISTORIC SITE

15588 History Lane, Illinois Route 97 (2 miles south of Petersburg, 20 miles NW of Springfield) **Petersburg** 62675

☐ Phone: (217) 632-4000 **www.lincolnsnewsalem.com**
☐ Hours: Wednesday-Sunday 9:00am-4:00pm
☐ Admission: FREE, suggested $2.00-$4.00 donation.
☐ Note: Diner on site except winters. They serve up some good sandwiches with lots of extras. Bike/hike trails, boat launch, picnic areas and campgrounds are here, too. Educators: Online Classroom handouts & activity sheets available under Students.

This site is a reconstruction of the village where Abraham Lincoln spent his early adulthood. The six years Lincoln spent in New Salem formed a turning point in his career. What changed him? His victories, his failures, his friendships? The stories you hear - are they fact or gossip? Although he never owned a home here, Lincoln was engaged in a variety of activities while he was at New Salem. He clerked in a store, split rails, enlisted in the Black Hawk War, served as postmaster and deputy surveyor, failed in business, and was elected to the Illinois General Assembly. In 12 log houses costumed interpreters re-create pioneer life. The Rutledge Tavern, ten workshops, stores, mills and a school where church services were held have been reproduced and furnished as they might have been in the 1830s. Rent a "bed and breakfast" for 37¢. Chat about the weather or politics with a storekeeper or go to "blab" school. From June through August (generally Friday-Sunday) make plans to come back for an evening of entertainment at New Salem's outdoor theater — Theatre in the Park. Or, attend an event like the Music Festival or Candlelight Tours each fall.

This park should be proud of its work to keep the village lively and the characters interesting. Bravo for the State Park to administer such a great site yet only take donations from the public.

BEAVER DAM STATE PARK

14548 Beaver Dam Lane (Travel on 108 west through Carlinville, three miles
north of Plainview) **Plainview** 62685
Phone: (217) 854-8020
www.dnr.state.il.us/Lands/Landmgt/PARKS/R4/beaver.htm

Fishing, picnicking, hiking, winter sports and tent and trailer camping are
among the most popular activities. Although the beaver is virtually gone
from this area, the park is named for a beaver dam that created its lake.
Approximately 8 miles of hiking trails are found in the park. These trails
encircle the lake, lead past the marsh, and extend through various wooded
areas in the park. An archery range is located across from the concession and
may be used free of charge. Archers must bring their own bow and arrows
(age 16 and under, must be with adult).

RAMSEY LAKE STATE PARK

Route 51/State Park Road **Ramsey** 62080
Phone: (618) 423-2215
www.dnr.state.il.us/Lands/Landmgt/PARKS/R5/RAMSEY.HTM

Rolling hills, timbered shoreline and beautiful Ramsey Lake make this park a
popular recreation spot. People who want to relax or energetic outdoor people
who want to hike, fish or camp can visit. A one-mile trail winds through
the park. Visitors also often use the unmarked fire lanes which make good
paths for easy walking. A 13-mile horse trail is located in the north end of
the area along with a small campground for horses. This area is one mile
north of the park entrance. Ice fishing, snowmobiling, cross-country skiing,
sledding and ice skating are among recreational activities for the cold weather
sports enthusiast. The 13-mile designated snowmobile trail provides a winter
wonderland view of the park when snow cover and weather permits.

SANGCHRIS LAKE STATE PARK

9898 Cascade Road (I-55 North to Exit 82 (Route 104). Route 104 east
6.1 miles through Pawnee and turn left, north, at Sangchris Lake sign)
Rochester 62563

|| Phone: (217) 498-9208

www.dnr.state.il.us/Lands/Landmgt/PARKS/R4/SANGCH.HTM

Nestled in native forests and brimming with a record bass population, the three-fingered lake extends into both Sangamon and Christian counties, earning it the name "Sangchris". Enjoy camping, fishing, and power boating on the lake. Wildflowers and song birds abound along 3 miles of scenic nature trails, and there are several unique albino deer living in the area. For the equestrian, there is a 5-mile horse trail, and for those preferring greater horsepower, there is an 11-mile snowmobile trail for winter use.

AIR COMBAT MUSEUM

835 South Airport Dr., Capital Airport **Springfield** 62670

|| Phone: (217) 698-3990 **www.aircombatmuseum.org**
|| Hours: Monday-Friday 9:00am-4:00pm (April-September). Call to arrange tours. Closed during lunch: Noon-1:00pm.
|| Admission: Donations suggested.

The Air Combat Museum was established to recognize, remember and pay tribute to both men and women veterans who operated, maintained and otherwise directly supported America's military aircraft, through the display of a dozen or so military aircraft. The ACM owns and operates two aircraft, one each from WWII and one from the Vietnam conflict. Notable examples include a Beechcraft AT-11 used to train bombardiers in WWII, a P-51 Mustang, a B-25 Mitchell, and a Soko G-21 Galeb, the first Yugoslavian jet.

ABRAHAM LINCOLN PRESIDENTIAL MUSEUM & LIBRARY

212 North 6th Street **Springfield** 62701

|| Phone: (217) 558-8844 **www.alplm.org**
|| Hours: Daily 9:00am-5:00pm. Last ticket sold one hour before closing. Closed: New Year's Day, Thanksgiving Day, Christmas Day.
|| Admission: $15.00 adult (age 16+), $6.00 child (5-15); $12.00 senior (62+)

and students, $10 military (ID required).
Educators: detailed lesson plans (esp. focused on Lang Arts): *www.illinois. gov/alplm/museum/Learning/Pages/Resource-Guides.aspx* Note: The museum exhibits are designed for children grades 4th and up, some small children may be frightened by the myriad of sights and sounds inside the special effects theaters (cannons fire, seats rumble). A Café and Museum Store are on site, too.

Curious about who Lincoln really was? The museum has taken what could be boring artifacts, and magically turned them into historical entertainment. The site uses several galleries to bring Honest Abe to life using the high-tech interactive methods of ghostly images, live actors and high action. A trip through The Whispering Gallery in this museum might change people's perspective about old politics. The Treasures Gallery showcases personal effects, such as the original handwritten Gettysburg Address. Other "Exhibit Journeys" lead guests through dioramas of key events in Lincoln's life, including a reproduction of the Old State Capitol where Lincoln practiced law and where he lay in state after his April 1865 assassination. The multi-screen, multi-stage special effects theater presentation, "Lincoln's Eyes" tells Lincoln's story through the eyes of an artist painting Lincoln's portrait (do you know what color his eyes were? This video has some loud noises and seat rumblings for effect). The Holavision® Theatre's "Ghosts of the Library" presentation aims to answer the question: "Why save all that stuff?" This theatre takes the idea of "boring history" and brings historical figures back to help us understand (a teacher's dream)! Is the narrator real or a holo-ghost? In Mrs. Lincoln's Attic, kids can play with a model of the Lincoln Home, try on period clothing, perform chores from the 1800s, and play with reproduction historic toys. They can also have their photos take with life-size models of Abraham Lincoln as a boy and an adult, as well as with Mary Todd and the Lincoln children (excellent photo ops). Daniel's favorite area: Ask Mr. Lincoln - this unique interactive theater is a chance to ask our 16th President a question and receive the answer in his own words. Our daughter Jenny's overall reaction, as she silently wept, "I feel like I knew him…" This place is that well done to elicit such a response from youth!

LAKE SPRINGFIELD

(I-55 exit 88) **Springfield** 62701

Phone: (217) 757-8660 or (217) 483-DOCK (marina)
www.lakespringfieldmarina.com
Hours: Daily 9:00am until 5:00pm or 7:00pm (seasonally).

Swimming - Lake Springfield Public Beach, Open Memorial Day through early August. Small Admission. Boating - Boats allowed on Lake Springfield include canoes, motorboats, pontoons, rowboats and sailboats. Fishing - About 15 sport fish species can be caught in Lake Springfield, including Channel Catfish, White Crappie, Bluegill, Largemouth Bass, Flathead Catfish, Carp, Striped Bass and Tiger Muskie. Marine Point and the bridge spanning East and West Forest Parks are accessible fishing areas for people with disabilities.

LINCOLN DEPOT

10th and Monroe **Springfield** 62701

Phone: (217) 544-8441 **www.abrahamlincolnonline.org/lincoln/sites/depot.htm**
Hours: Daily 10:00am-4:00pm (April-August). The Lincoln Depot is privately owned by a law firm, but the lower level is open to visitors.
Admission: FREE

"No one, not in my situation, can appreciate my feelings of sadness at this parting." Bittersweet words spoken by President-elect Abraham Lincoln as he departed his beloved Springfield to lead the country and change the course of history. The Depot contains restored waiting rooms (one for ladies and one for the luggage and tobacco-spitting men), exhibits of people and places dear to Lincoln, and a state-of-the-art video presentation recreating farewell address and the 12-day journey to his inauguration.

LINCOLN HOME NATIONAL HISTORIC SITE

413 South Seventh Street (8th and Jackson, I-55 exit 92A @ Sixth Street (Bus I-55) heading 4 miles to downtown. Right on Capitol, right on Seventh) **Springfield** 62701

Phone: (217) 492-4241 **www.nps.gov/liho/index.htm**
Hours: Daily 8:30am-5:00pm. Closed: New Year's Day, Thanksgiving Day,

Christmas Day.
   Admission: Free tickets are required and may only be obtained at the Lincoln Home Visitor Center.
   Note: Nearby (321 South Seventh Street) you can view Lincoln's Family Pew at the First Presbyterian Church. Educators: outstanding lesson plans, written with kids in mind: *www.nps.gov/liho/learn/education/curriculummaterials. htm*

A great starting point for your tour of Springfield. Upon entering, check in and get your timed tickets for the house tour. While waiting, visit the theatre showing short videos about different aspects of this neighborhood. The Quaker-brown residence where the Abraham Lincoln family lived for seventeen years (1844-1861) is a national treasure. It's located in the midst of a four-block historic neighborhood. Your 15-minute guided tour of the only home the Lincoln's ever owned will be conducted by friendly, entertaining National Park Service rangers. Stand in the room where Lincoln accepted the nomination for President. Did you know Mary Todd was a party girl? - her favorite - Strawberry Parties. And, the closest you'll ever come to shaking Lincoln's hand? Wrap your hand around the same handrail Lincoln used every day. We really liked this place - especially stories about the Lincoln boys and the family life.

DEAN HOUSE & ARNOLD HOUSE -Visit permanent exhibits located in two restored historic houses in the Lincoln Home neighborhood. Both exhibits are located across from the Lincoln Home, admission is free, and can be toured on a self-guided basis. Dean House: "What a Pleasant Home Abe Lincoln Has," explores the history of the Lincoln Home and Family. Arnold House: "If These Walls Could Talk: Saving an Old House" explains the preservation and restoration process of a historic house and tells the story of the residents that occupied the house.

LINCOLN TOMB STATE HISTORIC SITE

1500 Monument Avenue (Oak Ridge Cemetery, 1 mile west of 9th Street (old Rte 66, BL55) **Springfield** 62701

   Phone: (217) 782-2717 **www.illinois.gov/ihpa/Experience/Sites/Central/ Pages/Lincoln-Tomb.aspx**
   Hours: Daily 9:00am-4:00pm (5:00pm summer). Closed most Federal holidays and Sunday & Monday (Labor Day-April).
   Admission: FREE

Visit president Lincoln, his wife and three of their sons last resting place. Be sure to see the statuary inside the tomb that shows Lincoln at different periods of his public career. Abraham Lincoln was buried in Springfield's Oak Ridge Cemetery at the request of Mrs. Lincoln after his assassination in 1865. The original receiving vault in which Abraham Lincoln was buried can be seen on a tour of the cemetery. (Ask about the special Civil War Retreat Ceremony held at the Tomb each Tuesday evening during the summer.) In the tomb, they request silence or quiet conversation - not a problem - the mood will sober you.

LINCOLN PILGRIMAGE

Springfield - *New Salem. Lincoln's Tomb, www.alincolnbsa.org. Parade to the New State Capitol. Walk in Lincoln's footsteps as you follow where he walked through New Salem village as a young man, traveled from courthouse to courthouse in central Illinois as a circuit-riding attorney, climbed the steps of the Old State Capitol as a state legislator, and was carried to his final resting place at Lincoln Tomb. FREE. (last full weekend in April)*

LINCOLN-HERNDON LAW OFFICES STATE HISTORIC SITE

1 Old State Capitol Plaza (Sixth and Adams Streets, one-half block east of the Old State Capitol) **Springfield** 62701

- Phone: (217) 785-7289 **www.illinois.gov/ihpa/Experience/Sites/Central/Pages/Lincoln-Herndon.aspx**
- Hours: CURRENTLY CLOSED FOR RENOVATIONS!
- Otherwise: Monday-Saturday 9:00am-5:00pm (May to Labor Day week); Tuesday-Saturday 9:00am-5:00pm (rest of year). Closes: Daily Noon-1:00pm. Closed winter holidays.
- Admission: Donation suggested.
- Note: Next door is Del's Popcorn. Freshly popped and flavored popcorn, ice cream cones and candies are yummy and the atmosphere is playful. The place to go with the younger set as the Law Office tour may be boring for young ones.

Abraham Lincoln practiced law in the offices above Tinsley's store. The Law Offices have been restored to appear as it may have looked from 1843 until about 1852, when Abraham Lincoln practiced law on the building's third floor. It was an ideal location for a rising young law firm — near the Capitol and Springfield's finest hotel of the day and just above the local post office and Federal Courtroom. Stephen Logan (1843-44) and William Herndon (1844-52) were his partners during this time. This is the only surviving structure in which Lincoln maintained working law offices. Today, the first floor features an orientation center where visitors may view exhibits and a video describing the site's history. Guided tours are the only way to go upstairs. Hear the story of the "trap door" and how Lincoln used it.

OLD STATE CAPITOL STATE HISTORIC SITE

Old State Capitol Area (I-55 exit SR 29 north to Sixth Street and Adams Streets) **Springfield** 62701

Phone: (217) 785-7960 **www.illinois.gov/ihpa/Experience/Sites/Central/ Pages/Old-Capitol.aspx**

Hours: Wednesday-Saturday 9:00am- 5:00pm.

Admission: FREE guided tours.

"A HOUSE DIVIDED against itself cannot stand." These immortal words were spoken by Abraham Lincoln in the historic Old State Capitol Hall of Representatives in the turbulent days preceding the Civil War. He tried several hundred cases in the Supreme Court, borrowed books from the state library, and read and swapped stories with other lawyers and politicians in the law library. Around historic downtown, you'll notice "HERE I HAVE LIVED" EXHIBITS - View over 30 outdoor interpretive exhibits placed throughout the downtown area to experience Springfield as Abraham Lincoln knew it. Each exhibit is intended to capture a moment in time for Lincoln and how he was affected by the people, places and events he encountered in his hometown. Each story is accompanied by graphics or photographs and a medallion that is symbolic of that particular story. Visitors are encouraged to collect rubbings of each medallion.

SPRINGFIELD TROLLEY - An old-fashioned, open-air trolley (closed and heated in the winter) with regular stops at the major historic attractions. Tickets sold at several downtown locations ($5.00 Circle tour, $5.00-$10.00 for all day reboarding tour). For a list of stops, ticketing locations and days of operation, call (217) 528-4100.

SPRINGFIELD THEATRE CENTRE

420 S. Sixth Street (Hoagland Center for the Arts) **Springfield** 62701

Phone: (217) 523-2787 **www.springfieldtheater.com**

The Springfield Theatre Centre, originally called The Springfield Theatre Guild, is a not-for-profit organization incorporated in 1947 to provide Central Illinois with quality theatre, educational opportunities, and a creative outlet for live theatrical arts. Their White Rabbit Series includes titles like Alice in Wonderland, Aladdin and Santa Claus.

ILLINOIS STATE MILITARY MUSEUM

1301 N. MacArthur Blvd. (Camp Lincoln) **Springfield** 62702

Phone: (217) 761-3910 **www.facebook.com/Illinois.State.Military.Museum**
Hours: Tuesday-Saturday 1:00-4:30pm or by appointment. Closed government holidays.
Admission: FREE. Donations accepted.

On the grounds of the headquarters of the Illinois National Guard, the museum is committed to collecting, preserving, interpreting, and exhibiting the military artifacts associated with the citizen-soldier of Illinois. The exhibit includes rare items such as the artificial leg of Mexican General Santa Anna, a target board shot at by President Lincoln, as well as vehicles, weapons, uniforms, equipment and photographs. The Citizen-Soldier exhibit features the military experiences of famous Illinois soldiers such as Carl Sandburg, Robert McMormick, John A. Logan and Abraham Lincoln. All displayed in a WWII-era Civilian Conservation Corps barracks.

COMFORT SUITES - SPRINGFIELD

Springfield - *2620 S Dirksen Pkwy, 62703. Indoor Pool, micro/frig in each room and big complimentary continental breakfast. Within 10 minutes of all Springfield/Lincoln attractions. Most nights under $99. (217) 753-4000.* **www.comfortsuites.com/hotel-springfield-illinois-IL127.**

COZY DOG DRIVE IN

2935 South Sixth Street **Springfield** 62703

☐ Phone: (217) 525-1992 **www.cozydogdrivein.com**
☐ Hours: Monday-Saturday 8:00am-8:00pm.
☐ Note: In the morning they have fresh cake donuts and other breakfast items such as eggs, pancakes, and french toast.

For Illini, the nostalgia, charm and spirit of Route 66 can still be found in the secret corners of this Midwestern community. Take the Cozy Drive In for instance. A familiar Springfield landmark on old Route 66 since 1949, the original owners, the Waldmire family, are still serving up the same friendly atmosphere. Their specialty: a home-cooked recipe of Cozy Dogs (hot dogs deep fried in a secret bread batter - corn dogs) that travelers from around the world have come to love. For lunch or dinner they serve world famous Cozy Dogs along with fresh cut french fries, hamburgers, homemade chili and homemade bean soup, pork tenderloins and other delicious food items. Inside the diner, you'll find an amusing array of Route 66 memorabilia and souvenirs. Most everything is under $4.00.

DANA-THOMAS HOUSE

301 E. Lawrence (I-55 take Clear Lake Ave exit, head west. Turn left (south) onto 9th Street. Turn right onto Cook) **Springfield** 62703

☐ Phone: (217) 782-6776 **www.illinois.gov/ihpa/Experience/Sites/Central/Pages/Dana-Thomas-House.aspx**
☐ Hours: Thursday-Sunday 9:00am-5:00pm. Closed major winter holidays.
☐ Admission: Suggested donation $3.00 adult, $1.00 children (under 17).
☐ Educators: Education activities on simple structures: **www.illinois.gov/ihpa/Experience/Sites/Central/Pages/Dana-Thomas-House-Education.aspx**

It was 1902 in Victorian Springfield when local socialite and activist, Susan Lawrence Dana, hired a rising young architect from Chicago to remodel her family home. What resulted and remains today is one of Frank Lloyd Wright's finest prairie-style homes, complete with original furniture, art glass doors, windows and light fixtures. Frank Lloyd Wright (1867-1959) was thirty-five in 1902, the year he began work on the Dana House. Already well known for his innovative design, Wright was revolutionizing American domestic architecture in the Midwest.

DANA-THOMAS HOUSE CHRISTMAS

Springfield - *Dana-Thomas State Historic Site. Recall the splendor of a bygone era as you tour this spectacular Frank Lloyd Wright designed home completely bedecked in turn-of-the-century finery for the holiday season. Suggested donation. (month-long in December)*

ILLINOIS STATE MUSEUM

502 S. Spring Street (corner of Spring & Edwards Streets, south side of State Capitol complex) **Springfield** 62706

Phone: (217) 782-7386 **www.museum.state.il.us**

Hours: Monday-Saturday 8:30am-5:00pm, Sunday Noon-5:00pm. Closed New Year's Day, Thanksgiving Day, Christmas Day.

Admission: FREE.

Educators: Online lesson plans: ***www.museum.state.il.us/ed_opp/lessonplans.html***

Permanent and changing exhibits tell the story of Illinois' land, life, people, and art. The attendant will give each guest an ID badge that can be used to reveal answers and activate sound stations within the 1st floor exhibit halls. A completely new natural history hall, Changes: Dynamic Illinois Environments, reveals the exciting changes in Illinois environments over time. Interactive elements, audio and video effects, life-sized dioramas and thousands of authentic fossils and specimens illustrate the processes that shaped and continue to transform Illinois' diverse environments. In Changes, you can walk through a Fluorite (used in welding and to get fluoride for toothpaste) Mine; travel through an Ice Age tunnel and limestone cave - all within a few feet of each other. Explore French Illinois and meet the people who lived here. Native American heritage dioramas are in Peoples of the Past.

The Play Museum is a free children's area at the Illinois State Museum. Load a jeep; crawl through a cave; dig for fossils; put together a baby mastodont puzzle; frame art; explore collections of fossils, insects, artifacts; and toys; and play museum! The Play Museum is designed for children ages 3-10 and their families. Hours are Monday-Saturday (9:30 a.m.-4:00 p.m.) and Sunday (1:00 to 5:00 p.m.).

HENSON ROBINSON ZOO

1100 E. Lake Drive **Springfield** 62707

Phone: (217) 753-6217 **www.hensonrobinsonzoo.org**

Hours: Monday-Friday 10:00am-5:00pm, Saturday-Sunday 10:00am-6:00pm (April-October); Daily 10:00am-4:00pm (November, December, March). Weekends only January & February. Closed winter holidays.

Admission: $4.00-$5.75 (age 3+).

Note: Facilities include a gift shop, concessions and a petting area.

The Zoo is home to more than 300 animals native to Australia, Africa, Asia and North and South America. Over 90 species of native animals are housed here among naturalistic exhibits. Enjoy the relaxing atmosphere of the lagoons and watch mischievous spider monkeys at play on monkey island. Delight at the river otters. Marvel at the grace of the cheetahs and the deceivingly cuddly appearance of the Asiatic black bear. Then take a walk on the wild side with cougars, gibbons, lemurs, and more.

KNIGHT'S ACTION PARK / CARIBBEAN WATER ADVENTURE / ROUTE 66 DRIVE IN

1000 Recreation Drive (I-55 Sixth Street Exit, follow signs to Chatham Road & Recreation Dr.) **Springfield** 62707

Phone: (217) 546-8881 **www.knightsactionpark.com**

Hours: Action Park: Opens Daily 9:00am-dusk (weather permitting). Water Park: Opens Daily 10:00am-7:00pm (Memorial Day-Labor Day)

Admission: Action Splash Pass - $32.95. Action Park: Pay as you Go ($3.00-$5.00 per activity). Water Park: $22.00+ pass, $4.00 infants (2 & under w/ swim diapers). $4.00 discount on pass after 3:30pm and for $10.00 off for Landlubbers. This price includes all the water attractions in the water area except the games, such as water wars. There is no additional charge for tubes or parking.

In this 60-acre family fun park, you can splash down a giant waterslide or sprayground, test your mini-golf putts, or catch a flick. With two parks at one location, the water park offers its newest attraction - "The Devil Ray" (thrill ride, G forces giant halfpipe) along with a wave pool (one of our favorites), Bermuda Triangle waterslides, and action river ride (an awesome lazy river with gentle geysers and waves), pedal boats, activity pools and children's water-theme area (Seal Bay). The dry attractions include a golf practice range, miniature golf courses, batting cages, go karts, and their newest attraction,

"The Big Wheel" (ferris wheel). What a clean, compact, fun day to be had! Next door...load up the car and throw in the lawn chairs. It's time to head back in time to the Route 66 Drive In. Newly restored, located on an original alignment of Route 66 in Springfield, it shows double features (G, PG or PG13 only) nightly (beginning around 9:00pm) from Memorial Day weekend through Labor Day and on weekends through September ($5.00-$7.50). www.route66-drivein.com. Concession stand featuring all your drive-in favorites.

LINCOLN MEMORIAL GARDEN
2301 East Lake Shore Drive Springfield 62707

Phone: (217) 529-1111 www.lincolnmemorialgarden.org
Hours: Daily sunrise-sunset. Nature Center: Tuesday-Saturday 10:00am-4:00pm, Sunday 1:00-4:00pm. Closed several major holidays.
Admission: FREE

A nature center with five miles of wooded trails lead you on a journey through the Illinois landscape Lincoln walked. Depending on the season you visit, you could discover springtime dogwoods in full bloom, colorful wildflowers of summer, burnished autumn leaves, or snow-covered maple trees bursting with sap. All the plants found at the Garden are native to the three states Lincoln lived in - Kentucky, Indiana and Illinois. The oaks, maples and hickories, as well as the prairie grasses and forbs, would have been known by Lincoln, and reflect the landscape of his time. Located on the shores of Lake Springfield, it was designed as a "living memorial" to Abraham Lincoln.

MAPLE SYRUP TIME
Springfield - *Lincoln Memorial Garden. Visitors can experience the entire maple syrup process from tapping trees to collecting sap to actually cooking the sap into syrup. Demonstrations are held each Saturday and Sunday. FREE. (weekends mid-February thru early March)*

HIGHLAND GAMES & CELTIC FESTIVAL
Springfield - *Illinois State Fairgrounds. Join the fun of this traditional Scottish & Irish country fair, complete with bagpiping, ancient athletic competitions, Scottish Highland dancing, Irish Step Dancing, and a variety of Celtic foods and gifts. www.springfieldhighlandgames.com. Admission. (third Saturday in May)*

ILLINOIS STATE FAIR

Springfield - *Fairgrounds along Sangamon Avenue and Peoria Road.* ***www.agr.state. il.us/isf.*** *Hundreds of thousands of people flock here for the rides – both mechanical and living – games, hands-on exhibits, and entertaining demonstrations such as highdivers, birds of prey, lumberjacking, and more. Music, food, car and horse races. Adventure Village is a small carnival next to the main entrance open all summer. Conservation World is a 22 acre setting that offers family activities, fishing with exhibits, large fish tank, and a lumberjack show. Step back in time inside the Old Firehouse Building #7 and see antique fire service memorabilia, art works, equipment, and sculptures. Admission. (mid-August for 10 days)*

INTERNATIONAL ROUTE 66 MOTHER ROAD FESTIVAL

Springfield - *Downtown. Hundreds of vintage cars, entertainment, and celebrity guests from the U.S. and Canada fill the streets of historic downtown Springfield for a three-day celebration of cars, food, music, and friends of the heyday of US Route 66.* ***www.route66fest.com*** *Rte 66 Authors & Artists, and the World's Largest Sock Hop. FREE. (first weekend in October)*

PRAIRIE'S EDGE FARM

(20 minutes from Downtown Springfield) **Springfield (Rochester)** 62563

Phone: (217) 498-8251 **http://prairiesedgefarm.com**
Hours: By reservation only.

Join in the farm activities! From collecting eggs to feeding the livestock, this family owned and operated farm is the perfect hands-on experience for the family. Fees start at $40.00 for a group of 4 to 5.

POTAWATOMI TRAIL POW WOW

Taylorville - *Christian County fairground. Annual American Indian Pow Wow with authentic artifacts and wares, dancers in full regalia, authentic food, gourd dance to honor Veterans.* ***www.goflo.com/powwow***. *(first weekend in June)*

Chapter 2
*Chicago &
Chicagoland (CL)*

FAVORITES...

Food Factories & Farms

Prairies, Beaches, Aquariums & Zoos

Skyscrapers & Boardwalk Pier

Tours by boat, canal, trolley, firetruck

Giant-sized Science

Arlington Heights
- Doubletree Hotel Chicago & Birch River Grill
- Pappadeaux Seafood Kitchen

Aurora
- Phillips Park & Zoo
- Blackberry Farm's Pioneer Village
- Hampton Inn & Suites
- Scitech Hands On Museum
- Splash Country Water Park
- Aurora Regional Fire Museum

Aurora (Batavia)
- Fermilab Science Center

Aurora (North)
- Red Oak Nature Center

Beecher
- Plum Creek Nature Center

Big Rock
- Big Rock Plowing Match

Bolingbrook
- Johansen Farms

Brookfield
- Brookfield Zoo

Buffalo Grove
- Long Grove Confectionery Company Tour

Chicago
- Chicago Professional Sports Teams
- Chicago Trolley & Water Taxi Tours
- Giordano's
- Grant Park & Buckingham Fountain
- Art Institute Of Chicago
- Adler Planetarium & Astronomy Museum

Chicago (cont.)
- Chicago Playworks
- Field Museum, The
- Shedd Aquarium/ Oceanarium
- Federal Reserve Bank Of Chicago
- Skydeck Chicago
- McCormick Bridgehouse & Chicago River Museum
- Noble Horse Theatre
- American Girl Place
- Bubba Gump Shrimp Company
- Chicago Children's Museum
- Hancock Observatory
- Navy Pier
- O' Leary's Chicago Fire Truck Tours
- SherAton Chicago Hotel & Towers
- Spirit Of Chicago Cruise
- Wrigley Field Tours
- Chicago History Museum
- Lincoln Park Zoo
- Notebaert Nature Museum
- Garfield Park Conservatory
- Eli's Cheesecake World
- Museum Of Science And Industry (Msi)
- Oriental Institute Museum, The
- Chicago Kids Company
- Taste Of Chicago
- Chicago Air And Water Show

Des Plaines
- McDonald's #1 Store Museum

Elgin
- Children's Theatre Of Elgin
- Elgin Public Museum
- Elgin Historical Museum Holiday Tea

Elk Grove Village
- Pirate's Cove Theme Park

Evanston
- Grosse Point Lighthouse

Geneva
- Fox Valley Folk Music And Storytelling Festival

Glen Ellyn
- Willowbrook Wildlife Center

Glencoe
- Chicago Botanic Garden

Glenview
- Kohl's Children's Museum

Gurnee
- Six Flags Great America And Hurricane Harbor

Hoffman Estates
- Hilton Garden Inn

Itasca
- Spring Brook Nature Center

Joliet
- Joliet Area Historical Museum
- Joliet Iron Works Historic Site
- Splash Station Waterpark
- Harvest Days
- Candlelight Reception

Libertyville
- Lambs Farm

Lisle
- Morton Arboretum
- Lisle Eyes To The Skies Balloon Festival
- Polar Express Santa Train

Lockport
- Gaylord Building Historic Site & Restaurant
- Bengston Pumpkin Farm

Long Grove
- Strawberry Festival

Maple Park
- Kuipers Family Farm

Minooka
- Dollinger Family Farm

Naperville
- DuPage Children's Museum
- Naper Settlement

Oak Brook
- Fullersburg Woods Environmental Educational Center & Graue Mill

Oak Forest
- Gaelic Park Irish Fest

Oak Park
- Frank Lloyd Wright Home And Studio
- Hemingway Birthplace Home And Museum
- Wonder Works

Palos Park
- Pumpkin Patch

Prairie View
- Didier Pumpkin Farm

Romeoville
- Isle A La Cache Museum

Schaumburg
- Rainforest Café
- Atcher Island Water Park
- Spring Valley Nature Center & Heritage Farm
- Medieval Times Dinner & Tournament

Skokie
- Skokie Northshore Sculpture Park

South Barrington

26   KIDS LOVE ILLINOIS

- Goebbert's Pumpkin Farm

South Elgin
- Fox River Trolley Museum

South Holland
- Sand Ridge Nature Center

St. Charles
- Pheasant Run Resort And Spa
- Scarecrow Festival

Volo
- Volo Auto Museum

Wauconda
- Lake County Discovery Museum

Wheaton

- Billy Graham Center Museum
- Kline Creek Farm

Willow Springs
- A River Thru History: The Des Plaines Valley Rendezvous

Willowbrook
- Dell Rhea's Chicken Basket

Yorkville
- Raging Waves Waterpark

Zion
- Illinois Beach Resort
- Illinois Beach State Park

Window Washing Fun! - Hancock Building

Sites and attractions are listed in order by City, Zip Code, and Name. Symbols indicated represent: 🍽 Restaurants   🛏 Lodging

---

DOUBLETREE HOTEL CHICAGO & BIRCH RIVER GRILL

75 W. Algonquin Road (Rte 62 & I-90) **Arlington Heights** 60005

Phone: (847) 364-7600 **www.chicagoarlingtonheights.doubletree.com**
Note: If you want, you can take the complimentary local area shuttle to the nearest Metra station and board the transit into downtown Chicago without the fuss (and expense) of parking. Overnights stays start at $109.

As you enter the lobby and check-in, you'll be greeted by friendly staff, yes, but even better – the smell of warm chocolate chip cookies! Each evening around check-in time, they bake their famous cookies to give guests as a welcome gift. If that doesn't "grab" the kids attention, maybe the Fluffy bed and pillows in your room or the nice indoor atrium pool area and walking courtyard green space will. Just outside the fitness and pool area is a snack bar called Cravings - open 24 hours for late-night snack craving purchases.

The Birch River Grill Restaurant serves breakfast, lunch and dinner daily. When you first walk in, it gives you a cozy, homespun feel…with a glowing fireplace. They serve inspired American dishes in generous portions. Everyone is sure to find something that they would enjoy to eat, from Granny Apple & Onion Soup (topped w/ cheese & fresh baked apples - $6) to even the simplest and cheesiest Mac & Cheese. Signature meat entrees include Grilled Pork Tenderloin served with real smashed potatoes and rustic cranberry apple sauce ($16) or grilled, rubbed steak served au jus. Even the desserts are amazing, from a yummy carrot cake for two (which is a three tiered creation with cream cheese frosting) to the chocolate lover's favorite Chocolate Temptation Cake. And, the Doubletree Cookies & Milk ($5) is the classic ending to Doubletree dining. Who would think a city known for pizza and beef would also have so many Southern twists (ex. Sweet potato fries or fried green tomatoes) and East Coast turns (crab cakes).

28   KIDS LOVE ILLINOIS

PAPPADEAUX SEAFOOD KITCHEN

798 W. Algonquin Road **Arlington Heights** 60005

Phone: (847) 228-9551 **www.pappadeaux.com**
Serving lunch (entrees $10-15) and dinner (entrees ~$20).

The relaxed, fun-loving atmosphere of Louisiana is recreated in the cruise-ship designed restaurant. Parts of it feel like the elegant Titanic plus they have several aquarium bays with fresh fish (ready to be prepared fresh for you) and a tropical fish aquarium to gaze at while you wait to be seated. Find classic seafood specialties like fried shrimp, etouffee, grilled Gulf fish and fresh Gulf oysters. Can we suggest you get crazy? Maybe try Crispy Fried Alligator, Seared Frog Legs or fondue – blackened Shrimp & Crawfish Fondeaux in a creamy sauce with sautéed veggies to die for! Other specialties to try: Shrimp Brochette wrapped and filled (amazing – our fav of all selections); anything Cajun, Dirty Rice as a side – a flavor burst; and their crab legs come with special crab pickers that easily manage the tedious job of getting that luscious meat out. Steak and chicken dishes, too. The Kids Menu also doubles as an activity sheet. Kids twelve and under have choices of Corn Dog bites, Chicken Tenders, Fried Catfish, Fried Shrimp or a Combo Platter (avg. $5). The chef promises no spicy foods on the kids menu. Finish your festive meal with a signature dessert: Godiva Chocolate Mousse cake – chocolate heaven on a plate! We think their Cajun influences are just the right spice and their sauces are really worth trying in any dish.

PHILLIPS PARK & ZOO

828 Montgomery Rd (accessible from Smith Boulevard, Parker Avenue, or Howell Place off of Montgomery Road. Zoo is 901 Ray Moses Drive) **Aurora** 60505

Phone: (630) 898-7228 (park) or (630) 978-4700 (zoo), **www.phillipsparkaurora.com**
Hours: Daily 9:00am-5:00pm (zoo). Mastodon Island & Visitors Center open same hours, weekdays only.
Admission: FREE
Tours: Tours of the Zoo are offered during the hours of 9:00am and 2:00pm, Monday-Friday. All tours must be scheduled at least 2 weeks in advance.
Educators: Guides and Lesson Plans: **www.phillipsparkaurora.com/dnn/zoo/ZooInformation/ParentTeacherResources.html**. FREEBIES: Activities and Scavenger Hunts are on the online Kids Zone: **www.phillipsparkaurora.com/kids-zone-activities.html**

For updates & travel games visit: **www.KidsLoveTravel.com**

Zoo exhibits include: Bald Eagles "Kenai" and "Denali"; the Gray Wolves "Dakota" and "Cheyenne"; "Fly" the fox; "Graycie" the Artic Fox; "Snowflake" the Platinum Red Fox; North American River Otters "Teeter" & "Totter"; Llamas "Dahlai" & "Socks"; "Hank" the Elk Bull and his herd; Goats; a Pot-bellied Pig; Reptiles; Swans; Ducks; Turkeys; Peacocks and more.

- MASTODON ISLAND: The Mastodon Peninsula site features a tusk maze and a mastodon slid The mastodon bones that were unearthed in the park during a 1934 Civil Works Administration Project. The skull being the largest of the artifacts, weighs 188 pounds, and greets visitors at the entrance. The bones, estimated to be between 10,000 to 20,000 years old, include a 92-pound lower jaw, a 6-foot-long tusk, ribs and vertebrae.

- WEST RECREATION AREA: located southwest of the lake, features a playground for youngsters, sand volleyball courts, horseshoe pits and a pavilion. On-site parking is available off of Parker Avenue. In addition, you'll find three fishing piers located around the lake.

ZOO HOLIDAYZE

Aurora - *Phillips Park Zoo. Stroll the illuminated path at Phillips Park Zoo and enjoy the sights of over 6,000 holiday lights and the sounds of carols. (month long December)*

BLACKBERRY FARM'S PIONEER VILLAGE

100 South Barnes Road (I-88 Orchard Road exit, head south. West on Galena Blvd, left on Barnes) **Aurora** 60506

   Phone: (630) 892-1550 **www.foxvalleyparkdistrict.org/facilities/**
   blackberry-farm/
   Hours: Monday-Friday 9:30am-3:30pm, Weekends/Holidays 11:00am-5:00pm
   (May-August). later hours on Saturdays. Friday-Sunday only (September).
   Saturday/Sunday 11am-4pm (October).
   Admission: $4.50-$8.00 adult.
   Note: Food service is available at the outdoor pavilion, the Summer Kitchen,
   overlooking one of the ponds with a spraying fountain. Visitors may also
   bring a picnic lunch to enjoy along the lake shore. The paths are very stroller/
   wheelchair friendly.

Part amusement park and part museum, this Village is a great place for kids to have fun and learn a little American history along the way. Take a train ride or wagon ride through this 54-acre pioneer village and see an 1840s farm, an authentic depot, a carriage collection, a carousel and a petting zoo. Ever seen a Snow Roller used to compact the snow for sleighs? Recite a lesson from your McGuffey Reader with the Schoolmarm or try to figure out how to use the "contraptions" displayed around the Farm Museum (look like something from Chitty, Chitty, Bang, Bang).

Little ones have their own play area called Discovery Farm where kids can ride pedal tractors, load corn or pick apples. Kids especially enjoy the general store and the toy store. Many period craft demonstrations bring the Village to life. They are blacksmithing, spinning, weaving, sewing & pottery, as well as a one room schoolhouse, an Aurora home from the 1840s and a farm cabin. With a lake, ponds and a meandering stream, the Park allows families to wander, at leisure, through local history.

FALL HARVEST FESTIVAL

Aurora - *Blackberry Farm's Pioneer Village. Find out what harvest time was like on an 1800s farm. Costumed pioneers will prepare food, shell corn and press cider. Admission. (third Saturday in September) Pumpkin Weekends in October.*

HAMPTON INN & SUITES

Aurora - *2423 Bushwood Drive (I-88 exit Orchard Rd.) 60506.* **www. hamptoninnandsuitesaurora.com.** *This is a wonderful place for kids to stay with their parents when staying overnight in Chicagoland. Not only are the rooms spacious, but they have a frig, microwave and huge free breakfast offering fresh pastry, fruit and hot items that change each morning. The staff serves fresh coffee cake just out of the oven. The best part, though, is the pool area. They have a gated area just for kids - a mini water park with a soft frog slide, a water umbrella and water spouts. The other warm pool is for laps or noodle fun (they supply the noodles) with a large, adjoining hot tub for parent relaxation. Most rooms around $99 per night. Family Value Packages.*

SCITECH HANDS ON MUSEUM

18 West Benton Street (Take I-88 to Aurora, exit at 31 South. Proceed south on 31 until you reach Benton St. (one block after 31 becomes one way.) Turn East (left) **Aurora** 60506

- Phone: (630) 859-3434 **www.scitech.mus.il.us**
- Hours: Tuesday-Saturday 10:00am-3:00pm.
- Admission: $6.00-$8.00 (age 2+).
- Note: Discovery Zone has "experiments" for little tikes. Across the street is the Swimming Stones kinetic water sculpture. Does it look like magic or an earthquake?

Colors are Chemistry: Try mixing two colors is one thing, then UN-mixing them? In the Chromatography exhibit you can separate black ink into different colors - pretty cool. They have bubble science areas (did you know there were physics involved in making bubbles?), exploring light and magnetism, or motion and chemistry. Who's older, jellyfish or dinosaurs? Find out or just play with prehistoric and modern toy animals on the Era Staircase. See tiny live animals wiggling and swimming and find out the different ways they do it in Microscopic Movement. Investigate the inside of a tornado and anchor the weather today. The Outdoor Science Park has giant experiments like the Human Yo-Yo, Bike on a Tightrope, or Hoist the Large Lever (kids, can you lift your parents?)

SPLASH COUNTRY WATER PARK

195 S. Barnes Rd. (across from Blackberry Farm) **Aurora** 60506

- Phone: (630) 906-7981 **www.foxvalleyparkdistrict.org/facilities/aquatics/ splash-country-water-park**
- Hours: Monday-Friday 10:30am-6pm, Saturday & Sunday 11:00am-6pm.
- Admission: $7.00-$9.00 per person (age 2+). Twilight reduced rates.
- Note: Full concession stand with umbrella tables, Sand play area with seating and shade, Lap lane swimming available at designated times. Both the facility and the staff have won state and national awards for safety, operations and facility design.

Splash Country Water Park features: Six lane zero depth pool with children's play features, the 2nd largest lazy river in Illinois (with 1,100 feet winding through dumping buckets, sprayers, jets and a bubbling rapids), and one winding (enclosed tube/flume) slide & one winding (open tube/flume) slide. An enclosed kid-friendly area with spray guns, waterfall, and other interactive features for kids under 48 inches tall. 2 regulation sand volleyball courts.

AURORA REGIONAL FIRE MUSEUM

53 North Broadway (downtown, near America's Roundhouse) **Aurora** 60507

- Phone: (630) 892-1572 **www.auroraregionalfiremuseum.org**
- Hours: Thursday, Friday, Saturday 1:00-4:00pm.
- Admission: $3.00-$5.00 per person
- Educators & FREEBIES: **www.auroraregionalfiremuseum.org/education/educational_links.htm**.

This museum is housed in the old Central Fire Station. What would a fire museum be without fire trucks? The Aurora Regional Fire Museum has nine pieces of fire apparatus in the collection dating from an 1850s hand pumper to a 1960s aerial ladder truck. Different exhibits focus on topics such as equipment and uniforms. Don't some of those old engines look silly?

FERMILAB SCIENCE CENTER

(Exit I-88 at the Farnsworth exit, north. Farnsworth becomes Kirk Road. Follow Kirk Road to Pine Street) **Aurora (Batavia)** 60510

Phone: (630) 840-3351 or (630) 840-5588 **www.fnal.gov**

Hours: The Lederman Science Center is open Monday-Friday from 8:30am-4:30pm and on Saturday from 9:00am-3:00pm.

Tours: Self-guided: The Center can accommodate groups of five or less on a walk-in basis. Walk-in visitors can use the Visitor's Guide to explore more than 30 experiments.

Note: Fermilab visitors are allowed to go into the Lederman Science Center and the first and ground floor of Wilson Hall. Ask-a-Scientist program on selected Sunday afternoons. Behind the scenes tour and crazy questions answered. Exhibits are geared towards 5th-12th graders but younger ones will have fun playing with balls (although they won't get the science behind it). FREEBIES: games: **http://ed.fnal.gov/projects/labyrinth/games/**.

This physics research center has the highest energy accelerator in the world! Visitors are welcome to visit the "Quarks to Quasars" exhibits to gain hands-on experience as they experiment with exhibits that demonstrate how Fermilab physicists understand nature's secrets. Start at the Intro Videos to orient. Then, follow cartoons as they introduce each exhibit. Now, play (actually, experiment). Learn how accelerators "kick" energy in linear, circular and bending modes. Race cars, balls and yourself - scientists show you how. Now, kick it up a notch. Next, discover how to detect Invisible Particles (like uranium in stoneware or plastic). What material shields you from harmful radiation? Catch cosmic rays. Even play pool ball or pinball and see exactly where the energy from the cue ball goes. Patterns are the secret. Play nature's piano (can you hit the right keys?). The Margaret Pearson Interpretive Trail is a quarter mile self-guiding nature trail through a portion of Fermilab's restored prairie. See insects, fungi and geese that live in the prairie. Visitors are welcome to view Fermilab's herd of about sixty buffalo, too. Awesome!

RED OAK NATURE CENTER

2343 S. River St. (Route 25, 1/2 mile north of Rte. 56) **Aurora (North)** 60542

Phone: (630) 897-1808 **www.foxvalleyparkdistrict.org/facilities/red-oak-nature-center**

Hours: Monday-Friday 9:00am-4:30pm, Saturday/Sunday 10:00am-3:00pm.

Admission: FREE

Nestled on the east bank of the Fox River is a museum surrounded by forty acres of woods called Red Oak Nature Center. Choose between several trails with side signage to learn about the sights you see. One trail takes you to "Devils Cave" which is rich in folklore. Done hiking? Stop a while on the new observation deck overlooking the Fox River or explore the nature center. Displays invite "hands-on" participation and lead you to a better understanding of the natural world.

PLUM CREEK NATURE CENTER

27064 Dutton Road (1.25 miles east of IL 1 and I-394 on Goodenow Road, south of Crete) **Beecher** 60401

Phone: (708) 946-2216
www.reconnectwithnature.org/visitor-centers/pcnc

Hours: Tuesday-Saturday 10:00am-4:00pm, Sunday Noon-4:00pm.

Admission: FREE

Nestled among forests, fields, cattail marshes, and a small pond, the Nature Center is the perfect place for discovering the outdoors. It offers something for little children who like to touch feathers and rocks, school children who marvel at the structure of animal skulls, adults who wonder how to attract butterflies in their gardens, and seniors who enjoy watching winter birds at the feeders. A large window provides an observation area for the bird feeding station. Surrounding the bird feeders is a butterfly garden which demonstrates plants that attract a variety of wildlife. Picnicking, hiking, and camping await those looking for summer fun. In winter, enjoy cross-country skiing and ice-skating. Stop by the nature center to rent an inner tube ($1.00/all day with a valid ID) or bring your own sled (no snowboards or sleds with runners) and try sledding on their 30-foot hill. Afterwards, warm up in the Nature Center by the crackling fire. Enjoy a warm cup of coffee while viewing birds at the bird feeding area.

BIG ROCK PLOWING MATCH

Big Rock - *Plowman's Park, Hinkley Road, south of Rte 30. The only event of its kind in the state. This plowing competition began in 1894. Steel-or rubber-wheeled tractors, pedal tractor pull, parade, food and miniature train rides.* **www. bigrockplowingmatch.com** *(mid-September weekend)*

JOHANSEN FARMS

Bolingbrook - *710 W. Boughton Road. www.johansenfarms.com. Hayrides, two-story airslides, train rides (weekdays after 3:00pm), hold baby chicks, Amazing Corn Maze, Hay Tunnel, Goat Mountain, Rabbit hotel, pony rides (Oct. only), Jump in the Giant Castle, Toddlers Jumping Jail, Noah's Ark Challenge, and concessions. Admission. (daily, mid-September thru October)*

BROOKFIELD ZOO

3300 S. Golf Road (I-290 exit 20, follow signs from 1st Avenue)
Brookfield 60513

- Phone: (708) 485-3509 **www.czs.org/czs/Brookfield/Zoo-Home.aspx**
- Hours: Open 365 days a year. Daily 10:00am-5:00pm. Extended hours in summer and on weekends.
- Admission: $16.95 adult, $11.95child (3-11) and senior (65+). Tuesdays & Thursdays are FREE from October thru February. Parking $9.00 per vehicle. Extra $3.00-$5.00 added admission for Dolphin show, Family Zoo, Motor Safari and Butterflies!
- Tours: The zoo offers free Zoo Chats several times each day in several areas. Children and parents learn about animals and the keepers get to tell you how they care for their animals - and also share some funny stories about their work. "Ride all day" on the narrated tram, Motor Safari. One ticket lets you hop on and off at any of four stops. They give you the scoop on each area, especially pointing out where the baby animals are.

The largest zoo in the Chicago area (3000+ animals), Brookfield was the first in America to exhibit animals in natural settings vs. cages. Kids love the Dolphin show and Tropic World. Monkeys of all sorts are hilarious to watch here - this was our favorite exhibit area and nice that it's all-weather indoors. Stingray Bay and Wild Encounters are interactive. Other unique areas are Fragile Kingdom, Seven Seas, Habitat Africa, and The Swamp. Babies are born (even porcupine!) and displayed to the delight of guests (check their website for baby reports). Why are zoo keepers glad the sloth bears are tearing up the place? Heard of animal acupuncture? How about a monkey makeover? There is even an unusual smell in some of the zoo's exhibits - the zoo uses fragrant substances like cinnamon and garlic as part of the enrichment program to keep all of the animals stimulated and active. In the Family Play Zoo, youngsters can dress up and pretend to be animals, veterinarians and zookeepers. They even have face-paint and clever outfits to really let the kids get into it. We even pet an albino rat here - even its tail!

HOLIDAY MAGIC

Brookfield - *Brookfield Zoo. Twinkling lights create a winter wonderland, with fun for all ages, including carolers, ice-craving demonstrations, crafts and games (on weekends). Each night, stroll walkways illuminated by millions of twinkling lights. Enjoy magicians, music, storytellers and photo ops with Children's Zoo animals. Restaurants and gift shops will be open. Admission. (Thanksgiving weekend thru days before, then after, Christmas)*

LONG GROVE CONFECTIONERY COMPANY TOUR

333 Lexington Drive **Buffalo Grove** 60089

┃┃ Phone: (847) 459-3875 **www.longgrove.com/Factory-tours/**
┃┃ Admission: $2.00 per person (Handicapped accessible)
┃┃ Tour days: Weekdays-year 'round. Hours of operation: 10:00am to Noon. Length of tour: about one hour. RESERVATIONS REQUIRED.

IN TOWN: Here in Historic Buffalo Grove, the Grosswiller School House, a nostalgic red schoolhouse reminiscent of the one-room variety that once served the village, was built as the first candy kitchen and retail store of the Long Grove Confectionery. One of the store's unique features is a vintage beveled glass window, which still allows visitors today to view some candy production; mostly notably fresh strawberries being dipped in creamy milk chocolate.

FACTORY TOUR: Gather under the Antique Stained Glass Dome in the 85,000 square foot Long Grove Confectionery to begin your tour of our specialty chocolate kitchen. The tour guide will present a short video on how cacao (ca-cow) is grown and processed into "chocolate". It will also include a brief history of the family-owned business (presented by a grandpa talking to his granddaughter, very effective and endearing). Following the video, guests will see the giant sculpted chocolate on display before entering the walkway to view production and packaging of chocolates. The first thing you'll notice - the strong chocolate scent wafting in the air. They say that workers are always happy here because they get to sample all the time. Highlights are the chocolate painted Monets and watching the ladies hand-decorate seasonal "pops". The best part are the samples! Finally, stop at the factory store where purchases can be made with great discounts. This is really a delightful tour.

CHICAGO PROFESSIONAL SPORTS TEAMS

- **CHICAGO CUBS BASEBALL** - (Wrigley Field, home games - see Listing for Wrigley Field for directions). www.chicagocubs.com. (800) THE-CUBS. The Chicago Cubs' mission is to put the most competitive team on the field, continually reaching toward the goal of a World Series title for the city of Chicago. Off the field the Cubs are dedicated to making a positive impact on Chicago through Cubs Care and the community programs it funds. (April-September)
- **CHICAGO WHITE SOX BASEBALL** - (US Cellular Field, 333 West 35th Street). www.whitesox.com or (312) 742-PLAY. Join the White Sox Kids Club, the official youth fan club of White Sox Baseball. Look for the mascot, South Paw, at the games. (April-September)
- **CHICAGO BEARS FOOTBALL** - (Soldier Field, 1600 S. Lake Shore Drive, just south of the Museum Campus). (847) 615-BEAR or www.chicagobears.com. (September-December)
- **CHICAGO BULLS BASKETBALL** - (United Center, 1901 W. Madison). www.nba.com/bulls. (312) 559-1212 or (312) 455-4000. Meet Benny the Bull and watch his antics and the BullsKidz dancing. (October-April)
- **CHICAGO BLACKHAWKS HOCKEY** - (United Center, 1901 W. Madison). www.chicagoblackhawks.com, (312) 559-1212, (312) 445-4500. Family Nights (kids free with adult ticket). (October-April)
- **CHICAGO FIRE SOCCER** - (Bridgeview Stadium) (312) 559-1212, (888) MLS-FIRE. www.chicago-fire.com. Meet HUMO (Spanish for "Smoke"), a live Dalmatian dog, perform his tricks to entertain the fans. (June-early September)

CHICAGO TROLLEY & WATER TAXI TOURS

- **CHICAGO TROLLEY** - www.coachusa.com/chicagotrolley Hop on, Hop off. Day-long fully narrated tour stops at all of Chicago's top attractions every 15-20 minutes. See the highlights of downtown and lakefront areas including Museum Campus, Magnificent Mile and Navy Pier. Unlimited boarding. Admission: $18-$33 downtown Day Pass. $4-$10 more for 2 day passes.

- **SHORELINE WATER TAXI** - www.shorelinesightseeing.com. (312) 222-9328. For $4-$8 per person, you can taxi to/from the Navy Pier and the Museum complex without having to walk that distance. Another taxi boats between Willis Tower and Navy Pier. They also offer sightseeing tours that only last 30 minutes. Daily summer and border months, weekends only early spring and late fall.

GIORDANO'S
Chicago http://giordanos.com

Throughout town (more than 40 locations- if you're visiting the (Sears) Willis Tower, there's one across the street on Jackson that really captures the aura of the city). Pioneer of the famous stuffed pizza. You have to try this pizza! Be sure to order more than just cheese. Try to order something like their Special or another choice with several fresh ingredients. Pastas, sandwiches and assorted salads, too. Open for lunch and dinner. $

GRANT PARK & BUCKINGHAM FOUNTAIN
(Grant Park at Congress Parkway - up to Millennium Park on Michigan Avenue) www.chicagoparkdistrict.com/parks/grant-park Chicago 60601

Dubbed "Chicago's Front Yard," Grant Park consists of the Museum Campus to the south and Millennium Park to the north. The site of many annual festivals, the park is also home to Buckingham Fountain and many huge sculptures (must see is the "Bean"). The Fountain is modeled after Latona Fountain basin at Versailles in France, but twice its size. During the summer, evening light shows enhance the spectacle of view and rushing water. They also have plentiful Night at the Parks live music events with specialty food vendors. These parks, and the greenery found plentifully on many downtown streets, adds beauty to the swarm of skyscrapers. You'll be surprised how comfortable this big city feels as you wander from site to site!

ART INSTITUTE OF CHICAGO

111 South Michigan Avenue **Chicago** 60603

- Phone: (312) 443-3600 **www.artic.edu**
- Hours: Daily 10:30am-5:00pm. Until 8:00pm on Free Thursdays (Illinois residents only).
- Admission: $25.00 adult, $19.00 senior, child. Children under 14 are FREE. Chicago and Illinois resident discounts available.
- Note: Family Guides are available at admission desk.

The museum is one of the world's leading art museums with a great impressionist and post-impressionist collection of works by Monet, Renoir, Degas, Van Gogh, and others. Other collections include sculpture; photography; textiles; and arms and armor. Kids may really like the Thorne Miniature Rooms and Picture Gallery. The Family Room helps young visitors appreciate art from around the world with interactive computers, videos and games or "touch" art.

ADLER PLANETARIUM & ASTRONOMY MUSEUM

1300 Lake Shore Drive (Museum Campus) **Chicago** 60605

- Phone: (312) 922-STAR **www.adlerplanetarium.org**
- Hours: Monday-Friday 10am-4pm, weekends open half-hour later. Summer hours extended.
- Admission: $8.00-$12.00 (age 4+). Shows extra. Free days September-December (listed online).

The first museum of its kind in the Western Hemisphere has three floors of exhibits on astronomy, space exploration, telescopes and navigation. Best exhibits include the Night Sky @ Hidden Wonders and Planet Explorers adventure playspace. The museum also allows guests to lean back and relax as the Planetarium sky show takes them on a journey into outer space. The Sky Theater and StarRider Theater shows transport visitors to planets, moons, and distant galaxies, and cover the latest topics in space news. They offer a special Sky Show for Kids. Learn about the secrets of giants in space.

CHICAGO PLAYWORKS

60 E. Balbo Drive (just off Michigan Avenue, DePaul's Merle Reskin Theatre) **Chicago** 60605

- Phone: (312) 922-1999 **http://theatreschool.depaul.edu**

K BRIDGEHOUSE & CHICAGO RIVER MUSEUM (cont.)

loors of the bridgehouse to educate visitors on the Chicago
y and value to the area. Learn about natives, explorers and
once lived in what is now skyscraper Chicago. About 100
, the Michigan Avenue bridge lifts to the sky to allow large
through. It's a sight to see (go online for dates/times, usually
. The museum houses the gears and visitors are treated to a
he interworkings of the bridge that is lifted by (2) 100-horse
s. Great physics lesson. Every warm season, a water garden is
rving as a Fish Hotel. An abundance of fish meander to it to

NOBLE HORSE THEATRE

1410 N. Orleans **Chicago** 60610

(312) 266-7878 **www.noblehorsechicago.com**

Dinner performances are 1 hour and 45 minutes. The dinner is
d. The matinees are 70 minutes and there is no meal served. A snack
pen for the matinees. Shows are generally on Fridays and weekends.
sion: $22.00-$35.00 per person. Dinner is optional with evening
nances (extra charge).

castle enhances the mood as you experience the beauty and
elegant dancing horses performing shows like Cinderella or the
he horses perform indoors all year round in this elegant site in
d Town (restored 1871 stables). All the guests are close to the
ery seat provides a clear view of the show.

AMERICAN GIRL PLACE

higan Avenue (just a few feet west of shopping district, Water
Tower Place) **Chicago** 60611

: (877) AG-PLACE **www.americangirlplace.com**

Generally open 10:00am-7:00pm daily, except Thanksgiving and
nas.

sion: $19.00-$23.00 per person for either brunch, lunch, tea or dinner.
uled, reserved meals. Packages available.

Boys tagging along? They loan out Game Boys (when available) to
visitors - FREE. Photo Studio (get you picture put on the cover of AG
zine) and AG Movies behind-the-scenes.

Each season they produce plays for families and young audiences. It may be
an adaptation from favorite children's books (ex. Boxcar Children or Grimm's
Tales). Some are original cultural productions.

FIELD MUSEUM, THE

1400 South Lake Shore Drive (Roosevelt Rd. at Lake Shore Drive)
Chicago 60605

☐ Phone: (312) 922-9410 **www.fieldmuseum.org**
☐ Hours: Daily 9:00am-5:00pm. Open every day except Christmas.
☐ Admission: $18.00 adult, $15.00 senior (65+) or student (w/ ID), $13.00 child
(ages 3-11). $2.00 discount for Chicago residents. Add $7-$12.00 for upgrade
packages (more exhibits). The Field Museum offers 52 days a year when
admission is discounted for all visitors.
☐ Parking lots charge from $8.00-$13.00 per day. On the FREE Trolley route
(Museum Campus stop).
☐ Tours: Free Highlights Tours - Get the inside stories on some of the fascinating
objects on display at the Museum. Monday-Friday: 11:00am & 2:00pm.
☐ Educators: Educator guides for every age and exhibit space:
www.fieldmuseum.org/educators/resources.

Dinosaur buffs will be impressed with "Sue" - the largest, most complete,
and best preserved Tyrannosaurus rex discovered yet, at the Field Museum.
Considered one of the world's greatest natural history museums, they offer
a variety of permanent exhibit spaces. Inside, Ancient Egypt explores two
of the original chambers from a real tomb; experience the rich culture of the
Pawnee people of the central Plains in the Pawnee Earth Lodge; Traveling
the Pacific is where you enter a whole new world - a vessel navigating the
ocean swells; or, the Laboratory features research visible to the public while
experts study artifacts from the Pacific Ocean island regions. Kids get to be a
scientist for the day in Playlab. Parents, you'll enjoy taking your kids through
the many rooms full of taxidermied animals behind glass - looking like they
did in museums when we were kids. We even found skeletons of our beloved
guinea pigs.

SHEDD AQUARIUM / OCEANARIUM

1200 S. Lake Shore Drive Chicago 60605

- Phone: (312) 939-2438 **www.sheddaquarium.org**
- Hours: Daily 9:00am-5:00pm. Open later summer holidays and weekends.
- Admission: $21.95-$30.95 general admission (age 3+). Add $5.00 per person for the Aquatic show. Discount Days occur about 50 days/year.
- FREEBIES: Games & Activities: **www.sheddaquarium.org/Learning-Experiences/Fun-Games/**

The Shedd offers the world's largest indoor collection of aquatic mammals, reptiles, amphibians, invertebrates and fish. Wild Reef - Sharks at Shedd totaling more than 750,000 gallons of water, this exhibit allows guests to have an intimate encounter with more than 30 sharks, one of the largest and most diverse shark exhibits in North America, and a coral reef exhibit housing more than 500 aquatic species demonstrating the crucial role coral reefs play in the health of oceans. Guests can watch one of the Aquarium's daily feedings in the Caribbean Reef exhibit, where a diver feeds the fish by hand and describes their different species. Amazon Rising takes guests on a journey through time in the Amazon River. Also, the museum's magnificent Oceanarium is the world's largest marine mammal pavilion. The Oceanarium is home to Beluga whales, dolphins, Alaskan sea otters, seals and penguins in habitats replicating their natural environments. The Dolphin and Beluga whale "shows" are a must see! Although they were educating (snuck it in!), these shows are very entertaining and the mammals were so amusing!

FEDERAL RESERVE BANK OF CHICAGO

230 S. LaSalle Street Chicago 60606

- Phone: (312) 322-2400 **www.chicagofed.org/webpages/education/money_museum/index**
- Hours: Monday-Friday 8:30am-5:00pm. Closed major holidays.
- Admission: FREE.

Visit the Chicago Feds Visitors Center and see what a million dollars looks like. You can try your skill at detecting counterfeits. Learn how money and banking have evolved in the United States or take the 30-minute guided tours at 1:00pm each weekday.

SKYDECK

233 W. Wacker Drive (bounded by
Street, Jackson Entrance of

- Phone: (312) 875-9696 **www.the**
- Hours: Daily 10:00am-10:00pm (M
  (October-April). Last ticket sold on
- Admission: $19.50 adult, $12.50 c
  $6.00.
- Educators: Teachers Guide: **http:/
  schoolyouth-groups/teachers-g
  for-kids/**

Get up here and view the world! Breat
America's tallest building (1,450 fe
Tower consists of black aluminum ar
steel frame. The skydeck, which was r
the 103rd floor and includes the "Reac
presentation movie. Really, this is an
exhibits both share highlights of histor
They even have "Knee-high" peep hol
learn about each side of the tower and

THE LEDGE: It's a walk on the high si
step into glass enclosures that extend 4
their feet in dizziness-inducing splendc
with an inch and a half of glass betweer
in outcroppings on the west side of the V
like they're floating over the city belov
decks at the Grand Canyon and Toronto

This might be a good place to start your
a strong interest in history.

MCCORMICK BRIDGEHO
MUSE

376 N. Michigan Avenue (Michigan

- Phone: (312) 977-0227 **www.bridge**
- Hours: Thursday-Monday 10:00am-5
- Admission: $5.00 (age 5+).

MCCORMIC

Utilizes five
River's histo
wildlife that
times per ye
boats passag
late evening
rare look at
power engin
replenished s
"vacation."

- Phon
- Hours
  cater
  bar is
- Admi
  perfo

The Theatre
grace of the
Nutcracker.
Chicago's O
horses and e

835 N. Mi

- Phor
- Hour
  Chris
- Adm
  Sche
- Note
  male
  Mag

For

A destination that celebrates everything that's great about being a girl. Dine in the café, see a live musical in the theater, have your doll's hair styled in the doll hair salon, or browse the many entertaining displays and stores about dolls and places/times in history. This is a sweet, feminine place where girls can be girls (moms, too) as they immerse themselves in the art of female-ess" for several hours.

• CAFÉ: A fun and fanciful place for girls and their families to dine with their dolls (doll-sized Treat Seat) in a whimsical setting. The café serves family-friendly full meals (brunch, lunch, dinner) or afternoon tea daily. Start with warm cinnamon buns and end with Chocolate Mousse Flowerpot and cakes/cookie. Everything is mildly flavored. They have party favors you get to take home as a souvenir. Conversation starters at each table prompt girls and their guests to share stories.

• DOLL HAIR SALON: Let their specially trained stylists give your doll a new hairdo. $10.00-$20.00. Watch them brush out the "rats" and style the doll's hair into a silky, shiny "do".

BUBBA GUMP SHRIMP COMPANY

Chicago - *700 E. Grand Avenue, Navy Pier area. 60611 www.bubbagump.com. (312) 252-GUMP. Step into the world of Forrest Gump and enjoy barbeque ribs, fish and chips, and lots of shrimp! Casual, fun atmosphere with down-home southern bayou cookin'. Order the Hush Pups as an appetizer and finish your meal with the Warm, Giant Chocolate Chip Cookie dessert (share as a family). Order anything Cajun or with shrimp as an entrée. See how many "words of wisdom" you can catch while viewing Forrest Gump movie or looking for sayings around the themed restaurant. Kids menu is around $5.00. Daily lunch and dinner. $$*

CHICAGO CHILDREN'S MUSEUM
700 East Grand Avenue at Navy Pier **Chicago** 60611

⑂ Phone: (312) 527-1000 **www.chicagochildrensmuseum.org**
⑂ Hours: Sunday - Wednesday & Friday: 10:00am-5:00pm; Thursday: 10:00am-8:00pm. Extended summer weekend hours.
⑂ Admission: $13.00-$14.00 per person. Kraft Free Thursday nights and Target Free First Sundays - look on website for details. Teachers, police officers, firefighters, veterans and active military receive free admission every day.

CHICAGO CHILDREN'S MUSEUM (cont.)

    Note: Kids on the Fly, a satellite Children's Museum has been created at O'Hare International Airport to entertain and educate children during layovers or anytime they are waiting at the airport. Educators: Activities & Vocab guides: **www.chicagochildrensmuseum.org/index.php/education/resources-activities**

This museum is a "don't miss" destination for families with children. "Hands-on" is the logo and the logic for this museum. Children can explore the Climbing Schooner; take the Flying Machine Challenge in The Tinkering Lab (make your wings and test them on the flight tower); become junior paleontologists on a Dinosaur Expedition; PlaySpace and WaterWays; and KidsTown urban neighborhood playground. Play it Safe has enticing displays like the Bathroom Theatre. Do you remember your first crawl? Check out Treehouse Trails for preschoolers. We liked the clean, well-maintained exhibit spaces and the diversity of each station - you can even play giant chess and checkers here.

360 CHICAGO (HANCOCK OBSERVATORY)

875 North Michigan Avenue (John Hancock Center) **Chicago** 60611

    Phone: (888) 875-VIEW **www.360chicago.com**
    Hours: Daily 9:00am-11:00pm.
    Admission: $19.00 adult, $13.00 youth (3-11). Tilt: add $7.00.
    Note: Educators can find Activity Sheets - **www.360chicago.com/educators/**

A 39-second elevator ride takes you to the 94th floor observatory of the John Hancock Center for a panoramic view of Chicago, Lake Michigan, and up to four surrounding states. The large panel windows allow a tremendous view of the city. We also loved the Sky Walk area - a screened in outdoor walk where you can see and hear the city. Or TILT outward 1,000 feet above The Magnificent Mile! Count how many roof-top pools you see. Includes two innovative, interactive features: Windows of Chicago and Soundscope (extra $1.00 fee) using virtual reality technology and virtual audio experience. Finally, pose as a Big John construction worker or window washer with amusing trick photography backgrounds and props - go ahead, ham it up! This is the best tower for views.

NAVY PIER

600 East Grand Avenue (off Lakeshore Drive) **Chicago** 60611

|| Phone: (312) 595-PIER **www.navypier.com**
|| Admission: To individual activities, FREE to roam around.
|| Note: Fireworks displays take place every Wednesday and Saturday from Memorial Day to Labor Day.

Navy Pier, a mile-long complex of shops and restaurants, juts into Lake Michigan near the south end of the Magnificent Mile. With an old-fashioned Ferris wheel spinning overhead, the massive old military dock is buzzing all year long with concerts, fireworks and special events. The pier is home to the Chicago Children's Museum and many sightseeing boat docks. You can also roam the children's indoor maze of mirrors, attend an IMAX film, or ride an old-style "swing" carousel. Even kids enjoy the Stained Glass walk-thru museum admiring the art of painted or mosaic glassworks for FREE. You can spend hours here - grab a treat and walk and play in the old-fashioned carnival atmosphere.

CHICAGO INTERNATIONAL TOY AND GAME FAIR

Chicago - *Navy Pier. www.chitag.com. One of the only shows in the Western Hemisphere to provide consumers with the opportunity to preview, play and purchase the widest selection of toys and games offered directly by manufacturers before the fourth quarter when the hot new products are introduced. (Labor Day Weekend)*

WINTER WONDERFEST

Chicago - *Navy Pier. Features sparkling lights, hundreds of decorated trees, and Santa Claus with his toy-making elves. Activities will include an indoor ice skating rink, a musical carousel, a unique model train display and entertainment. FREE, admittance to activities require purchase of a wristband. (mid-December through day after New Years)*

O' LEARY'S CHICAGO FIRE TRUCK TOURS

505 N. Michigan Avenue **Chicago** 60611

|| Phone: (312) 287-6565 **www.olearysfiretours.com**
|| Admission: 90-minute tours run $20-$25.00 adult, and $10-$15.00 child. Firework night tours are the higher price because of extra stop at Navy Pier. Scheduled Summer & Fall. Groups only Winter & Spring. You may ask for your family to be part of another groups tour that has unpaid space.

Take a 1965 Mac Pumper (or another old model) real fire engine truck tour with REAL firemen! What a great way to learn about the sites and the history behind the great Chicago Fire - stories from firemen who know the scoop. At one stop, you can actually stand on the spot where Mrs. O'Leary's infamous "Betsy the cow" accidentally tipped over the lantern. Besides the many views of great architectural buildings, you'll pass several engine houses (even the oldest one in Chicago). Occasionally, the driver will blow one of many sirens he has on board. You'll learn about fire safety advancements, too. And, how the fire pole and Fire Safety Week initiated at the Chicago fire department. What a unique and special tour!

SHERATON CHICAGO HOTEL & TOWERS

Chicago - 301 E. North Water Street (& Columbus Street) 60611. Gorgeous view of Navy Pier, Lake Michigan and the Chicago River! Indoor pool and very puffy beds to come back to each evening. Several restaurants are on the property and Walgreens is across the parking lot. This location is within blocks of the Magnificent Mile and Navy Pier. Just a trolley or water taxi from the (Sears) Willis Tower and the Museum Campus. Great central location to base from. www.sheratonchicago.com. (312) 464-1000. $$$ - Specials $115.

SPIRIT OF CHICAGO CRUISE

600 E. Grand Street (docks at Navy Pier) Chicago 60611

Phone: (312) 836-7899 or (866) 211-3804 www.spiritofchicago.com

Admission: Highly recommended for families, the Lunch Cruise rates from $30.00-$50.00 per person. Daily Noon-2:00pm departures. Walk ups welcome but reservations are strongly recommended.

The luxurious way to view Chicago's skyline on city's most entertaining cruise ship. Lunch, brunch and sunset cruises. They have a DJ playing oldies, in between sightseeing pointers and live entertainment. Their singers and dancers put on a Celebration Show. Diners can dance, too. Get your "groove on" or head up the stairs and out on the deck. By the way, the food (chicken, beef and fish) is very good. This was one of the best lunch boat cruises we've done!

WRIGLEY FIELD TOURS

1060 W. Addison Street (Lake Shore Drive to Irving Park Rd. Head west to Clark. Turn left (south). Wrigley Field is ahead on the left (east) **Chicago** 60613

Phone: (773) 404-CUBS
http://chicago.cubs.mlb.com/chc/ballpark/wrigley_field_tours.jsp
Admission: Tickets are $25 per person.
Tours: Limited to 46 people per tour. Tours are scheduled every half-hour, beginning at 10:00am with the last tour scheduled for 4:30pm on each date. Basically offered 14 days/month. Tours do sell out. To ensure your tour, tickets must be purchased in advance.
Note: The Cubs Gift shop will be open during tours. Personal cameras and video cameras are welcome. If traffic is heavy on Lake Shore Drive, take Broadway or Clark to Addison.

Each 90-minute tour provides an insider's look at 90 years of history in this legendary ballpark. Tour stops include: Cubs Clubhouse, Press Box, Visitors Clubhouse, Bleachers, Dugouts, Playing Field, And Mezzanine Suites. The Wrigley Field bleachers and scoreboard were constructed in 1937 when the outfield area was renovated to provide improved and expanded seating...the original scoreboard remains intact...the score-by-innings and the pitchers' numbers are changed by hand. One of the traditions of Wrigley Field is the flying of a flag bearing a "W" or an "L" atop the scoreboard after a game ... a white flag with a blue "W" indicates a victory; a blue flag with a white "L" denotes a loss. Most importantly, this is a behind-the-scenes look at the famous history of the oldest MLB ball field.

CHICAGO HISTORY MUSEUM

1601 N Clark Street (North Avenue and Clark Street) **Chicago** 60614

Phone: (312) 642-4600 **www.chicagohistory.org**
Hours: Monday-Saturday 9:30am-4:30pm, Sunday Noon-5:00pm.
Admission: $14.00 adult, $12.00 senior (65+) and student (13-22), FREE for children 12 and under. Admission includes audio tour. Illinois resident discount days each month offer free admission.
FREEBIES: online games: **www.chicagohistory.org/mychicago/03games.html**. Educators: My Chicago activities: **www.chicagohistory.org/education/resources**

The Chicago Historical Society is the oldest cultural institution and keeper of Chicago memories. Visit the museum to trace Chicago's growth from wilderness outpost to the architectural, cultural and social mecca of the midwest. Through artifacts, photographs, paintings and video presentations, the museum tells the story of this town using Hands-on History Galleries with "please touch" artifacts; an exhibit on the Great Chicago Fire; and an American History wing that ties in U.S. history with Chicago. In Sensing Chicago kids are invited to participate by riding a high-wheel bicycle down a wood-paved street, follow the Great Chicago Fire, catch a fly ball at Comiskey Park, use a Smell Map and even be a Chicago-style hot dog.

LINCOLN PARK ZOO

2200 N. Cannon Drive (Lake Shore Dr. and Fullerton Pkwy.) **Chicago** 60614

- Phone: (312) 742-2000 zoo or (312) 742-4838 **www.lpzoo.org**
- Hours: Daily 10:00am-5:00pm.
- Admission: FREE. Parking $20.00 plus.
- Educators: **http://lpzoo.org/pdf/education/curriculumguide.pdf**

One of the last free zoos in the country. Where else can you see so many animals right in the center of a city? Thousands of exotic and endangered species fill animal houses, habitats, pools and exhibits. Visit the African Journey exhibit featuring elephants, rhinos, giraffes, wild dogs and hissing cockroaches. Other favorites are the penguins and the primates. The Children's Zoo includes live animal presentations, a petting zoo, a zoo nursery, and a hands-on learning center for kids. Families will get a taste of country life at the Farm-in-the-Zoo, a model Midwest farm in the heart of the city or the nature boardwalk around the pond at the southern end of the zoo.

ZOOLIGHTS

Chicago - *Lincoln Park Zoo. Zoolights is a free event that features more than one million holiday lights, a spectacular water laser show, live ice carving, Santa's workshop and of course, zoo animals. FREE. (weekend after Thanksgiving through first week of January)*

NOTEBAERT NATURE MUSEUM

2430 North Cannon Drive, Lincoln Park (I-90 to northwest corner of Fullerton Parkway and Cannon Drive in Lincoln Park) **Chicago** 60614

Phone: (773) 755-5100 **www.naturemuseum.org**

Hours: Weekdays 9:00am-5:00pm, Weekends 10:00am-5:00pm. Closed on major winter holidays only.

Admission: $9.00 adult, $7.00 senior (60+) or student w/ID, $6.00 child (3-12). Thursdays – FREE.

Set along the lakefront in Lincoln Park, this indoor and outdoor museum invites guests to reconnect with nature. This state-of-the-art museum explores the biodiversity of the Midwest through interactive exhibits. From the Great Lakes to the prairies - natural to the urban areas. Hands-on Habitat: This engaging two-story hands-on, body-on exhibit takes budding naturalists (age 3 to 7) on an exploration of the secret world of animal homes. Examine your relationship with nature and the impact humans have on the environment in the Butterfly Haven, River works, Marsh and Wilderness.

GARFIELD PARK CONSERVATORY

300 North Central Park Avenue (I-290 exit at Independence Blvd (Exit 26A), head north. Turn east (right) onto Washington Blvd. Turn left (north) onto Central Park (3600W) **Chicago** 60624

Phone: (312) 746-5100 **www.garfieldconservatory.org**

Hours: Daily 9:00am - 5:00pm, Wednesdays till 8:00pm.

Admission: FREE. Free Parking is just south of the Conservatory's main entrance.

Visit the Children's Garden, which is open during all conservatory hours, or visit during weekend Discovery Area hours, and let the staff introduce you to the giant soil table. Inside the Garden, a gigantic vine beckons children to trace it from root to blossom, while a 7-foot-tall seed waits to be climbed. The adventurous can hunt for some of the most unusual specimens found in the Garfield Park Conservatory (some of which are included on their downloadable Eye Spy Conservatory Hunt). Young explorers will encounter the Sensitive Plant, so shy that it cringes when touched, and the Balsa Tree, which emits a hollow sound when the trunk is tapped. Up on the mezzanine, children can befriend a larger-than-life bee and assist it in pollinating the largest flower in the room before taking a ride down the twirling stem of a green slide. Young toddlers and babies are invited to explore the colors and textures of soft-form blocks and play rings in the special permanent Crawling Area, and can slip down their own miniature green slide. Jungle climate and a botanical garden under glass.

ELI'S CHEESECAKE WORLD

6701 West Forest Preserve Drive (follow website directions, corner of
Montrose) **Chicago** 60634

- Phone: (800) ELI-CAKE **www.elicheesecake.com/tours.aspx**
- Hours: Monday-Friday 8:00am-6:00pm, Saturday 9:00am-5:00pm, Sunday 11:00am-5:00pm.
- Tours: Tasting & Traditions experience is offered daily at 1 PM in the cafe. This experience is a PowerPoint and video presentation of the history of the company and how they make cheesecake. At the conclusion you sample a selection of delicious desserts. Price: FREE. Closed on most holidays. Please call ahead (773) 308-7000 or check website for additional dates. Space is limited. Guests will be taken on a first come first serve basis. This presentation takes approximately 30-45 minutes. Special educational tours available for school and scout groups.
- Note: Afterwards, shop for Sweet Imperfections discounted product in the café store or enjoy lunch at the bakery cafe offering soups and sandwiches.

Eli's huge cheesecake bakery, retail store and dessert café is the only place where you can see Chicago's favorite dessert being made. Begin a tour watching an informative slide show that reviews all the cake-making stations. Did you know they bake an average of 30 new styles of cheesecake each year (some are not for retail, but wholesale customers). We discovered their number one ingredient is cream cheese - their most expensive ingredient is vanilla from overseas. Watch pans filled with cookie-crust bottoms and topped with cake batter travel through a 70-foot-long baking tunnel (look at all those cakes!). The desserts then spiral slowly up a dizzying two-story tower to give them time to cool (it looks like a spiral parking lot). The cakes are then decorated by hand. Tiramisu cakes are dunked in giant coffee vats. Can you believe those workers do most everything by hand? Oh does it smell good in there!

CHEESECAKE FESTIVAL

Chicago - *Eli's Cheesecake World, During this annual festival, enjoy an entire weekend of cheesecake samples, cooking demos, a cheesecake eating contest, live performances and games. FREE. (first weekend in August)*

MUSEUM OF SCIENCE AND INDUSTRY (MSI)

5700 South Lake Shore Drive (57th St. & Lake Shore Dr.) **Chicago** 60637

- Phone: (773) 684-1414 **www.msichicago.org**
- Hours: Monday-Friday 9:30am to 4:00pm. Extended hours until 5:30pm on weekends & school break days.
- Admission: $18.00 adult, $17.00 senior (65+), $11.00 child (3-11). Discounts for residents. Special exhibits, Omnimax, and on-board submarine extra fee. Parking $16.00. Fifty or more FREE Days are offered each year - list online.
- Educators: Classroom activities: **www.msichicago.org/education/educator-resources/classroom-activities/**.

This museum invites children to push buttons and pull levers on its exhibits which explore contemporary science and technology. Families can walk through a beating heart, tour a captured German submarine, and visit a subterranean coal mine. The Submarine exhibition features audio narratives from war veterans as well as the discovery of two original periscopes, which were hidden beneath one of the Navy's most secret research facilities. Let your imagination run wild at the museum's Idea Factory, Feel the physics of tornados and avalanches, or see how toys are made. In the Space Center, visitors can blast off in a simulated space shuttle ride and view the Apollo 8 spacecraft. Before you leave peak inside the Fairy Castle or gaze at the world's largest pinball machine.

CHRISTMAS AROUND THE WORLD & HOLIDAY OF LIGHT

Chicago - *Museum of Science & Industry. Showcases more than 50 trees in an enchanted forest, decorated by Chicago's ethnic communities with traditional ornaments. Holiday of Light explores holiday traditions that celebrate light in this season of the year. Workshops and performances including a reading of the classic holiday tale, The Polar Express. (weekend before Thanksgiving through the first full weekend in January)*

ORIENTAL INSTITUTE MUSEUM, THE

University of Chicago, 1155 East 58th Street **Chicago** 60637

- Phone: (773) 702-9514 **www.oi.uchicago.edu**
- Hours: Tuesday-Sunday 10:00am-6:00pm. Open until 8:00pm on Wednesdays.
- Admission: FREE. Suggested Donation: $10.00 for adults, $5.00 for children under 12.

FREEBIES: Kids Corner archeology games: **http://oi.uchicago.edu/OI/MUS/ ED/kids.html**. Educators: for $5.00, you can access self-guided audio tours; especially the Kid's Tour of Ancient Egypt.

The Oriental Institute Museum is a showcase of the history, art and archaeology of the ancient Near East. The galleries display artifacts that illustrate the power of these ancient civilizations, including sculptural representations of tributes demanded by kings of ancient empires, and some sources of continual fascination, such as a fragment of the Dead Sea Scrolls - one of the few examples in the United States. Visitors begin in Assyria, move across Anatolia and down the Mediterranean coast to the land of ancient Israel. In Mesopotamia: A wealth of objects from what may be the world's first urban civilization are displayed, including pottery, clay tables, stone sculptures, and vessels made of luxurious stones and metals. It includes exhibits explaining how scholars from the Oriental Institute have conducted excavations and research since the end of the nineteenth century until today, plus two computer kiosks that currently house interactive programs for visiting families. Artifacts from Persia, Egypt and Iraq, too.

CHICAGO KIDS COMPANY

5900 W. Belmont / 11th & Western (St. Patrick's Performing Arts Centre-N/ Beverly Arts Center - S) **Chicago** 60641

Phone: (773) 205-9600 **www.ChicagoKidsCompany.com**
Showtimes: Weekdays at 10:30am, Weekends at 1:00pm.
Admission: $12.00 per person.

Celebrating 15 years of Fairy Tale Fun, this company performs at a North Side and South Side location. Productions like fables of the Tortoise and the Hare or Little Red Riding Hood are done with comical costumes and scenery for the kids ages 2 to 12 to enjoy.

TASTE OF CHICAGO

Chicago - Grant Park. What began as a one-day event on Michigan Avenue that featured a few dozen restaurants has grown to a multi-faceted, multi-day event highlighting more than 65 restaurants every year. Festival fans can watch food prep by Chefs from around the world and around Chicago – then, receive a copy of the recipes to take home to try out new cooking ideas. Local bands of every musical genre can be heard. Family Village located at the south end of Taste right next to the Water

Flume and the Ferris Wheel. Here, kids have their own entertainment stage and crafts to do. FREE www.tasteofchicago.us (five days early July, after July 4th)

CHICAGO AIR AND WATER SHOW

Chicago - *Along the lakefront centered at North Avenue Beach. The oldest and largest free admission air exhibition of its kind in the United States, featuring civilian and military aircraft and watercraft. FREE* **www.chicagoairandwatershow.us** *(third weekend in August)*

MCDONALD'S #1 STORE MUSEUM

400 N. Lee Street (Des Plaines exit towards downtown off I-194 toll road)
Des Plaines 60016

- Phone: (847) 297-5022
- Hours: Open Seasonally (Memorial Day to Labor Day). Call for hours.
- Admission: FREE
- Note: An operating McDonald's restaurant is located across the street from the museum.

McDonald's #1 Store Museum is a recreation of the first McDonald's Restaurant opened in Des Plaines, Illinois by McDonald's Corporation founder, Ray Kroc, on April 15, 1955. The original red and white tiled restaurant building featuring the Golden Arches underwent several remodels through the years and was finally torn down in 1984. The present facility was built according to the original blueprints with some modifications to accommodate Museum visitors and staff. The "Speedee" road sign is original. The customer service and food preparation areas contain original equipment used in the days when fresh potatoes were peeled, sliced, blanched and fried; milkshake mix and syrup were whipped up on the Multi-mixers; Coca-Cola® and root beer were drawn from a barrel, and orangeade from the orange bowl. The all male crew is represented by mannequins dressed in the 1955 uniform - dark trousers, white shirts, aprons and paper hats. The basement features a historical display of photos, memos, early advertising, memorabilia, and a short video presentation. Because the museum is hardly ever open to go inside, just a quick walk around, peering in the windows, may be your closest view of the original setup.

CHILDREN'S THEATRE OF ELGIN

1700 Spartan Drive, VPAC 141A (Hemmons Cultural Center
performance hall) **Elgin** 60123

Phone: (847) 214-7152 www.cteelgin.com

Their mission is to provide high quality theatrical experiences for children and young adults...by children and young adults. They encourage family support and participation in theatre with familiar productions like Sleeping Beauty and Cinderella. Most performances are $10.00 admission, making live theatre affordable and accessible.

ELGIN PUBLIC MUSEUM

225 Grand Boulevard (Lords Park area) **Elgin** 60123

Phone: (847) 741-6655 www.elginpublicmuseum.org

Hours: Tuesday-Sunday Noon-4:00pm (summers). Weekends only (rest of year).

Admission: $1.00-$2.00.

This 1907 building is the oldest building in the state built as a museum and still serving as a museum. Its exhibits focus on natural history and anthropology with highlights of TyRex, fossils, Ice Age and Native Americans. You will also learn the process of fossilization and view a fossil of the Tully Monster, the state fossil. A discovery room allows for hands-on learning and they have weekly programs for kids and groups. Puppet theater, puzzles, blocks, books, microscope, musical instruments from around the world, and lots of hands on objects from furs and antlers to starfish and turtle shells can be found in the Discovery Room. Lords Park is the 120-acre park, adjoining, and host to several festivals (Bubblefest, Native American Fest) and Bison Feedings.

ELGIN HISTORICAL MUSEUM HOLIDAY TEA

Elgin - *360 Park Street. In the permanent exhibit rooms, children can get behind the wheel of a reproduction road race car or have their picture taken with Ralph Mulford, winner of the first road race held in 1910. The Watch Factory room features a wall mural of the clock face that once graced the watch factory tower and the 13th watch produced on the famed assembly line. Visitors are invited to view a 6-minute introductory video, treats and holiday cheer.* **www.elginhistory.org**. *Admission. (first Saturday in December)*

PIRATE'S COVE THEME PARK

999 Leicester Road (I-290 (IL-53): exit at Exit 4, Biesterfield Road, and head east 1/2 mile to Leicester Road and turn right) **Elk Grove Village** 60007

    Phone: (847) 437-9494 **www.elkgroveparks.org/pirates_Cove/**
    Hours: Monday-Saturday 10:00am-4:00pm (mid-June thru mid-August). Reduced hours Sundays/ Holidays and pre-post season.
    Admission: $9.00-$11.00 child. Adults get in FREE.

Take a train ride through the property on Safari Express. (Parents can ride, too). In the Castle of Camelot, children can climb through a maze of tunnels, nets, tires, and tubes ... or take a ride down the back of Misty, The Smoking Breathing Dragon. Scale the Smugglers Crag, Pirate's Coves 20-foot high climbing wall. The wall is designed with different skill levels in mind. The Eureka Train Ride directs you around a train track, through a dark tunnel, and past the old Eureka Mine. Paddle Boats take you through Pebble Pond, where you and your friends can ride and splash. There's also a carousel and an authentic 18th Century Pirate Ship - perfect for picnicking or just taking a gander at the Theme Park.

GROSSE POINT LIGHTHOUSE

2601 Sheridan Road (I-94 to the Old Orchard exit turning East to Crawford Avenue then North to Central St. & East to Sheridan Rd.) **Evanston** 60201

    Phone: (847) 328-6961 **www.grossepointlighthouse.net**
    Admission: $6.00 adult, $3.00 child (8-12). To go into the lighthouse tower, you must have a reservation and you must be at least 8 years old. You must also be able to hoist yourself up onto the final platform to reach the very top. School groups tours do not allow for the tower climb.
    Tours: Saturday and Sunday afternoons at 2:00pm, 3:00pm or 4:00pm (June - September). Grosse Point Lighthouse is not open on holiday weekends.
    Note: Evanston Beaches - five beaches (Clark St, Greenwood St, South Blvd, Lee St, and Central Street) with bike paths, swimming, boating, picnicking and tennis along Lake Michigan. www.cityofevanston.org.

Grosse Point Lighthouse was built by the United States Government in 1873 as the lead lighthouse marking the approach to Chicago after several shipwrecks demonstrated its need. While the grounds around the lighthouse are open on a daily basis, tours of the keepers' quarters museum are open only summer weekends.

As part of the tour, visitors get a chance to climb the 141-steps to the top of the light tower for a panoramic view of the Lake Michigan shore and Chicago's soaring skyline. Evanston Beach is just beyond the lighthouse and a popular spot. You may have trouble finding parking nearby on summer weekends.

FOX VALLEY FOLK MUSIC AND STORYTELLING FESTIVAL

Geneva - *Downtown. www.foxvalleyfolk.com. A barn dance, storytelling, hands-on music, a children's area, food and more than 30 acts. Admission (age 13+). (Labor Day weekend)*

WILLOWBROOK WILDLIFE CENTER

525 South Park Blvd (east side of Park Blvd. Across from College of DuPage, 1 mile south of Rte. 36, 1 mile north of Rte. 56) **Glen Ellyn** 60137

☐ Phone: (630) 942-6200 **www.willowbrookwildlife.com**

☐ Hours: Daily, except major holidays 9:00am-5:00pm. Winter hours end at 4:00pm.

When you visit the main building at Willowbrook Wildlife Center, you will be able to view close up over 30 native species of wild animals. Windows provide a view of the Center's kitchen and nursery where baby animals are cared for and fed during spring and summer. Children and adults will enjoy discovering an indoor museum where all the exhibits can be touched. Large permanently disabled animals are displayed outdoors along the nature trail including a golden eagle, bald eagle, hawks, owls, raccoons and foxes. The paved trail is open year-round.

CHICAGO BOTANIC GARDEN

1000 Lake Cook Road (I-94) and U.S. Route 41. Exit at Lake Cook Road and travel 1/2 mile east to the Garden) **Glencoe** 60022

☐ Phone: (847) 835-5440 **www.chicagobotanic.org**

☐ Hours: Daily 8:00am-sunset.

☐ Admission: FREE. Parking fee $25.00 per vehicle.

☐ Tours: The Grand Tram Tour is a tram tour around the perimeter of the Garden that provides an overview of all areas. Trams are wheelchair-accessible. (extra $3.00-$5.00).

The Garden's 385 acres are uniquely situated on nine islands surrounded by 81 acres of lakes, 23 gardens and three native habitats. Stroll or take a tram through the fragrant rose garden, the sensory garden and the stunning three-island Japanese garden. A walking and biking trail borders the gardens. To keep kids interested, visit during Wonderland Express or Walks, Trick or Treat or family camps.

KOHL'S CHILDREN'S MUSEUM

2100 Patriot Blvd (intersection of Patriot Boulevard and West Lake Avenue on The Glen in Glenview) **Glenview** 60026

- Phone: (847) 832-6600 **www.kohlschildrensmuseum.org**
- Hours: Monday-Saturday 9:30am-5:00pm, Sunday Noon-5:00pm. Closed Monday afternoons during school year.
- Admission: $8.50 adult and child. $1.00 discount for seniors.

This children's museum offers a smaller museum for kids ages 2 to 10 to easily manage. What you'll notice at each space is the interaction between kids trying to make something work together. For example, share brushes and paint as you design Adventures in Art or race cars in the Car Care raceway. Girls may gravitate to Doll Day Care but everybody is counting and experimenting in City on the Move, Hands on House, Music Makers, and Dominick's grocery store. Powered by Nature and Waterworks are really just giant science. There is such an emphasis on teamwork, one exhibit is even called Cooperation Station. Outside is a 2-acre nature park to get the willies out.

SIX FLAGS GREAT AMERICA & HURRICANE HARBOR

1 Great America Pkwy (I-94 and Grand Avenue, IL 132 east) **Gurnee** 60031

- Phone: (847) 249-INFO **www.sixflags.com/greatAmerica/index.aspx**
- Hours: Generally the park opens at 10:00am and closes between 8:00-10:00pm summers. Water park hours are 11:00am-7:00pm (Memorial Day weekend - Labor Day weekend only). Spring and Fall weekends only, closing at dusk. Fridays in October are 5:00-11:00pm only.
- Admission: Generally $47.00 per person (age 4+) if purchased online. Admission to add waterpark is $7.00 more. Discounts and season passes available. Parking is $20.00.

SIX FLAGS GREAT AMERICA & HURRICANE HARBOR (cont.)

Six Flags Great America boasts 13 world class coasters, exciting shows spread throughout the day (relax and cool off) and over 100 rides or attractions. Hurricane Harbor is a lush, tropical setting featuring 25 water slides, the world's largest interactive water playground, a massive wave pool, and a ½ mile long adventure river.

HILTON GARDEN INN HOFFMAN ESTATES

Hoffman Estates - *2425 Barrington Road (I-90 exit Barrington Rd). 60195. The hotel offers comfortable, spacious guest rooms, heated indoor pool and whirlpool, and a refrigerator/microwave in every room. Great location to base from for shopping/ dining at Woodfield Mall, Medieval Times, Nature Centers, waterparks and the zoo. Rooms start at $149. (847) 277-7889 or* **www.hoffmanestates.gardeninn.com**.

SPRING BROOK NATURE CENTER

130 Forest Avenue (behind the Itasca Library and Water Park at Catalpa Avenue and Irving Park Road) **Itasca** 60143

- ☐ Phone: (630) 773-2239 **www.itasca.com/index.aspx?NID=461**
- ☐ Hours: Nature Center Monday-Friday 2pm-7pm, Sat/Sun 11am-5pm (summer). Weekends (rest of year). Grounds open sunrise to sunset year round. Admission: FREE

Park at the Water Park and follow the path south across the bridge to the red barn. Visit their raptor aviary (bald eagles and barn owls) and Visitor Center with an aquarium and interactive displays. Over two miles of trails provide hiking opportunities through a marsh, prairie, woodland and arboretum.

JOLIET AREA HISTORICAL MUSEUM

204 N. Ottawa Street (I-55 exit Rte. 52 east on Jefferson to downtown. Over the Des Plaines Bridge, turn left on Joliet Street to Ottawa) **Joliet** 60432

- ☐ Phone: (815) 722-7003 **www.jolietmuseum.org**
- ☐ Hours: Tuesday-Saturday 10:00am-5:00pm, Sunday Noon-5:00pm. Closed on Mondays, except for School Holidays.
- ☐ Admission: $6.00 adult, $5.00 senior (60+) and $4.00 student w/ ID, $3.00 youth (4-17). Several FREE Days offered each year.
- ☐ Note: Free parking is available in the Museum parking lot located 1 block north of the Museum at the corner of Ottawa and Webster Streets. During your visit stop in the Route 66 Welcome Center.

Begin with a short orientation video. Walk through a life-size replica depicting the building of the historic Illinois Michigan Canal. Stroll down a turn-of-the-century street past store fronts. Take in a silent film at the Rialto Theatre (kids think this is hilarious). Take a virtual ride on a replica trolley that takes you on a tour of the city. Along the way, meet life-size models and interact with touch-screen visuals. Talk of the Town is the award-winning video interactive of virtual conversations with historical townsfolk. The past comes alive as you travel through distinct zones depicting the stages of this area's growth. They include: I&M Canal, City of Stone and Steel, and War history. Check out the Resource and Discovery Room which is packed with activities for children. Try an I Spy Game and loads of crafts. Just a city museum, this is an example of modernizing historical artifacts to engage the kids dramatically. Great job.

JOLIET IRON WORKS HISTORIC SITE

(Located .10 miles east of Route 53 (Scott Street) and .10 miles east of the Ruby Street Bridge, on Columbia Street in downtown Joliet) **Joliet** 60433

｜｜ Phone: (815) 727-8700
     www.reconnectwithnature.org/preserves-trails/Joliet-Iron-Works
｜｜ Hours: Summer 8:00am-8:00pm, Winter 8:00am-5:00pm.
｜｜ Admission: FREE
｜｜ Note: The site is also the access point for the 11.4 mile I & M Canal Trail. This trail - of which portions are paved or crushed stone - connects Joliet's City Center to the Centennial Trail at 135th street in Romeoville.

Joliet is known as the City of Steel and Stone. Rich deposits of limestone led to a thriving quarrying industry. In the years following the Civil War, a huge iron producing industry would employ thousands at the Joliet Iron Works until the 1930s. Follow a 1-mile walkway through the site on a self-guided tour through exhibits explaining the iron making process and describing the men who worked there. Walk among the ruins.

SPLASH STATION WATERPARK

2780 US Route 6 (I-80 E to the Houbolt Road exit. Turn right. Take Houbolt
to Route 6 and turn left) **Joliet** 60436

  Phone: (815) 741-7275 **www.jolietsplashstation.com**

  Hours: Friday & Saturday 11:00am-8:00pm (peak summer break). 11:00am-
  6:00pm (rest of summer days).

  Admission: $13.00 general, $9.00 under 48" tall (ages 4+). Resident discount
  about $4.00 each. Twilight (after 5:00pm) is half price.

Joliet is known as the City of Steel and Stone. Rich deposits of limestone led
to a thriving quarrying industry. In the years following the Civil War, a huge
iron producing industry would employ thousands at the Joliet Iron Works
until the 1930s. Follow a 1-mile walkway through the site on a self-guided
tour through exhibits explaining the iron making process and describing the
men who worked there. Walk among the ruins.

HARVEST DAYS

Joliet - *Garfield Farm Museum. www.garfieldfarm.org. A major event in the Fall
at Garfield Farm is Harvest Days which feature demonstration of pioneer farming
skills like the candle making shown here as well as a sheep dog demonstration, blacksmithing, and displays of farm and home items. There is also a story teller and guided
walk through the farm prairie areas. Admission. (first weekend in October)*

CANDLELIGHT RECEPTION

Joliet - *Garfield Farm Museum. www.garfieldfarm.org. Experience the tradition of winter
visiting as practiced by families like the Garfield's in their 1846 Brick Inn. Hospitality,
food, music, and bake-sale. Donations Accepted. (first weekend in December)*

LAMBS FARM

14245 West Rockland Road (intersection of I-94 and Route 176, you can
see it from the highway) **Libertyville** 60048

  Phone: (847) 362-4636 **www.lambsfarm.org**

  Hours: 10:00am to 5:00pm daily during season - closed during winter
  months. Restaurant closed Mondays.

Lambs Farm is a place that, most importantly, empowers an extraordinary
group of more than 250 people with developmental disabilities to lead
personally fulfilling lives. Uniquely, Lambs Farm is also a place where
families gather to enjoy their many shops and attractions. The fun, affordable

family destination features a Farmyard with animals to pet, a large Pet Shop, Country Store & Bakery, Thrift Shop, and the Country Inn Restaurant - serving breakfast and lunch. Enjoy a variety of attractions like mini-golf, a mini-train ride, cow bounce house and an Old World carousel. A great idea.

BUNNY BRUNCH

Libertyville - *Lambs Farm. For reservations. (847) 362-5050. Hop over to Lambs Farm for a delicious buffet and some fun with the Easter Bunny. Kids will enjoy a magic show, face painting, a wagon ride, a photo with the Bunny, and planting seeds in a flower pot they'll decorate themselves. Admission includes meal. (Friday & Saturday of Easter weekend)*

WINTER WONDERLAND

Libertyville - *Lambs Farm. Enjoy a delicious brunch! After brunch, kids will enjoy sleigh rides, crafts and a photo with Santa. Gather around the fireplace and grab a soothing mug of hot chocolate for some of your favorite winter stories. by reservation only. Admission includes meal. (second & third wkends in December)*

MORTON ARBORETUM

4100 Illinois Route 53 (I-88 Route 53 exit north) **Lisle** 60532

- Phone: (630) 968-0074 **www.mortonarb.org**
- Hours: Daily 9:00am-5:00pm. Closes one hour earlier in winter months.
- Admission: $14.00 adult, $12.00 senior (65+), $9.00 child (2-17). Seasonal Tram tours $5 extra. Winters and Wednesdays are discounted.

Morton Arboretum has a great Children's Garden and a new Maze Garden, focusing on trees and plants of the Midwest. The special garden is geared towards kids ages 2-10. Let kids lead you through the space after you enter the garden at the Kid's Tree Walk, which leads to Tree Finder Grove. Several of the garden areas include water play areas and play equipment to climb on. One garden highlights backyard nature, another encourages kids to look, listen, feel and smell plants. Play in a corn crop or sand and water play areas. The Adventure Woods highlight wetlands, prairie and forest settings. Kids can hop across a shallow pond on stepping stones or cross a kid-sized bridge leading to a tiny island. Play equipment, treehouses and netted bridges turn one garden into a climbing adventure. It leads to a secret stream where kids can play, then crawl in a net above. The prairie flows into another garden that gives kids access to a rope bridge nestled in the treetops.

FALL COLOR FESTIVAL

Lisle - Morton Arboretum. 1700 acres of trees ablaze in color. Hand-dipped taffy apples, pumpkin decorating and a corn maze. (month-long in October)

LISLE EYES TO THE SKIES BALLOON FESTIVAL

Lisle - Lisle Community Park. Twenty-plus hot air balloons float above the Community Park. Fireworks, food vendors, arts-and-crafts booths, a petting zoo and carnival complete with fun. Admission. **www.eyestotheskies.org** *(late June thru July 4th)*

GAYLORD BUILDING HISTORIC SITE & RESTAURANT

200 West Eighth Street (I-80; take Briggs Street north and turn left on Division Street, right on IL 171 (State Street), then left to the 8th Street parking lot) **Lockport** 60441

Phone: (815) 588-1100 **www.gaylordbuilding.org/index.php**
Hours: Monday-Friday 9:00am-5:00pm. Restaurant 11:00am-8:00pm.
Admission: FREE

Public Landing Restaurant is set within the old canal building museum and open for lunch and dinner. Kids Menu average $8.00. Here, more than 150 years ago, the Gaylord Building played a major role in creation of the Illinois & Michigan Canal. The I & M Canal linked Lake Michigan with the Mississippi River, creating a waterway that opened a prosperous trade route from New York to New Orleans. Shortly after its completion, the railroads dominated the transportation industry. Today the Gaylord Building is a gateway to the I&M Canal National Heritage Corridor. Explore the building's canal exhibits. Relax with a stroll or bike ride along the scenic canal trail.

BENGSTON PUMPKIN FARM

Lockport. 13341 West 151 Street. You'll experience hours of enjoyment including a relaxing Hayrack ride, a giggling animated Fun Barn, the famous action-packed Pig Races, the adorable Petting Zoo, Mr. Scarecrow's Corn Maze, The Pumpkin Launcher, a Train Ride, Bluegrass playing Skeleton Band, Farm Animals, Straw Tunnel, Pony Rides, the all new Frog Hopper Ride, delicious refreshments, eats & treats. Admission. www.pumpkinfarm.com (late September thru October)

STRAWBERRY FESTIVAL

Long Grove - *Long Grove Historical Village. Celebrate with strawberry treats, lots of great food, family entertainment and 101 ways to enjoy strawberries.* ***www.longgroveonline.com/strawberry.html.*** *(last weekend in June)*

KUIPERS FAMILY FARM

Maple Park - *1 N 318 Watson Road, 5 miles west of rte 47.* ***www.kuipersfamilyfarm. com*** *Take a Pony Ride, Run Through a Cornfield Maze, Feed Baby Animals, Sample Home-grown Squash, Enjoy a Horse-drawn Haywagon Ride, Get Lost in a Maze, Pick Pumpkins Right from the Patch, Giggle in a Cornstalk Tunnel, Roll in the Straw, Peddle in a Tractor Derby, Chat with a Scarecrow, Satisfy your hunger at the Corncrib Café, Stroll through the Nature Walk or Ride in the Johnny Popper Grain Train. Admission. (daily, except Monday, in October)*

DOLLINGER FAMILY FARM

Minooka - *7420 East Hansel Road (I-80 exit 122).* ***www.dollingerfarms.com.*** *Farm animals, petting zoo, corn maze, hayrides and train rides. Admission for some activities. (late September thru October)*

DUPAGE CHILDREN'S MUSEUM
301 North Washington Street Naperville 60540

 Phone: (630) 637-8000 **www.dupagechildrensmuseum.org**
 Hours: Monday-Saturday 10am-8pm, Sunday 11am-6:00pm.
 Admission: $7.50-$8.50 (age 1+).

The DuPage Children's Museum has 3 floors made up of different exhibit neighborhoods - each one special in its own way. Each neighborhood is packed with exciting ways to explore art, math, science and how they work together in the world. Young Explorers, Airworks, Waterways, Build It, Make It Move and Creativity Connections. There are also three Young Explorers neighborhoods (adjacent to other exhibit neighborhoods) designed for children up to 24 months.

NAPER SETTLEMENT

523 S. Webster Street (I-355 or I-88/290, follow signs to entrance located at Aurora Ave. and Webster St.) **Naperville** 60540

- Phone: (630) 305-4044 **www.napersettlement.museum**
- Hours: Tuesday-Saturday 10:00am-4:00pm, Sunday 1:00-4:00pm (April-October). Tuesday-Friday only (November-March). Closed New Year's, Thanksgiving and Christmas.
- Admission: $12.00 adult, $10.00 senior, $8.00 youth (4-17) - peak. $4.00 to $5.25 - winter (Nov-March). Only village exteriors are open in winter.
- Tours: Mobile Tour. Seasonal Geocache GPS unit $1.00 rental.
- FREEBIES: Fun At Home projects: **www.napersettlement.museum/index. aspx?nid=160**

Naper Settlement tells the story of how life changed for people in towns such as Naperville throughout the 19th century. From frontier to bustling town, costumed villagers interpret life and answer questions or tell stories that bring the past to life. The paths of the 13-acre village are dotted with more than 30 structures that range from an early log house to a Victorian mansion. Climb aboard a Conestoga wagon, visit Fort Payne, drop in for class at a one-room schoolhouse or tour a working print shop. Stop in the History Connection to participate in hands-on activities such as building a log cabin or dressing up in old-fashioned clothes.

FULLERSBURG WOODS ENVIRONMENTAL EDUCATIONAL CENTER & GRAUE MILL

3609 Spring Road (between York Road and 31st Street (Oak Brook Road) **Oak Brook** 60523

- Phone: (630) 850-8110 or 630-655-2090 (mill) **www.grauemill.org**
- Hours: The entry gate opens one hour after sunrise and closes one hour after sunset. The visitor center is open daily from 9:00am- 5:00pm except on the Fourth of July, Thanksgiving, Christmas Eve, Christmas Day and New Year's Day. Graue Mill is open daily except Monday 10:00am-4:30pm (mid April to mid-November).
- Admission: FREE for Visitors Center. Small FEE for Mill ($1.75-$4.00).

The Fullersburg Woods Visitor Center is a modern, interactive facility that provides an introduction to the local environment. Visitors can examine the reconstructed remains of a 13,000-year-old woolly mammoth to learn about DuPage County's natural history or can use microscopes and spotting scopes to examine some of the creatures that call the forest preserves home today.

- **INTERPRETIVE TRAIL** - Taking a self-guided tour of this 1.3 mile trail through lowland woods and restored prairies by foot, bicycle or cross-country skis is a good way to learn about DuPage County's natural history. Most of the trail follows Salt Creek, providing visitors with the chance to see beavers, various waterfowl and other creatures.

GRAUE MILL - Travel the 0.5-mile walk along the banks of Salt Creek to visit Graue Mill. Along the way, stop to read the signs that highlight the area's cultural history. The Mill is the only water-powered grist mill in Illinois that still grinds corn daily. Catch a live demonstration or look over exhibits. Iron clothes or try to decide what to purchase from old Sears and Roebuck catalogs. After the miller's demo, maybe purchase some ground corn meal to use at home (recipes included). The Mill opened an expanded exhibit entitled "The Graue Mill and the Road to Freedom." This exhibit, using a computer interactive system and additional displays relates the importance of the Graue Mill and DuPage County in assisting fugitive slaves to escape to freedom.

GAELIC PARK IRISH FEST

Oak Forest - *Chicago Gaelic Park, 6119 W 147th Street. Irish eyes can't help but smile at this annual four-day celebration. Irish dancing, foods and crafts, plus five stages full of Emerald Isle music and merriment. Children can enter freckle contests, see a magic show and ride ponies.* **www.chicagogaelicparkirishfest.org**. *Admission. (days before Memorial Day)*

FRANK LLOYD WRIGHT HOME AND STUDIO

951 Chicago Avenue (I-290 west to Harlem Ave/Rte 43 exit. Head northwest 1.5 miles to right on Chicago Ave. Head 3 blocks east) **Oak Park** 60302

- Phone: (708) 848-1976 **www.gowright.org**
- Hours: Closed Thanksgiving, Christmas, New Year's.
- Admission: $14.00-$17.00 per person (age 7+).
- Tours: Approximately every 20 minutes from 10:00am to 3:40pm. Tour length 45-60 minutes. All tours start at Gingko Tree Book Shop @ the Home. Interior photography is not permitted except with additional fee paid.
- Note: Historic District Self-Guided Exterior Audio Tour available for additional $6.00-$8.00.

Tour the place where Frank Lloyd Wright lived and worked for the first 20 years of his career. Wright used his home as an architectural laboratory, experimenting with design concepts that contain the seeds of his architectural philosophy. Here he raised six children with his first wife, Catherine Tobin. In 1898, Wright added a studio, described by a fellow-architect as a workplace with "inspiration everywhere." In the Studio, Wright and his associates developed a new American architecture: the Prairie style, and designed 125 structures, including such famous buildings as the Robie House, the Larkin Building and Unity Temple. The restored early 1900s building has a light-filled octagonal drafting room and an adorable barrel-vaulted playroom. We'd recommend this for older kids who have studied architectural styles or the Design Detectives Family Tour every Saturday (1:30pm). Junior interpreters reveal family life stories and how America's most famous architect broke the rules of design.

VICTORIAN CHRISTMAS TOURS

Oak Park - *Frank Lloyd Wright Home and Studio. Special tours led by junior interpreters featuring stories of how the Wright family celebrated the holidays at the turn of the last century. A wonderful holiday tradition for the family. FREE. (second and third Sunday in December)*

HEMINGWAY BIRTHPLACE HOME AND MUSEUM
339 N. Oak Park Avenue Oak Park 60302

☐ Phone: (708) 848-2222 **www.ehfop.org**
☐ Hours: Sunday- Friday 1:00pm-5:00pm, Saturday 10:00am–5:00pm. Closed Federal holidays.
☐ Admission: $13.00-$15.00 per person (age 6+).

HOME: Take a moment and stand in front of this beautiful Queen Anne style residence, with its expansive porch and grand turret and be prepared to take a small step back into time. The museum and home focus on Hemingway's first 20 years spent in Oak Park through the collection of photographs, letters, memorabilia and his earliest writings. The home, designed by architect Wesley Arnold and built around 1890 for Ernest Hall, Hemingway's maternal grandfather, maintains many of its original features that even Ernest would find familiar.

MUSEUM: Just a short walk from the birthplace, the Ernest Hemingway Museum is host to permanent and temporary exhibits that explore the author's life. Kiosks fashioned from historic doors hold exhibits of rare photos and artifacts, including Hemingway's childhood diary and the famous letter from nurse Agnes von Kurowsky-later portrayed in "A Farewell to Arms" - terminating their engagement.

WONDER WORKS

6445 West North Avenue (Harlem Avenue North. Turn east on North Avenue and go approximately 0.4 miles) **Oak Park** 60302

Phone: (708) 383-4815 **www.wonder-works.org**

Hours: Monday & Wednesday-Saturday 10:00am-5:00pm, Sunday Noon-5:00pm.

Admission: $6.00 per person.

Wonder Works is a children's museum with permanent exhibits such as Lights, Camera, Action; Farm to Market; Build it; Arts Area; and the Great Outdoors. Become royalty, a dancer or a wild animal on stage or man the lights and sounds to create a never-before-seen production. Pick apples and buy, sell and barter fruits and vegetables the farm stand. Camp out in a tent or climb up in the tree house as you experience the secrets of the great outdoors.

PUMPKIN PATCH

Palos Park - *The Center Children's Farm, 12700 Southwest Hwy. Experience life down on the farm with guided family tours or hike on the peaceful nature trail. Hayrack rides out to the pumpkin patch allow groups to be lead through the farm by a guide who will teach the children about each of the animals and invite the children into the animal pens for a close look and feel. **www.palospark.org/center.htm.** FREE. (October weekends)*

DIDIER PUMPKIN FARM

Prairie View - *16678 W Aptakisic Road. **www.didierfarms.com.** Pick your own pumpkin and explore the corn maze. At the Great Pumpkin Weigh Off, locals weigh in their product – some pumpkins weigh over 700 pounds. Then, take the kids for a pony ride before visiting the farm animal zoo and scarecrow alley. Admission. (last weekend in September through October)*

ISLE A LA CACHE MUSEUM

501 E. Romeo Road (.5 miles east of Route 53) **Romeoville** 60441

- Phone: (815) 886-1467 **www.reconnectwithnature.org/visitor-centers/icm**
- Hours: Tuesday-Saturday 10:00am-4:00pm, Sunday Noon-4:00pm.
- Admission: FREE

"Island of the Hiding Place" - this mysterious title is the translation of the French phrase Isle a la Cache. Inside the Museum, explore exhibits of the French fur trade. Find out about a voyager's day on the river; examine a real birch bark canoe; see the trade items of metal, beads, and cloth that changed the Native American's lifestyle. Step inside a Native American wigwam where you can play native games or dress-up in period clothing. Touch the soft, silky fur of a beaver and realize for yourself why Europeans desired this waterproof coat. Children can take part in a "trade" and understand the value of items for different cultures and experience Native American life while visiting an 18th Century replica longhouse. Isle a la Cache Museum. Find out how cultural history shaped the region and you can picnic, fish and canoe on the property.

RAINFOREST CAFÉ

Schaumburg - *Woodfield Mall, D121. 60173. A theme restaurant and wildlife preserve filled with live and mechanical animals; ongoing rainstorms; hand-sculpted cave-like rock; a cage of tropical birds; many colored live fish (in tanks) and watch out for the large animals "rumbles." Order anything tropical (we especially recommend chicken and the Appetizer Adventure) and save room for the Sparkling Volcano dessert! They even give groups (pre-arranged) educational tours uncovering misconceptions and mysteries about the rainforest. Educators - they offer discount meals for groups and curriculum, too! (847) 619-1900 or www.rainforestcafe.com.*

ATCHER ISLAND WATER PARK

730 S. Springinsguth **Schaumburg** 60193

- Phone: 847-985-2135
  www.parkfun.com/facilities/pools/Atcher-Island
- Hours: Monday-Friday 11:00am-8:30pm, Weekends Noon-8:00pm (mid-June thru 3rd week in August).
- Admission: $7-$9.00 per person. $2.00 per person discount for resident.

Each summer, spend some time relaxing on a tropical island. Atcher Island is the Schaumburg Park District's tropical themed water park with water slides, a unique circular drop slide (we call them toilet bowls), children's spray ground (doesn't that just sound like fun?) and more. Remodeled from the ground up with a Polynesian feel, forget your worries and lounge poolside, or feel the rush of plunging down a slide. Refreshments and concessions are available on site.

SPRING VALLEY NATURE CENTER & HERITAGE FARM

1111 E. Schaumburg Rd (farm @ 201 S. Plum Grove Rd) **Schaumburg** 60194

Phone: (847) 985-2100 **www.parkfun.com/Spring-Valley**
Hours: Trails open 8:00am-5:00pm (open until 8:00pm summers). Farm open/Visitors Center Daily 9:00am-5:00pm
Admission: FREE

Step back in time and see the landscape as the first pioneers saw it...tall grass and wildflowers. Listen to the sounds of frogs and gliding blue heron at the edge of the marsh...help to milk a cow...prepare a meal on a wood cookstove. Walk the 3 miles of accessible trails viewing wildflower-studded prairies, quiet woodlands, and wetlands bustling with wildlife. We'd highly recommend the .7 mile trail between the Farm and Nature Center. You feel immersed in a tall prairie - probably the best example we've seen in the whole state - that you could walk through. The nature center (open 9:00am-5:00pm) museum contain exhibits and trail guide booklets and nature backpacks for rent. On a visit to Volkening Heritage farm, you can help with seasonal farm chores, participate in family activities and games of the 1880s or simply visit the livestock and soak in the quiet. Authentically dressed interpreters welcome and guide visitors through the site. Many programs are held at the re-created 19th century farm, complete with antique farm equipment and a furnished farmhouse.

SUGAR BUSH FAIR

Schaumburg - *Spring Valley Nature Sanctuary. A celebration of nature's sweet gift of maple syrup featuring historical demonstrations, activities and a pancake breakfast. (mid-March)*

AUTUMN HARVEST FESTIVAL

Schaumburg -*Spring Valley Nature Sanctuary & Farm. An old-fashioned harvest festival featuring hayrides, 19th century farm life demonstrations, food, games, and music. (first Sunday of October)*

MEDIEVAL TIMES DINNER & TOURNAMENT

2001 North Roselle Rd (I-90 Roselle Rd, north of tollway) **Schaumburg** 60195

☐ Phone: (847) 882-0202 or (888) WE-JOUST **www.medievaltimes.com**

☐ Shows: Generally Wednesday-Friday at 7:30pm (summers). Evening and/or Matinee show on weekends and holidays. School year only weekends and holiday shows.

☐ Admission: Adults: $61.95 adult, $36.95 child (12 and under). Tax and Gratuity not included. Includes dinner, beverages,and live show.

☐ Note: Due to some choreographed fighting scenes in the tournament, small children may be frightened by the bashing sounds of sword against sword (it appears very real).

You'll know you've arrived when the European-style castle front appears on the horizon. This show transports guests back 900 years to a time when chivalry was honored and knights performed daring feats to entertain the lords and ladies of the court. As you are assigned seating, you'll also be assigned a knight to cheer for and a "take home" crown to wear to show your support. You will sit with others who join cheers of support for your chosen knight of the realm. Serfs and wenches dressed in period costumes serve guests a feast of fresh vegetable soup, roasted chicken, spare rib, herb basted potato, a pastry and beverages. In order to honor medieval tradition, guests eat their meals without silverware (your kids will love having to eat with their hands!). As the lights dim, the story begins with the battle-weary King and his Knights returning to the Castle. The King calls for a grand tournament to determine the realm's new champion. As everyone is feasting, the Knights spar in tournament games and jousts. As the plot unfolds - we all hope truth, honor and love will eventually triumph over evil, and peace restored. The villain is revealed in the final minutes of the show bringing the crowd to their feet - cheering for the brave hero who defends the castle! The beautiful Andalusian horses and quick displays of choreographed sword and jousting ability make this show so engaging!

SKOKIE NORTHSHORE SCULPTURE PARK

(east side of McCormick Blvd btw. Dempster St and Touhy Ave) **Skokie** 60076

   Phone: (847) 679-4265 **www.sculpturepark.org**
   Hours: Daily during daylight hours. Admission: FREE

This unique facility combines recreational features with an outstanding exhibition of large scale contemporary sculpture. Plan a visit to walk, bike or jog on their two miles of pathways and enjoy the more than 72 world class sculptures you will see along the way. Is it a plant, an animal, or a robot? What materials were used? Many of these are made (recycled) from found objects put in the trash. With names like "Weee" and the terribly unusual shapes - your kids will run to see the name of the next sculpture on the trail.

GOEBBERT'S PUMPKIN FARM

South Barrington - *40 W Higgins Road. Pumpkins, animal land (barnyard and exotic), corn stalk maze, strawtown maze, wagon rides, camel rides, pony rides, and weekend pig racing. Café and group tours. Admission.* ***www.pumpkinfarms.com*** *(last weekend in September through October, daily)*

FOX RIVER TROLLEY MUSEUM

361 South LaFox Street (IL 31) (I-90 or US Route 20 west to Elgin. Exit on Illinois Route 31 southbound) **South Elgin** 60177

   Phone: (847) 697-4676 **www.foxtrolley.org**
   Hours: Saturdays, Sundays and Holidays - seasonally, afternoons.
   Admission: $2.00-$4.00.

Celebrating more than 100 years of electric trolleys, experience the sights and sounds of this unique part of American history aboard a genuine old-time trolley car which takes you on a four mile trip along the banks of the scenic Fox River and the Blackhawk Forest Preserve. The museum operates a variety of antique trolleys, many from lines long vanished, over tracks that once connected Carpentersville, Elgin, Aurora, and Yorkville.

PUMPKIN TROLLEY

South Elgin - *Fox River Trolley Museum. Enjoy hay rides, trolley rides, pumpkins, food and some evening movies. The trolley rides mid-month on take you out to the pumpkin patch to pick a pumpkin and then enjoy a small treat. Admission. (month-long in October)*

POLAR EXPRESS

South Elgin - *Fox River Trolley Museum. Board the all reserved "Polar Express" at Blackhawk Forest Preserve for a ride north to meet Santa and experience the magic of the season. Reservations and admission only. (first Sunday in December)*

SAND RIDGE NATURE CENTER

15891 Paxton Avenue (On Paxton Ave. two blocks north of 159th St)
South Holland 60473

Phone: (708) 868-0621
http://fpdcc.com/nature-centers/sand-ridge-nature-center/
Hours: Daily, except Fridays. Basically 9:00am-4:00pm. Later hours in the summer. Closed Fridays in winter.

Sand Ridge Nature Center is a 235-acre preserve with four well-marked trails offering easy hiking, from under a mile to 2 miles long. Each trail features different habitats, including prairies, oak savannas and woodlands, marshes, a pond, and ancient sand dunes. Within the modern Nature Center building, the Exhibit Room houses interpretive displays, as well as native local wildlife including snakes, turtles, and fish. A Kids Corner features hands-on activities, displays and animal puppets, and puzzles. Outside, visitors can stroll through a colorful butterfly garden, and enjoy a vegetable garden and herb garden displaying plants used by pioneers and Native Americans. There are several reproduction log cabins on site, which depict the lifestyles of early 19th century settlers in Illinois. Pioneer demonstrations are held most Wednesday mornings (May-November).

PHEASANT RUN RESORT AND SPA

St. Charles - *4051 East Main Street (Rte 64). (800) 474-3272* **www.pheasantrun.com**. *60174. There's a wide range of activities on the 250-acre grounds including golf and indoor/outdoor pools. Guests can enjoy strolling down Pheasant Run's indoor replica of New Orlean's Bourbon Street and Noble Fool Theatrical ranging from classic plays to improve to musicals. All wonderful, but the Specialty and Seasonal Packages is what really caught our attention. All packages include overnight accommodations as well as access to the pools. Try a Spring Fling – go fly a kite, Frisbee contests and other outdoor activities. Bubble toys and poolside games. Their Summer Splash is similar but also features barbeques, DJ and music, breakfast and moonlight movies. At Smores-N-More you can warm up on fall and winter nights with your family as you* *enjoy a bonfire with smore kits and live entertainment (maybe a storyteller or cowboy singer). Again, crafts and a meal are included. The Theatre and Kids Club require an additional fee.* 📖 _____

SCARECROW FESTIVAL

St. Charles - *Downtown. More than 100 handmade scarecrows strut their stuff(ing) at this huge arts-and-crafts show. Children can make their own scarecrows to take home. Carnival, entertainment. FREE. www.scarecrowfest.com (second weekend in October)*

VOLO AUTO MUSEUM

27582 Volo Village Road (Route 12 on Highway 120, 13 miles west of I-94)
· **Volo** 60073

- Phone: (815) 385-3644 **www.volocars.com**
- Hours: Daily 10:00am-5:00pm except Easter, Thanksgiving and Christmas.
- Admission: $14.95 adult, $12.95 senior, veteran, military (w/ ID), $8.95 child (5-12). FREE for any kid 4 and under or military personnel in uniform.

After purchasing tickets, the first building you walk is the Kids Hollywood Museum, which is probably the kids favorite space (Scooby Doo Mystery Machine, Flintstone Mobile, Batmobile, General Lee and such). They claim the world's largest collection of muscle cars on exhibit and they have a nice growing tribute to military called Military Adventure.

LAKE COUNTY DISCOVERY MUSEUM

27277 N Forest Preserve Rd (Lakewood Forest Preserve, Fairfield Road & IL 176) **Wauconda** 60084

- Phone: (847) 968-3400 **www.lakecountydiscoverymuseum.org**
- Hours: Monday-Saturday 10:00am-4:30pm, Sunday 1:00-4:30pm.
- Admission: $6.00 adult, $2.50 youth (4-17), $3.00 students and seniors (62+). Online coupon.

Visit the Discovery Museum and take a ride through 10,000 years of Lake County history at the Vortex Roller Coaster Theater. This award-winning museum provides the same experience you'd expect from a big-city museum. Hands-on interactive exhibits educate and entertain. Learn about the Native American and pioneer families who first settled the area. Be sure to look for the nation's largest public collection of postcards.

74 KIDS LOVE ILLINOIS

BILLY GRAHAM CENTER MUSEUM

500 East College Avenue (I-355 south at Schaumburg. West on Roosevelt Road thru Glen Ellyn, past President Street, to Washington Street. Turn north towards campus) **Wheaton** 60187

- Phone: (630) 752-5909 **www.wheaton.edu/bgcmuseum**
- Hours: Monday-Saturday 9:30am-5:30pm, Sunday 1:00-5:00pm. Closed Thanksgiving Day and between Christmas & New Years. Call on other holidays.
- Admission: $1.00-$4.00 suggested donation. $10.00 family.

As you journey through the Museum, your first stop will be in the Rotunda of Witnesses, which houses nine displays of great witnesses for the Gospel. From here, you'll proceed to the History of Evangelism in America section, where you will see an array of historical images and artifacts that the museum has collected over the years. At the end of this section, you'll encounter the lovely presentation of the basic Christian message in the Cross of the Millennium. From here, you'll enter a major section of the Museum which highlights the Life and Ministry of Billy Graham. As you leave the Billy Graham display, you'll encounter a powerful depiction of the needs of our world and be challenged to personal evangelism. A final theater presentation in this section captures the highlights of crusades from around the world. What path will you choose? The last leg of your journey through the Museum takes you on a Walk through the Gospel, with a stirring three dimensional presentation of the Christian message. A small chapel and bookstore greet you as you end your tour.

KLINE CREEK FARM

600 S County Farm Road (Entrance on County Farm Rd., north of Geneva Rd. on west side (just south of St. Charles Rd.) **Wheaton** 60187

- Phone: (630) 876-5900
  www.dupageforest.com/Education/Centers/Kline_Creek_Farm.aspx
- Hours: Thursday-Monday 9:00am-5:00pm.
- Admission: FREE, donations accepted.
- Tours: The house and summer kitchen are available for guided tours only. Those tours are available from 10:00am-4:00pm daily when the farm is open.

The Forest Preserve District of DuPage County has combined original structures, authentic re-creations, livestock and historically accurate activities

For updates & travel games visit: **www.KidsLoveTravel.com**

into a realistic 1890's DuPage County working farm. Costumed interpreters depict lifestyles around each building. The self-guided tour brochure is available at the entrance. Kline Creek Farm offers 50 weekends of theme-based programs and activities each year. Activities include sausage and butter making; canning and processing garden produce; hay-making; and the social occasions of holidays.

A RIVER THRU HISTORY: THE DES PLAINES VALLEY RENDEZVOUS

Willow Springs - *Columbia Woods Forest Preserve (I-294 exit 75th St West). Step into the 19th-century fur-trade era along the Des Plaines River at the Forest. Revelers can sip homemade root beer, as they cheer the canoe races and listen to Native American storytellers. Early American food, tomahawk exhibitions, music and games. Admission.* ***www.ariverthruhistory.com*** *(second weekend in September)*

DELL RHEA'S CHICKEN BASKET

Willowbrook - *(I-55 & Rte 83). 60527. "Get you chicks on Route 66." It got its humble beginnings sometime in the late 1930s or early 1940s in an old gas station lunch counter. One day two local farm women came in and overheard the owner talking about selling more food. Having a wonderful recipe for fried chicken, they approached him and offered to teach him their recipe if he bought his chickens from them. Because the fried chicken was so good and the highway so busy, the Chicken Basket outgrew its lunch counter and the 2-car repair bays were turned into a dining room. The Chicken Basket as it is today opened in the summer of 1946 on Illinois Route 66. Burgers and fried fish are on the menu but the people come for the chicken, on the bone or off, breaded, fried and served with homestyle sides. Avg $9.00 meal or $5.00 kids meal. Lunch and dinner served every day but Mondays. (630) 325-0780 or* ***www.chickenbasket.com.***

RAGING WAVES WATERPARK

4000 N. Bridge St. (Rt. 47) (one hour SW of Chicago) **Yorkville** 60560

     Phone: (630) 882-6575 **www.ragingwaves.com**
     Hours: Generally 10am-5pm (Memorial Day - Labor Day wkend)
     Admission: Full Day Passes run $19.99-$29.99. Tubes extra.

Billed as the state's largest water park, this Down Under Australian-themed attractions covers 45 acres and features splashy options like a three-story head-spinning contraption called the Tornado, 18 slides, a wave pool, a raft ride and massive replicas of marsupials. They offer Summer Family Fun Value packages including admission, tube rental and meals.

ILLINOIS BEACH RESORT

Zion - *Illinois Beach State Park, 1 Lake Front Drive. 60099. The Illinois Beach Resort has been renovated and is located on a portion of the South Unit beach to provide guests with a beautiful view over the waters of Lake Michigan. It offers a restaurant (with great view), large indoor pool, whirlpool, and exercise room. Resort guests also have 24-hour access to the beach. We recommend morning and early evening walks. Note: Even in the summer, the water only gets to about 70 degrees - too cold for most adults to swim but a great way to cool off. Other amenities include a gift shop, game room, in-room movies and games, miles of nature trails, sandy beach, and bicycle trails. Rooms run around $100 per night. They offer many special value packages. (866) IL-BEACH or* **www.ilresorts.com.**

ILLINOIS BEACH STATE PARK
Lake Front (Take I-94 to Rt.173 east. Follow Rt. 173 to Sheridan Rd.)
Zion 60099

☐   Phone: (708) 662-4811
     http://dnr.state.il.us/lands/landmgt/parks/r2/ilbeach.htm
☐   Note: North Point Marina, located north of the state park, is a full-service marina. Considered one of the finest/ largest floating docks in North America, the site also has restaurants, swimming beaches, charters, sport courts, picnic areas and access to bike or hiking trails. (847) 746-2845.

Illinois Beach stretches for six and a half miles along the sandy shore of Lake Michigan in Northern Illinois. Illinois Beach State Park encompasses the only remaining beach ridge shoreline left in the state…including dunes. The Dead River winds through the preserve creating a unique wetland habitat for many endangered species. Nature walks and guided tours through the preserve are available to the public on the weekends all summer long. 4,160-acres of beauty provide visitors with an opportunity for swimming, boating, picnicking, hiking, fishing, or just enjoying the beauty of nature. Illinois Beach also offers camping in a beautifully wooded campground where both tent and RV camping are welcome. (see separate listing for the resort).

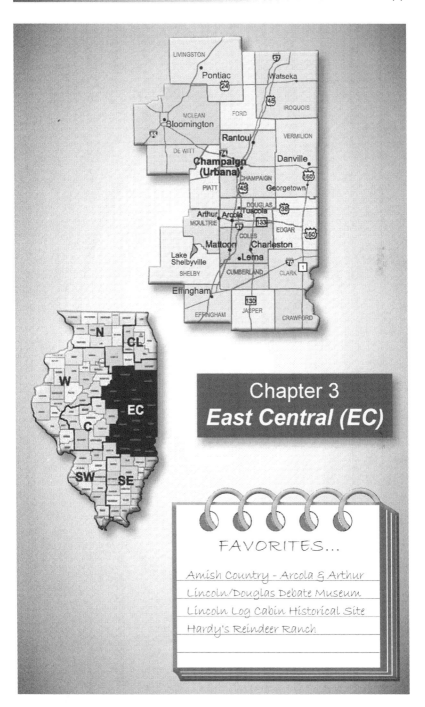

LIVINGSTON

Pontiac

Watseka

MCLEAN   FORD   IROQUOIS

Bloomington

Rantoul   VERMILION

DE WITT

Champaign
(Urbana)

Danville

CHAMPAIGN

PIATT   Georgetown

DOUGLAS

Arthur Arcola Tuscola

MOULTRIE   EDGAR

COLES

Mattoon Charleston

Lake
Shelbyville   Lerna

SHELBY   CUMBERLAND   CLARK

Effingham

EFFINGHAM   JASPER   CRAWFORD

N

CL

W

EC

C

SW   SE

Chapter 3
East Central (EC)

FAVORITES...

Amish Country - Arcola & Arthur

Lincoln/Douglas Debate Museum

Lincoln Log Cabin Historical Site

Hardy's Reindeer Ranch

Altamont
- Ballard Nature Center
- Illinois High School Rodeo
- Millroad Steam Thresherman's Festival & Antique Tractor Show

Arcola
- Illinois Amish Interpretive Center
- Rockome Gardens
- Broom Corn Festival

Arthur
- Arthur's Visitor Information Center
- The Great Pumpkin Patch

Bement
- Bryant Cottage State Historic Site

Bloomington
- Miller Park Zoo
- Beer Nuts Factory
- American Passion Play

Bloomington (Normal)
- Children's Discovery Museum Of Central Illinois
- Illinois State University Museums

Champaign
- Orpheum Children's Science Museum
- Prairie Farm
- Staerkel Planetarium
- Curtis Orchard

Champaign (Urbana)
- Spurlock Museum

Charleston
- Fox Ridge State Park
- Lincoln-Douglas Debate Museum
- Red, White And Blue Days

Clinton
- Weldon Springs State Park
- Christmas Candlelight Tours

Danville
- Vermilion County Museum & Fithian Home
- Illinois Renaissance Faire

Dewitt
- Clinton Lake State Recreation Area

Effingham
- Lake Sara & Effingham Beach
- Sculpture On The Avenues

Findlay
- Eagle Creek State Recreation Area

Hoopeston
- National Sweetcorn Festival

Lerna
- Lincoln Log Cabin State Historic Site

LeRoy
- Moraine View State Recreation Area
- Grand Village Of The Kickapoo Pow Wow

Mahomet
- Early American Museum

Marshall
- Lincoln Trail State Park

Martinsville
- Moonshine Store Restaurant

Mattoon
- Bagelfest

Monticello
- Monticello Railway Museum

Oakland
- Dr. Hiram Rutherford's Home
- Walnut Point State Park

Oakwood
- Kickapoo State Park

Palestine
- Pioneer City Rodeo & Labor Day Festival

Rantoul
- Hardy's Reindeer Ranch
- Octave Chanute Aerospace Museum

Shelbyville
- Lake Shelbyville

Shirley
- Funks Grove Pure Maple Sirup

Strasburg
- Hidden Springs State Forest

Sullivan
- Little Theatre On The Square

Tuscola
- Amishland Red Barn Buffet & Shoppes
- Holiday Inn Express, Amish Country

Windsor
- Wolf Creek State Park

Sites and attractions are listed in order by City, Zip Code, and Name. Symbols indicated represent 🍽 Restaurants   🛏 Lodging

BALLARD NATURE CENTER

5253 East US Highway 40 (east of town) Altamont 62411

- Phone: (618) 483-6856 **www.ballardnaturecenter.org**
- Hours: Center open Monday-Friday 8:00am-4:00pm. Weekends Noon-4:00pm. Closed Mondays and Sundays in winter. Trails open daily dawn to dusk.
- Admission: Donation suggested.

The Ballard Nature Center consists of 210 acres, including 100 acres of woodland, 15 acres of restored prairie, 10 acres of shallow water wetlands and

85 acres of agricultural land. The 4,300 square foot handicapped accessible building includes a library, bird viewing area, and an exhibit room, featuring interpretive displays on various interesting "bits of nature" relevant to the area. Walking trails through prairie, woodlands, and wetlands are available, and interpretive trails are being developed.

ILLINOIS HIGH SCHOOL RODEO

Altamont - *Effingham County Fairgrounds. Illinois high school rodeo athletes compete for the glory, fun and the opportunity to advance to the Nationals. Rodeo sports are action packed including bull and bronco riding, barrel racing and calf roping. Little buckaroos can compete in mutton bustin' and the littlest cowpokes can saddle up for the stick horse events. Admission.* **www.ilhsra.org** *(second weekend in June)*

MILLROAD STEAM THRESHERMAN'S FESTIVAL & ANTIQUE TRACTOR SHOW

Altamont - *Effingham County Fairgrounds. Horse Pull, Antique Tractor Pull, Train Show, Free rides on Little Obie, Civil War living history reenactment. Lawn mower pull and steam engine display. www.millroadthresherman.org (fourth weekend in July)*

ILLINOIS AMISH INTERPRETIVE CENTER

(now located on Rockome premises) (I-57 exit 203, head west to town)
Arcola 61910

Phone: (888) 45-Amish **www.amishcenter.com**

Tours: Groups of 10 or more can make arrangements to tour the center (November-April). Families can arrange to tour Amish countrysides with packages and various fees charged per add-on.

Note: Curious still? Make your own tour by asking for the Amish Country map highlighted by staff here, or at the visitors center next door. Stop in at various Amish businesses, look around, watch them work, and maybe purchase items homemade.

This is the first museum in Illinois dedicated to the Amish culture. It traces the history of the Amish religion and provides a glimpse into the lives of the Illinois Amish. A fifteen minute video on the Amish helps to separate fact from myth about their culture. The Simple People feel the way to heaven is to be in this world, not of this world. The People of the Book cherish their books, especially the Bible. They use horses vs. machinery and keep their farming costs down. One of the oldest known Amish suits and a rare 100 year old buggy are on display along with a view of the inside of a typical Amish home. This is a good way to start a visit to Illinois Amish Country. Next, arrange for a group tour. The Amish work the rich farmland of the area with teams of six to eight horse hitches, and the Amish's horse-drawn, black buggies are a common sight around the Amish country. Sit at long tables as one big, happy family and enjoy the warmth of a country meal at a real Amish Home. Traverse the Countryside with a ride-along tour guide. Tour the Home of an Amish family. Check out hardwood floors, gas lighting, gas stove and refrigerator. Houses are sparsely furnished, furniture is plain colored, with no prints.

ROCKOME GARDENS

125 North Country Road 425 East (I-57 exit 203, head west) **Arcola** 61910

Phone: (217) 268-4106 **www.rockome.com** (currently under renovation)
Hours Daily 9:00am to 5:00pm (May-October).
Admission: $10.00 adult, $8.00 senior (60+), $6.00 child (5-12). Includes admission to most attractions including the Illinois Amish Museum.

Visitors aren't likely to have seen anything like the "stones" at Rockome Gardens. Using native rock and cement, as well as some odds and ends (old pop bottles and pieces of glass), the Yoders have crafted fences, archways, large hearts, cups and saucers, birdhouses, and a variety of other designs throughout the park to delight and amuse visitors. Guests to Rockome Gardens can experience that simpler life firsthand by visiting a house modeled after a true Amish home of the 1950's, with sparse furnishings and a focus on living for the Lord rather than for worldly things. Paths are provided throughout the park, perfect for a leisurely stroll, and children can spend the day riding a horse that provides power for the saw, petting animals in the petting zoo, watching cheese being made in the factory, creeping through the haunted cave (very scary, parents use caution...), or watching the G-gauge model train as it winds through the hills, flowers, and buildings. If your feet get tired, just hop on a horse and buggy for a ride through the park or climb aboard the train and wind your way through the fields and woods that border the east side of the park to the Amish Interpretive Center just down the path. Or, play a game of Tic-Tac-Toe with a chicken (be ready, the chicken is good).

BROOM CORN FESTIVAL

Arcola - *Main Street. The fest celebrates Arcola's legacy as the one-time broom corn capital of the world. Stroll Main Street to watch broom-making demos, carnival rides, country music and catch the rousing Lawn Ranger's Broom Brigade Parade.* **www. arcolachamber.com/arcola-broomcorn-festival/** *(second weekend in September)*

ARTHUR'S VISITOR INFORMATION CENTER

106 E. Progress Street **Arthur** 61911

Phone: (800) 72-AMISH **www.IllinoisAmishCountry.com**

Arthur has been central to life in Illinois' largest Amish Settlement for more than a century and offers you a year-round look at the way life was and how life is today. Explore the community, enjoy a homemade drumstick ice cream cone at Dick's Pharmacy (118 Vine Street, www.dicks-pharmacy.com) - an old-fashioned soda fountain displaying a collection of over six hundred painted soda bottles. Sample baked goods and cheese or sit down for pizza. All of this within easy walking distance downtown Arthur.

AMISH COUNTRY CHEESE FESTIVAL

Arthur - *Downtown.* **www.arthurcheesefestival.com**. *Free cheese sliced from huge wheels with crackers provides a free snack sandwich each day. National Cheese Curling Contest, Cheese Eating Contest, Kiddie Tractor Pull, sidewalk sales, live bands, kids games, rides, food and craft vendors. FREE. (Labor Day weekend)*

THE GREAT PUMPKIN PATCH

Arthur - *2 miles south and 1/2 mile west of town. Pumpkins, corn maze, straw maze, farm animals, concession, and historic One Room schoolhouse. Newer areas include: a unique Children's Garden, an history of The Great Pumpkin Patch and farm, and bird display. Admission.* www.the200acres.com *(daily, early September thru October)*

BRYANT COTTAGE STATE HISTORIC SITE

140 E. Wilson Street **Bement** 61813

Phone: (217) 678-8184 **www.illinois.gov/ihpa/Experience/Sites/Central/ Pages/Bryant-Cottage.aspx**

Hours: Thursday-Sunday 9:00am-4:00pm. Open until 5:00pm (March-October). Open Wednesdays also each summer.

Admission: FREE. Donations accepted.

In 1858, Bryant found himself playing a role in one of the country's most famous political debates. That summer, both Abraham Lincoln and Douglas planned to talk to area residents in nearby Monticello. The chance meeting turned into a discussion about their campaign plans and many believe the two politicians formed their platforms for the Lincoln-Douglas Debates, held later that year. The Cottage still stands in Bement and is a state memorial. Look and see a glimpse of a typical residence of that time and shows how Bement's early settlers lived and carried on with their daily activities.

PATRIOTIC SERVICE

Bement - *Bryant Cottage. Parade, tours and fireworks. (July 4th)*

BEMENT CHRISTMAS

Bement - *Library and Bryant College. Parade and holiday open house with luminaries set ablaze. (second weekend in December)*

MILLER PARK ZOO

1020 S. Morris Avenue (Morris Avenue exit off of Veteran's Parkway, turn right onto Wood St., and then take the first right) **Bloomington** 61701

- Phone: (309) 434-2250 **www.millerparkzoo.org**
- Hours: Daily 9:30am-4:30pm.
- Admission: $4.95-$6.95 (age 3+).

Miller Park Zoo offers many exhibits and Zookeeper interaction opportunities that are enjoyed by the whole family. Some highlights include: sun bears, reindeer, Sumatran tiger, sea lions, snow leopard, red panda, lynx, Galapagos tortoise, bald eagles, pallas cats, and red wolves. The Zoo features many large exhibits such as a Wallaby WalkAbout, Zoolab, Children's Zoo, Animals of Asia, and the animal building. The Zoo's newest exhibit is the Tropical America Rainforest.

BEER NUTS FACTORY

103 N. Robinson Street **Bloomington** 61704

- Phone: (309) 827-8580 **www.beernuts.com**
- Hours: Monday-Friday 8:00am-5:00pm.
- Admission: FREE

Originating in the 1930s by Edward and Arlo Shrink, this family-owned manufacturing plant produces redskin nuts, which are exclusive to the company Beer Nuts. The ancestors of today's BEER NUTS Peanuts were known as "Redskins" because they were prepared with their red skins intact. They were processed by hand in the back room of the store and sold over-the-counter by the scoop. "Redskins" were occasionally offered at no charge to entice patrons to buy homemade orange drink. Ten varieties of nuts are produced at this plant including original and glazed peanuts, almonds, cashews, macadamias, and pecans.

Visitors can observe the manufacturing process via a short video and can also participate in nut tasting at the gift store (the fun part!). The video is mostly educational explaining that peanut plants flower above the ground, but grow under the sandy soil. Watch as peanuts are washed, roasted and then coated with that special "lightly salty, slightly sweet." Please Note: No beer is ever used in the making of the product.

AMERICAN PASSION PLAY

Bloomington - *Center for Performing Arts, 110 E Mulberry Street. A historically accurate and emotionally touching performance detailing the ministry of Christ with over 50 amazing set changes, live animals and a choir. Admission. (all performances are Saturday (and some Sunday) matinees, starting one month before, leading to, Easter weekend)* **www.americanpassionplay.org**

CHILDREN'S DISCOVERY MUSEUM OF CENTRAL ILLINOIS

101 East Beaufort Street (downtown) **Bloomington (Normal)** 61761

| | Phone: (309) 433-3444 **www.childrensdiscoverymuseum.net**
| | Hours: Tuesday-Saturday 9:00am-5:00pm, Sunday 1:00-5:00pm. Open until 8:00pm on Thursday. Closed school year Mondays.
| | Admission: $6.00 per person (ages 2 & over).

Explore, imagine, create and play with three floors of easy hands-on exhibits. Visitors can: "Shop" the Main Street Market; Climb the two story Luckey Climber; Explore a Compost Pile in Oh Rubbish; pretend play on the Train Table or Water Play areas; or explore The Arts. My Place is an endless Brio Plan Table where children can create their own city and travel from place to place. Older children enjoy the simulated computer games where they create their own neighborhood or learn map-making skills using fun computer activities. Mr. Bones and the Medical Center might teach you a few science facts.

ILLINOIS STATE UNIVERSITY MUSEUMS
College Avenue **Bloomington (Normal)** 61761

Phone: (309) 438-INFO

ISU was founded in 1857 with much of the original legal work completed by Abraham Lincoln. ISU was the first public university in the state and the tenth oldest state teacher's school in the nation.

- **ISU ART GALLERIES**: 110 Center for the Visual Arts. (309) 438-5487. Three art galleries hold nearly 20 annual exhibitions .

- **ISU EYESTONE ONE-ROOM SCHOOLHOUSE**: corner of College Avenue and Adelaide Street. (309) 438-5415. Elementary students can experience a typical day in an authentic McLean County one-room schoolhouse as it was in 1899 (slate boards and wooden desks). Tours by appointment only.

- **ISU PLANETARIUM**: College Avenue and School Street. (309) 438-5007 or www.phy.ilstu.edu/planet.html. The majesty of a night sky is recreated in a celestial theater in the round. Tours by appointment. Public showings are 60 minutes.

- **ISU FARM RESEARCH FACILITY**: 25578 ISU Farm Lane. (309) 365-2211 or www.agriculture.ilstu.edu. Book your tours of a working farm. See dairy operation, beef cattle, swine, sheep and the Aquaculture Research Facility where they raise fish in an indoor, controlled environment. Computers feed animals here - How? FREE.

ORPHEUM CHILDREN'S SCIENCE MUSEUM
346 N. Neil Street, downtown **Champaign** 61820

Phone: (217) 352-5895 **www.orpheumkids.com**
Hours: Weekdays 10:00am-4:00pm, Weekends 1:00-5:00pm. Closed Mondays.
Admission: $4.00-$5.00 per person.

Walk through the doors of the 1914 Orpheum Theatre now converted to a museum with more than 20 interactive science exhibits. With a giant, 14-foot lever, children balance their body with 300 pounds of lead. A mirror takes the images of two and makes them one. At Castle Workalot simple machines cleverly bear the burden of all that hard labor. Meet Wendy the box turtle, a tarantula or Irene the Hissing Cockroach. The courtyard outside allows for a Dino Dig or searching for polished rocks at the Gem Mine.

PRAIRIE FARM

2202 W. Kirby Avenue (Centennial Park) Champaign 61821

|| Phone: (217) 398-2550 **https://champaignparks.com/project/prairie-farm/**
|| Hours: Daily 1:00-7:00pm (Memorial Day-Labor Day). Petting area 3-5:00pm daily.
|| Admission: FREE. Fee for trolley ride and some programs.

Traditional farm animals (like sheep, pigs, horses, cows, chickens) mixed with recreation. Visitors are welcome to pet the farm's animals in the petting area. Kids can cross the footbridge that spans the farm's miniature duck pond, then take a trolley ride around the farm. Recreation includes sport courts, picnic areas, waterslide, and pool.

STAERKEL PLANETARIUM

2400 West Bradley Avenue (Parkland College's Cultural Center) Champaign 61821

|| Phone: (217) 351-2200 **www2.parkland.edu/planetarium/**
|| Hours: The Staerkel Planetarium is open year-round on Friday and Saturday evenings. A variety of show types are presented.
|| Admission: $4.00-$5.00.

The second-largest planetarium in Illinois uses a Zeiss Star Projector to project thousands of visible stars on the 50-foot dome. State of the art audio visual equipment and special effects help visitors learn about the planets and stars of the universe. One popular program, Prairie Skies, delivers a live-night tour of the wonders of tonight's sky, accompanied by some of the legendary stories of the ancient sky. Find out what constellations and planets are visible tonight and how to find them. This show is updated seasonally and is intended for all ages. In addition to regular features, the dome offers children's shows, rock-and-roll light shows and seasonal presentations.

CURTIS ORCHARD

3902 S Duncan Road **Champaign** 61822

Phone: (217) 359-5565 **www.curtisorchard.com**

Curtis Orchard is an 80-acre apple orchard, pumpkin patch and entertainment farm. The bakery offers pies and donuts plus apple cider. Seasonal apple and pumpkin picking, kids play structures, a giant slide, several mazes including the Giant Jungle Maze, petting zoo, pony and horseback trail rides, and an orchard wagon tour. Admission is charged for activities and/or tours. The orchard is open late July to late December.

Tours are available Mondays, and Wednesdays - Fridays. Tours take 45 minutes and include: Honey bee presentation; Cider making presentation; Apple grading presentation. Refreshments for everyone include: Small Apple, Cinnamon-sugar donut, Apple sipper (8-oz of cider). Fee: $5.00 per person. Side Option: Pumpkin Patch picking.

SPURLOCK MUSEUM

600 S. Gregory (Univ. of Ill. Campus, I-74, Rte. 45 exit, south. East on University, south on Lincoln. Look for Krannart and you're there) **Champaign (Urbana)** 61801

Phone: (217) 333-2360 **www.spurlock.uiuc.edu**

Hours: Tuesday Noon-5:00pm, Wednesday-Friday 9:00am-5:00pm, Saturday 10:00am-4:00pm, Sunday Noon-4:00pm.

Admission: FREE, suggested donation is $3.00.

The museum highlights the lives of people from six continents through the exploration of food, clothing, shelter, communications, technology, conflict, art, religion, and ethics. Learn by looking at objects used by people around the globe and how it was used. See suites of armor or a 2,000 year old mummy of a young child in Ancient Egypt. Walk around a tipi in the American Indian Culture gallery. To engage the kids, make sure you've studied Ancient cultures and religions (esp. the Middle Ages). Also, be sure to pick up a scavenger hunt - be a Spurlock Sherlock - as there are really not any hands-on areas to interact with.

FOX RIDGE STATE PARK

18175 State Park Road (I-70, take Exit for Rt. 130 North. Go approximately
11 miles) **Charleston** 61920

- Phone: (217) 345-6416
  http://dnr.state.il.us/lands/Landmgt/PARKS/R3/FOX/FOX.HTM
- Miscellaneous: Fishing, boating and camping.

Fox Ridge State Park is known for its steep, thickly wooded ridges, broad,
lush valleys and miles of rugged, scenic hiking trails and covers 2,064 acres.
In sharp contrast to the flat prairies of most of this section of Illinois, Fox
Ridge is set amidst rolling hills along the forested bluffs of the Embarras
("Ambraw") River. Fox Ridge is a ravine of glacial moraine and many of
these trails are steep but has 18 picturesque wooden bridges and numerous
rest benches. The staircase to Eagle's Nest requires 144 steps to get you to
the deck overlooking the river, providing a wonderful view during the fall,
winter and spring.

LINCOLN-DOUGLAS DEBATE MUSEUM

416 West Madison Avenue/126 E. Street (Coles County Fairgrounds,
E. Street @ Madison Avenue) **Charleston** 61920

- Phone: (217) 348-0430 www.lookingforlincoln.com/debates/tours/charleston.
  asp
- Hours: Daily 9:00am-4:00pm.
- Admission: FREE, donations accepted.
- Note: The museum participates in a State of Illinois Heritage Tourism project
  called "Looking for Lincoln." While in downtown Charleston, view outdoor
  murals that have been created by local artists.

Tour the only museum in Illinois retracing the senatorial debates of 1858
between Abraham Lincoln and Stephen A. Douglas. Just a few hundred
feet away (signs direct you two hundred steps to the actual spot) from the
museum, 12,000 people gathered to hear Lincoln and Douglas debate their
positions on issues including slavery and interpretation of the Constitution.
They show a video of re-enactors creating scenes from the long debate. The
museum includes a Children's Hands-On Area, a Gift Shop, and a life-size
sculpture of Lincoln and Douglas. This is an absolutely awesome place for
Lincoln photo ops - indoors and out!

RED, WHITE AND BLUE DAYS

Charleston - *Morton Park (IL 16 / Lincoln Ave @ Division Street). Two days of family fun and top name concerts. Parades, Fireworks (Coles County Memorial Airport) simulcast on local radio. MTO Air Show will host military and civilian fly-bys and static displays, professional airshow performances airport firefighting and snow removal equipment on display. Central Illinois Air will be selling airplane and helicopter rides. A variety of food and beverages will be available. Bring your chairs and enjoy great music entertainment. FREE www.charlestonredwhiteandblue.com (Fourth of July weekend)*

WELDON SPRINGS STATE PARK

1159 County Road 500 North **Clinton** 61727

Phone: (217) 935-2644
http://dnr.state.il.us/lands/Landmgt/PARKS/R3/WELDONRA.HTM

More than a museum, Union School Interpretive Center is a "hands-on" learning center with a "please touch" philosophy. Both science and local history are emphasized. A collection of taxidermist-mounted mammals which make their homes in the park encourages visitors to pet a squirrel's tail, feel a badger's claws, or examine a beaver's teeth. Discovery boxes are filled with natural treasures grouped around a central theme to stimulate students' curiosity about the natural world. Insect cards demonstrate many of the basic concepts of ecology with magnified specimens. Additional natural history exhibits examine the park's variety of habitats, the eastern bluebird nestbox trail, forestry, animal builders, and raptors. During the milder seasons, you are invited to fish, boat, picnic, camp, hike, and view wildlife. Or, you might want to pitch horseshoes at the park's tournament-quality horseshoe pits. When the snow flies, hardier outdoors persons may add sledding and tobogganing on a one-eighth mile hill, ice fishing and cross-country skiing to the itinerary of their visit.

CHRISTMAS CANDLELIGHT TOURS

Clinton - *C.H. Moore Homestead. www.chmoorehomestead.org. Candlelight tours, sleigh rides, cookies and hot chocolate, entertainment, gift shop. Admission. (Friday evenings in December)*

VERMILION COUNTY MUSEUM & FITHIAN HOME
116 North Gilbert Street **Danville** 61832

- Phone: (217) 442-2922 or (800) 383-4386
  www.vermilioncountymuseum.org
- Hours: Tuesday-Saturday 10:00am-5:00pm.
- Admission: $1.00-$2.50 (age 13+). Add a little more to tour the Fithian Home, too.

The museum is a replica of the courthouse where Abraham Lincoln practiced law from 1841 to 1859. It houses an exhibit of the Lincoln Law Office, as well as natural history displays, a one room school house, and a coal mine shaft. Also on site is the 1855 Fithian Home. Dr. William Fithian was a friend of Lincoln's. You can see the original room where Lincoln spent two nights in 1858, and the balcony where he gave an informal speech.

LINCOLN'S BIRTHDAY OPEN HOUSE

Danville - *Vermilion County Museum. This event, which has taken place for well over 35 years, acquaints visitors with the time of Illinois history when Lincoln was traveling the Judicial Circuit. Admission. (first Sunday in February)*

CHRISTMAS WITH THE FITHIANS

Danville - *Vermilion County Museum. Tour of two historic Fithian homes, house of Dr. William Fithian 1890s; house of grandson early 1900s. Admission. (first weekend in December)*

ILLINOIS RENAISSANCE FAIRE

Danville - *Ellsworth Park. Step back in time to the 16th century and relive history with full scale live re-enactments, kings, queens, jugglers and jousters. There will be ribbons and flags waving the in wind, the sound of lutes, and the smells of exotic foods cooking. www.illinoisrenfaire.com Admission. (last weekend in August)*

CLINTON LAKE STATE RECREATION AREA
725 1900 East (Turn left at corner of Rt 54 and Co Hwy 14, three miles east of town) **Dewitt** 61735

- Phone: (217) 935-8722
  http://dnr.state.il.us/lands/Landmgt/PARKS/R3/CLINTON.HTM
- Note: Camping, horseback trails, boating and waterskiing.

If just getting out and about is your interest, try the park's three hiking trails. The 5 mile Houseboat Cove Trail north of the beach follows the shoreline and comes back through the woods. It is easy to moderate in difficulty. A beautiful, 1,000-foot white sand beach awaits swimmers in the warm waters of the lake. The beach is open from Memorial Day weekend through Labor Day. Located close to the swim beach or accessible by car, you will find Mascoutin Grill. This concession, with indoor and outdoor dining, serves sandwiches, beverages, snacks and its ever popular fish dinner. You can also purchase bait, camping supplies and ice. Mascoutin Grill is a seasonal operation open during warm weather. Ice fishing, ice skating and snowmobiling are allowed on the lake when the ice is thick enough.

LAKE SARA & EFFINGHAM BEACH

Lake Sara Road (Illinois Routes 32 & 33, exit 160) **Effingham** 62401

- Phone: (217) 868-2964
- Hours: Daylight
- Admission: FREE

Lake Sara offers the outdoor enthusiast water skiing, swimming, beaches, fishing, boating and camping. Large beach, picnic areas, docks, and pavilion rentals.

SCULPTURE ON THE AVENUES

201 E. Jefferson Avenue (begin here at Effingham CVB) **Effingham** 62401

- Phone: (800) 772-0750 **www.visiteffinghamil.com/restaurants/detail/ Sculpture%20on%20the%20Avenues/279**

In 1997, Effingham took the first steps to creating a popular public art event. The first piece was created by Leonardo Nierman, an internationally renowned sculptor, titled Flame of Hope - a work of polished steel. Eight sculptures by Midwestern artists later, Sculpture on the Avenues was born. There's fun, whimsy and stark lines and edges. The pieces are placed to be accessible, to be touched and viewed from every angle. A dozen sculptures have found permanent homes in Effingham and the surrounding area. Childlike pieces include Joy and Balancing Boy. An informative brochure, which facilitates a walking tour, is available at area hotels, downtown businesses, the tourism office at City Hall and in a convenient display outside City Hall.

WONDERLAND IN LIGHTS

Effingham - *Community Park. The winding road reveals a surprise at every turn. Follow the colorfully lighted road into every colorful fantasy. Reindeer fly, elves are busy decorating their home, and around the next turn, a forest of giant candy canes and gingerbread. Giant toys parade thru the hollow. The Nativity is nestled against a hillside and an American flag, complete with fireworks caps off the display. Visit with Santa and take a buggy ride or sip hot cocoa on the nearby Courthouse lawn. Admission, donations. (nightly, Thanksgiving weekend through New Year's Eve)*

EAGLE CREEK STATE RECREATION AREA

(Hwy 121 to Dalton City, then Hwy 128 south to east of Findlay)
Findlay 62534

Phone: (217) 756-8260 or (800) 876-3245 resort
http://dnr.state.il.us/lands/Landmgt/PARKS/R3/EAGLECRK.HTM

Nestled on the shores of Lake Shelbyville, Eagle Creek offers miniature golf, hiking, fishing, waterskiing, bicycling, archery, and horseback riding. The resort amenities include indoor and outdoor pools, pontoon rentals, boat docks, and sport courts. In addition to the small, friendly wooded campgrounds and the action on the lake, large herds of deer frequent these areas and are always an exciting and inspiring sight.

NATIONAL SWEETCORN FESTIVAL

Hoopeston - *McFerron Park, Route 1 & W Penn St. The festival boasts 29 tons of free corn on the cob, parade, carnival, demo derbies, and the National Sweetcorn pageant. Admission. **www.hoopestonjaycees.org/festival/** (extended Labor Day weekend)*

LINCOLN LOG CABIN STATE HISTORIC SITE

South 4th St/ 400 South Lincoln Hwy Road (I-70 exit 119. Route 130 north.
Follow signs. 8 miles south of Charleston) **Lerna 62440**

Phone: (217) 345-1845 **www.lincolnlogcabin.org**

Hours: Thursday-Sunday 9:00am-4:00pm. The Living History Program operates Wednesday-Sunday 9:00am-5:00pm (May-October). Closed winter holidays.

Admission: FREE, donations appreciated.

Note: Picnic shelters, playgrounds and restrooms available. One mile north is the Moore Home State Historic Site, a reconstructed frame home where Abraham Lincoln bid his stepmother farewell in January of 1861 before leaving to assume the Presidency. Also, many visit the Lincoln cemetery (open dawn to dusk) to see the burial site of Abraham Lincoln's father and stepmother, Thomas Lincoln and Sarah Bush Lincoln. The church is open to the public. Educators: Lesson Plans: *www.lincolnlogcabin.org/education-kits/Intro-Copyright-Notice.pdf*

Lincoln Log Cabin Historic Site was the 1840's home of Thomas and Sarah Bush Lincoln, father and stepmother of our 16th president. Abraham Lincoln was a lawyer living in Springfield by the time his parents lived here, but he did visit them periodically. The site includes a working, living history farm developed around a two-room cabin. A second farmstead, the Stephen Sargent Farm, has been moved to the site to help broaden visitors' understanding of 1840's rural life in Illinois. Be sure to watch the 14-minute film about the Lincolns, Sargents, 1840s life, and the site's living history program. This film prepares visitors for their visit to the farms. Compare the two types of farming: lifestyle farming (Lincolns) vs. profit farming (Sargents). The excellent Museum has many "TRY IT!" interactives. How many cords of wood do you need to stack? Design a pattern of scraps for a quilt. Even try running your own farm (by computer). Upland Southern dialect is spoken with first person interpreters in the outdoor village. They are really good actors!

1845 INDEPENDENCE DAY

Lerna - *Lincoln Log Cabin State Historic Site. Celebration of 1845 July 4th with militia activities, patriotic speeches, games and more. (Saturday after July 4th)*

HARVEST FROLIC & AGRICULTURAL FAIR

Lerna - *Lincoln Log Cabin State Historic Site. The Fair includes period cooking, applesauce making, food drying and preservation, quilting, grist milling, period music, and numerous hands-on activities. Visitors may also stroll the trades area which features period trades and craftspeople demonstrating their wares. These will include blacksmithing, pottery, wood carving, paper cutting (Scherenschnitte), weaving, broom making, candle making, and wood turning on the "Great Wheel." Many of the trades and crafts people will be selling their wares. FREE. (first weekend in October)*

CHRISTMAS ON THE PRAIRIE

Lerna - *Lincoln Log Cabin State. Christmas Candlelight Tours - Christmas as we* *know it today was not widely celebrated on the prairie in the early 1800s. At the Lincoln Cabin the family will gather around the hearth while the women are busy with their spinning and knitting. Meanwhile, at the Sargent Farm, members of the Sargent family will celebrate the holiday with good food, simple decorations, and readings from the Bible. Period music and song. FREE. (second weekend evenings in Dec)*

MORAINE VIEW STATE RECREATION AREA

27374 Moraine View Park Road (I-74, Exit #149 at LeRoy. Follow signs into LeRoy) **LeRoy** 61752

     Phone: (309) 724-8032
     http://dnr.state.il.us/lands/Landmgt/PARKS/R3/MORAINE.HTM

With fully developed facilities for picnicking, camping, hiking, swimming, fishing, boating, horseback riding, and winter sports, the 1,687-acre Moraine View State Recreation Area, with its 158-acre lake, is a beautiful, convenient and accessible locale for relaxation and recreation. The Black Locust picnic area includes a public, sandy beach where swimming is permitted from Memorial Day to Labor Day. The half-mile Tanglewood Self-Guiding Nature Trail winds around the lake finger in a wooded area and will take you within sight of a thriving beaver dam and lodge. Tall Timber Trail is a 1.5-mile backpack and hiking trail over moderate terrain. The Timber Point Handicapped Trail is a half-mile long opportunity for the disabled visitor to enjoy the pleasures of the woods as well.

GRAND VILLAGE OF THE KICKAPOO POW WOW

LeRoy - *Grand Village of the Kickapoo Park. Experience the Kickapoo Pow Wow in the Grand Village where the buffalo, native crops, native plants and grasses are being restored. Admission. www.grandvillage.net (first weekend in June)*

MUSEUM OF THE GRAND PRAIRIE

North Route 47 (1 mile north of I-74, Lake of the Woods Forest Preserve) **Mahomet** 61853

     Phone: (217) 586-2612 **www.museumofthegrandprairie.org**
     Hours: Daily 1:00-5:00pm (March-December); Monday-Saturday hours extended 10:00am-5:00pm (summer).
     Admission: Donations accepted.
     Note: Complemented by Mabry Gelvin Botanical Gardens.

See a full-size wigwam, the tooth of a wooly mammoth or crank the working model-T engine. With many hands-on exhibits and programs, the museum lets visitors experience life on the Grand Prairie in Champaign County during the 1800s and 1900s. Explore Abraham Lincoln's connections to Champaign County in this new exhibit. Ride in Lincoln's buggy, visit Kelley's tavern, see the photographer's shop where Lincoln's photograph was taken, listen to Lincoln's friend B.F. Harris talk about his "old friend Abe Lincoln". The Discovery Room offers hands-on opportunities to interact.

LINCOLN TRAIL STATE PARK

16985 East 1350th Road (just west of IL 1, 2 miles south of town)
Marshall 62441

Phone: (217) 826-2222
http://dnr.state.il.us/lands/Landmgt/PARKS/R3/LINCOLN.HTM

Within the thickly wooded land of this park lies a nature preserve with ravines holding a beech-maple forest just as they did in the pioneer days. The Lincoln passed through this area en route from Indiana to Macon County in 1830. The focal point of the park is Lincoln Trail Lake, which covers 146 acres in the southwest corner of the park. Enjoy camping, fishing and hiking trails and power boating, as well as an on-site restaurant. The Beech Tree Trail is just a half-mile long, extending from the boat dock parking lot and concession stand, past the large picnic shelter, and to Lakeside Campground. The trail includes a series of stairways and foot bridges, which provide an excellent view of the beech maple forest.

MOONSHINE STORE RESTAURANT

Martinsville - *6017 E 300th Road. 62442. **www.clarkcountyil.org/Communities/ moonshine.htm** Hours: Daily 6:00am-1:00pm except Sundays and major holidays. No credit cards. Roy Lee and Helen Tuttle bought the old-time (circa 1912) country store in 1982 and promptly made it the best eating house in town. Aside from cold cut deli-style sandwiches, drinks and snacks, Moonshine is the home of the world-famous Moonburger. You can get a double beef cheese Moonburger, you can get a bacon Moonburger, shoot, you can get a Moonburger just about any old way y'all want it. Helen only flips burgers until 12:30pm. After that, it's cold sandwiches. The store guest-book has visitors from all 50 states and around the world. The visitors get a chance to enjoy hospitality and ambience from days gone by, no fancy menus* *here, just give her your name when you order over the deli counter and pay as you leave. You can sit down on the inside benches or enjoy the picnic table right next to the kerosene pump.*

BAGELFEST

Mattoon - *Peterson Park. Family event with food vendors, major entertainment, World's Biggest Bagels, World's Biggest Bagel Breakfast, baby bagel and doggie bagel contests. FREE. www.mattoonbagelfest.com (third long weekend in July)*

MONTICELLO RAILWAY MUSEUM

P O Box 401 (I-72 at Market Street. Exit 166. Turn at the stoplight onto Iron Horse Place) **Monticello** 61856

- Phone: (217) 762-9011 **www.mrym.org**
- Admission: Fees charged based on trip. Basically $6.00-$10.00 per person.
- Tours: Trains depart the museum site on Saturdays and Sundays, three to four times per day, weekends and holidays May-October)

The train pulls up to the depot and the call "All Aboard" echoes in your ears and prepares you for your trip back to the olden days of railroading. Allow yourself to enjoy the sights of the Illinois countryside. As you travel, the conductor will punch your souvenir ticket, call attention to the points of interest along the way and answer any questions you might have. Make an afternoon of it with a picnic at the grove near Camp Creek Yard.

LUNCH WITH SANTA ON THE TRAIN

Monticello - *Monticello Railway Museum. Old Wabash Depot. Ride the train and enjoy lunch and a visit with Santa and elves. Reservations required. Admission. See website for Polar Express rides, too. (first weekend in December)*

DR. HIRAM RUTHERFORD'S HOME

Pike Street just north of Illinois Route 133, one block south of the Oakland square on Pike Street **Oakland** 61943

- Phone: (217) 346-2031 **www.drhiramrutherford.com/index.html**
- Hours: Fridays and Saturdays 10:00am-2:00pm (April - October).
- Admission: Small donation.

Some 110 years ago, rural folk with ailments came from miles around to see Dr. Hiram Rutherford in his Oakland home office. Rutherford was Oakland's first doctor. The interior of the home offers a look into 19th-century life, complete with a summer kitchen and drying shed. Largely because his life coincided with Abraham Lincoln's days as a lawyer – and because Rutherford played a part in a lawsuit that Lincoln lost – the doctor's house, and even his desk, have been preserved.

WALNUT POINT STATE PARK

2331 East County Road 370 North (within a few miles of Interstate 57, U.S. Highway 36 and Illinois Route 133, just north of town) **Oakland** 61943

Phone: (217) 346-3336

http://dnr.state.il.us/lands/Landmgt/PARKS/R3/WALNUTPT.HTM

Enjoy camping, fishing, hiking and boating in this park. Paddle-boat, row-boat and canoe rentals are available, as well as a concession store. Hear live music on weekends. The 59-acre, multi-fingered Walnut Point Lake is the focal point of the park. Hiking and nature-study enthusiasts will find 2.25 miles of trails weaving through the timber. By using the main park road and the Gray Squirrel-Twin Points connection trail, walkers and joggers can complete a 3-mile exercise loop. All trails are restricted to foot traffic only. The Lakeside Nature Trail (.5 mile) is handicapped accessible.

KICKAPOO STATE PARK

10906 Kickapoo Park Road (off I-74 near Danville) **Oakwood** 61858

Phone: (217) 442-4915

http://dnr.state.il.us/lands/Landmgt/PARKS/R3/KICKAPOO.HTM

This park was the first in the country to be built on strip-mined land. The park offers many types of camping, miles of hiking trails, fishing, canoeing, guided horseback riding, and more than 10 miles of mountain biking trails. The Middle Fork State Fish and Wildlife Area winds through a mixture of forests and prairies.

PIONEER CITY RODEO & LABOR DAY FESTIVAL

Palestine - *Main Street - Leaverton Park & Pioneer City Arena. Performances of the PRCA Rodeo, Lunch with the Rodeo Clowns, and Camping. Chuckwagon Breakfast –*

about 2000 other hungry people join you to share 800 pounds of whole hog sausage, 400 pounds of pancake batter, 1200 cartons of milk, and 200 gallons of coffee (free will donation only). Live bands, carnival, and parade. FREE for festival. Tickets required for rodeos. **www.pioneercity.com/rodeo/** *(Labor Day weekend)*

HARDY'S REINDEER RANCH

1356 CR 2900N (I-74 exit 184, Rte 45 N approx. 16 miles. Head west on Rte. 136. Just past I-57, turn left at Evans Rd & follow signs) **Rantoul** 61866

- Phone: (217) 893-3407 **www.reindeerranch.com**
- Hours: Open August 1-December 21, call for seasonal hours. Generally 10:00am-7:00pm, especially September, October, December.
- Admission: FREE (fee for corn maze, hayrack ride & pedal carts). Reindeer Tours are $3.00 per person.
- Note: Great place for groups to come - chuckwagon packages range from $6.00-$20.00. In the banquet hall, play dress up as the "characters" in your group dress for the wild west - great photo ops!

The North Pole has moved to Central Illinois! From August thru October the theme is "BEST IN THE midWEST." Pick a pumpkin in the pines, browse through the general store gift shop, or try your luck at figuring out the mysteries of the 6-acre Cornfusion maze. Experience the Kid's Corral, take a hayrack ride, play in a realistic Indian tepee or the straw fort, pedal your way through the new Grand Prix style race track, and of course, see the Reindeer! Wait until you see them! Try on some antlers (they shed them every year) and feed them apples. The staff will teach you so much. From November through December, the reindeer ranch is transformed into a Christmas wonderland. Hear that clicking sound? The reindeer do click when they walk (Up on the Housetop, click, click, click…) and they really do leap and dance (if it's snowing!) The general store is reminiscent of days gone by with a pot-bellied stove, period costumes, twinkling lights and wonderful smells. The western style banquet facility was recently renovated and is available for "Wild West" BBQ or outdoor weenie roast. "Howdy partner" - this place is so...o....o endearing!

OCTAVE CHANUTE AEROSPACE MUSEUM

1011 Pacesetter Drive (Rte 45 N to turn right at Welcome to Rantoul sign, follow around until you see planes by the side of the road) **Rantoul** 61866

- Phone: (217) 893-1613 **www.aeromuseum.org**
- Hours: Monday-Saturday 10:00am-5:00pm; Sunday Noon-5:00pm. Closes One hour earlier winter weekends.
- Admission: $10.00 adult, $8.00 senior, $5.00 child (over 5).
- Note: Skydiving events held on campus are a big thrill to watch or do! Educators: History of aviator pioneers - **www.aeromuseum.org/index. php/2013-02-06-20-03-42/historic-aviators.**

Located in and out of a hanger of the former Chanute Air Force Base, this museum is the largest aerospace museum in Illinois and home to more than 40 aircraft and missiles. From the old biplane, prop plane, and high performance World War II fighter planes right up through modern jet aircraft. In the hanger, kids will awe over the greeting from a giant planes! Ever seen an ejection seat? Go down to missile storage or see the missile platform base. How does a motor work? Push a button and watch. If you like memorabilia, check out the diaries and uniforms paying homage to all veterans, prisoners of war, and those missing in action. End indoors at the simulated repair shop with sight and sound. This place really appeals to the guys.

LAKE SHELBYVILLE

Rte 4, Box 128B (between Rtes 121, 32 & 128) **Shelbyville** 62565

- Phone: (217) 774-3951 **www.lakeshelbyville.com**
- Note: Folks tell us they love annual family reunions at Lithia Resort (217-774-2882 or **www.lithiaresort.com**). Air-conditioned rooms with refrigerator, rooms with kitchen or rooms with adjoining kitchen. Luxury Cabins: large kitchen and family room, bath and bedrooms - some are log cabins. The property has a large picnic shelter, grills, campfire rings, catch and release ponds, arcade, and are close to the Lithia Springs Marina.

The US Army Corps of Engineers lake offers sparkling waters, sheltered coves, and sandy beaches. Shelbyville Visitor Center is located in the Dam East Recreation Area. The center is one mile east of Shelbyville just off Rte 16. Tour the exhibit area, stay for an introductory video about the lake, or take a guided tour of the Lake Shelbyville Dam. All tours begin at the visitors center and are held each weekend from Memorial Day to Labor Day. The visitor center is open daily in the summer, weekends spring and fall. The

Corps offers trails ranging in length from 1/2 mile to the 11-mile Chief Illini Trail. As snow approaches, so do the sledders and cross-country skiers. Ice fishing and ice-skating are also very popular activities.

FIREWORKS OVER THE LAKE

Shelbyville - *Lake Shelbyville beach. Food, band, fireworks over the lake. (July 4th)*

SCARECROW DAZE

Shelbyville - *Games for kids, pumpkin carving contest, make and take scarecrows, bingo, scavenger hunts and a parade. FREE. (second weekend in October)*

SHELBYVILLE FESTIVAL OF LIGHTS

Shelbyville - *Forest Park. (800) 874-3529. Share the music of the holiday season as you drive through light displays in town and then experience the Starflake Trail throughout the county. Donations. (daily mid-November thru New Years nights)*

FUNKS GROVE PURE MAPLE SIRUP

Shirley - *5257 Old Route 66 (15 min south of Bloomington). There's more than maple sirup at Funk's Grove. Since 1824, the Funk family has been producing its special brand of pure maple sirup (yes, it's spelled that way on purpose) from more than 6,000 taps in this grove of maple trees. Leave time for a timber walk and visit to the mineral museum on the property. FREE (early spring, daily except Sunday/Monday daytime).* **www.funksmaplesirup.com/index.html**

HIDDEN SPRINGS STATE FOREST
Rural Route 1, Box 200 (5 miles southwest of town, Illinois Route 32)
Strasburg 62465

Phone: (217) 644-3091
http://dnr.state.il.us/lands/Landmgt/PARKS/R3/HSFOREST.HTM
Note: Timbers Restaurant and Lodge (adjacent) features a dining room and accommodations in a log building, horse-drawn surrey rides and pony leads for kids. Chuckwagon dinners for groups. (**www.timberslodge.com**)

The name Hidden Springs was selected to designate this particular state forest because of the seven known springs on the property which were used for drinking water by the early settlers. Most of the springs are covered over with vegetation but two spring trails remain: Rocky Spring and Quicksand Spring. Possum Hollow Nature Trail, 3/4 mile in length, provides access to Park

Pond and the pine seed orchard. Trail guides, available at the headquarters, campground, and picnic area, guide the visitor to the 35 interpretive stations. The Big Tree Trail, one mile in length, features a sycamore 78 inches in diameter, one of the largest to be found in Illinois. Facilities for picnicking, camping, fishing, and wildlife watching are here, too.

LITTLE THEATRE ON THE SQUARE

12 E. Harrison Street **Sullivan** 61951

- Phone: (217) 728-7375 or (888) 261-9675 **www.thelittletheatre.org**
- Hours: Matinees: Wednesday & Sunday at 2:00pm; Saturday at 4:00pm. Theatre for Young: 6 days each month (summer) at 10:30am.
- Admission: $28.00-$30.00 per person for matinees. Theatre for Young Audiences: $10-12.50 per person.

The Little Theatre features name artists and many talented amateurs. In addition to traditional theatre and musicals (ex. Beauty and the Beast), the Theatre produces children's theatre (ex. Sleeping Beauty) and a Christmas holiday show.

AMISHLAND RED BARN BUFFET & SHOPPES

Tuscola - *(I-57 exit 212, across from the Holiday Inn Express) 61953. The Amishland Red Barn is the north gateway to the largest Amish community in Illinois. The Amish Style buffet serves great chicken and homestyle foods. Oh, and the pies! The quiet, indoor "streets" with cobblestone sidewalks, street lamps, and several individual specialty stores are a great way to walk off your meal. If you still have room, sample Aunt Sarah's Cheese - many varieties. Meals run $13.00 for adults (all you can eat buffet). Children have a reduced rate. Lunch daily, sometimes dinner.*

HOLIDAY INN EXPRESS, AMISH COUNTRY

Tuscola - *1201 Tuscola Blvd (I-57 & US 36 exit 212) 61953. A family-friendly hotel close to Amish attractions, restaurants and shopping. The spacious rooms include micro/frig units and high-speed internet. The hotel offers guests a free deluxe Breakfast Bar each morning and a heated indoor pool and spa. (217) 253-6363 or* **www.hiexpress.com/Tuscola**

WOLF CREEK STATE PARK

Rural Route 1 (on Lake Shelbyville's eastern shore) **Windsor** 61957

Phone: (217) 459-2831
http://dnr.state.il.us/lands/Landmgt/PARKS/R3/Wolfcrek.htm

The Wolf Creek/Eagle Creek sites, facing each other across the central portion of Lake Shelbyville, provide the perfect setting for outdoor recreation and natural relaxation. This 2,000 acre park offers camping, fishing, horseback riding, hiking trails, swimming and power boating. For refreshing walks in the forests, Wolf Creek contains seven hiking trails. For invigorating winter time activity there is a 16½ mile snowmobile trail, and for the equestrian there is a scenic 15-mile equestrian trail.

Travel Journal & Notes:

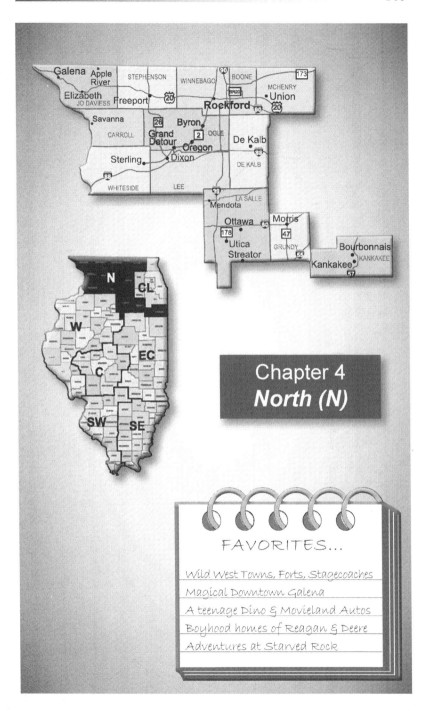

Chapter 4
North (N)

FAVORITES...

Wild West Towns, Forts, Stagecoaches

Magical Downtown Galena

A teenage Dino & Movieland Autos

Boyhood homes of Reagan & Deere

Adventures at Starved Rock

Amboy
- Depot Days

Apple River
- Apple River Canyon State Park
- Stagecoach Trails Livery

Bourbonnais
- Exploration Station Children's Museum
- Kankakee River State Park
- Strickler Planetarium

Byron
- Byron Forest Preserve/ Jarrett Prairie Center

Caledonia
- The Pumpkin Patch

Channahon
- Channahon State Park & I&M Canal Trailhead

Crystal Lake
- Johnny Appleseed Festival

Dekalb
- Glidden Homestead And Historical Center
- Stage Coach Theatre

Dekalb (Sycamore)
- Old Sycamore Farm Pumpkin Patch

Dixon
- Ronald Reagan Boyhood Home

Dixon (Grand Detour)
- John Deere Historic Site

Dubuque (IOWA)
- National Mississippi River Museum & Aquarium

Elizabeth
- Apple River Fort Site

Franklin
- Franklin Creek State Natural Area & Grist Mill

Franklin Grove
- Chaplin Creek Historic Village Harvest Festival

Freeport
- Silver Creek And Stephenson Railroad Antique Steam Train Rides

Fulton
- Christmas In The Canyon

Galena
- Chestnut Mountain Resort Activities
- Desoto House Hotel
- Eagle Ridge Inn Resort
- Galena History Museum
- Galena Trolleys
- Ulysses S. Grant Home & Old Market House State Historic Sites

Harvard
- Royal Oak Farm Orchard

Huntley
- Toms Farm Market Fall Festival

Lena
- Lake Le-Aqua-Na State Park
- Torkelson Cheese Company

Malta
- Jonamac Orchard

Manteno
- Bethlehem Walk

Marseilles
- Illini State Park

McHenry
- Moraine Hills State Park
- Harms Farm
- Shades Of Autumn Festival

Mendota
- Sweet Corn Festival

Morris
- Gebhard Woods State Park
- Goose Lake Prairie Area

Morrison
- Morrison-Rockwood State Park

Mt. Morris
- White Pines Forest State Park

Oregon
- Castle Rock State Park
- Lowden State Park
- White Pines Ranch

Ottawa
- Buffalo Rock State Park & Effigy Tumuli
- Illinois Waterway Visitors Center

Prophetstown
- Prophetstown State Recreation Area

Rockford
- Beef-A-Roo
- Mary's Market
- Klehm Arboretum & Botanic Garden
- Burpee Museum Of Natural History
- Discovery Center Museum
- Olympic Tavern
- Trolley Station & Forest City Queen Rides
- Midway Village
- Coco Key Water Resort
- Illinois Snow Sculpting

Rockford (Cherry Valley)
- Magic Waters Waterpark

Rockford (Loves Park)
- Ski Broncs Water Ski Show
- Rockford Speedway
- Rock Cut State Park

Rockford (Roscoe)
- Historic Auto Attractions

Savanna
- Mississippi Palisades State Park

Shabbona
- Shabbona Lake State Park

Spring Grove
- Chain O'lakes State Park
- Richardson Adventure Farm & Corn Maze

Tampico
- Ronald Reagan Birthplace

Union
- Donley's Wild West Town
- Illinois Railway Museum

Utica
- Starved Rock State Park

Woodstock
- Challenger Learning Center
- Groundhog Days
- All Seasons Orchard
- Old Fashioned Harvest Fest
- Red Barn Farm Fall Festival

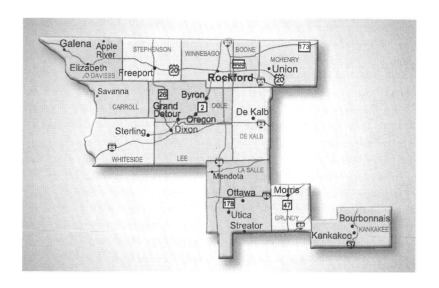

A Real Stagecoach Ride - Stagecoach Trails

Sites and attractions are listed in order by City, Zip Code, and Name. Symbols indicated represent: 📵 Restaurants   🛌 Lodging

DEPOT DAYS

Amboy - *East Main Street & South East Ave, Depot Museum. Built in 1876, this depot was headquarters for the Illinois Central Railroad. Tour the Depot and Schoolhouse, have a old-time soda at the Amboy Pharmacy, or glance at wood carvings (three presidents from IL) made from tree trunks at City Park. Also carnival, food, parade, entertainment and a vehicle show.* ***www.depotdays.com*** *(last few days of August)*

APPLE RIVER CANYON STATE PARK

8763 E. Canyon Rd (U.S. Highway 20 at Illinois Highway 78, 1 mile east of Stockton. Travel north 6 miles on Illinois 78 and turn west at the park signs)
Apple River 61001

Phone: (815) 745-3302
http://dnr.state.il.us/lands/landmgt/parks/R1/APPLE.HTM

This scenic canyon area was formed by the action of the winding waters of Apple River.   Limestone bluffs, deep ravines, springs, streams and wildlife characterize this area which was once a part of a vast sea bottom that stretched from the Alleghenies to the Rockies. Five hiking trails rated moderately difficult to strenuous wind through the woods and along the scenic river bluffs. Watch for white-tailed deer, raccoons and hawks. Eagles are sometimes seen in winter. Forty-seven varieties of birds, some 14 different ferns and 165 varieties of flowers, including the rare bird's-eye primrose, are found here. The park has four picnic areas along the Apple River and three picnic shelters. Fishing is popular, and Apple River is stocked with trout in the spring. There are 47 primitive campsites (without showers or electricity); reservations are not accepted.

STAGECOACH TRAILS LIVERY

5656 Stagecoach Trail (1/2 mile west of town) **Apple River** 61001

Phone: (815) 594-2423
Admission: $75.00 per hour per group of eight.
Note: Also available: wagon train trips, hayrides and sleigh rides. Bunkhouse warming room. Call for reservations.

Stagecoach Trails Livery near Galena, Illinois offers stagecoach rides in a replica of an original Concord Stagecoach. They offer covered wagon trips with or without authentic "chuck wagon" meals. You choose the length of all trips. First, visit the Bunk House looking through pictures of the family of horses; see the goat who rides horseback; pick up a piece of real lead; or try to pick up a stagecoach robbery strong box - filled with gold and such - can you imagine trying to carry it? R.J. Spillane (the proprietor) will weave lots of cowboy tails as he shares his memories! The trails are located on some of the old original stagecoach and wagon trails. It used to take 5 days (1820s) to go from Galena to Chicago. On the trails you may find all kinds of wildlife including small game, deer, or perhaps the magnificent wild turkey. Maybe you'll take the trail over a bridge or cross the racking Apple River and right through prairie tall grass. Sometimes, you may catch a glimpse of an old church, school, barn and general store. Come along, relax, and enjoy God's country. This is truly one of the most unique settings and "historical" tours we've ever taken! Well worth the effort to make the trip out to literally "feel" like you're out west in the early 1800s…and, you get to meet a modern-day cowboy – R.J. Spillane is quite a character!

EXPLORATION STATION CHILDREN'S MUSEUM

459 Kennedy Drive **Bourbonnais** 60914

 Phone: (815) 935-5665 **www.btpd.org/exploration_station.php**
 Hours: Monday-Saturday 10:00am-5:00pm, Sunday 1:00-5:00pm. Closed most major holidays and Fall/Winter Mondays.
 Admission: $7.00 (age 1+). Discount for township residents.

Inside the multi-level castle, visitors can experience medieval life in a number of ways. They can dress up in royal garb in the dressing room, hide out in the dungeon, explore secret tunnels and keep an eye out for royal enemies by using real periscopes that view out over the Perry Farm Park. At Exploration Station, children can be a clerk in the new grocery store, climb inside the tower of a medieval castle, work in a kid's size emergency room, man an ambulance, create a flying machine, sit in the cockpit of a fighter jet behind the controls, connect pipes and elbows in Airways, view the planets and star constellations, learn about fossils, create their own art project, dance on the floor keyboard like Tom Hanks in "BIG", paint their faces and much more.

KANKAKEE RIVER STATE PARK

5314 West Illinois Route 102 (I-55 north to Dwight Exit (Rte.17 east). Go approximately 20 miles to Warner Bridge Rd. north) **Bourbonnais** 60914

- Phone: (815) 933-1383
  http://dnr.state.il.us/lands/landmgt/parks/R2/KANKAKEE.HTM
- Admission: FREE. No reservations for camping. Concessions fees.

Anglers, canoeists, hunters, campers, hikers, bicyclers, horseback riders (rentals) and other outdoor enthusiasts find the park's recreational opportunities unsurpassed. The naturally channeled Kankakee River is the focus of the park's popularity. The park's Rock Creek Café and Trading Post, near Rock Creek Canyon and the suspension bridge, offers meals and camping supplies. The park's trail system stretches for miles along both sides of the river. Hiking, biking and cross-country ski trails are on the river's north side, while horse and snowmobile trails can be found on the south. A 3-mile route along Rock Creek lets hikers take in the beauty of limestone canyons and a frothy waterfall. A bicycle trail begins at Davis Creek Area and travels 10.5 miles of trails in the form of a linear trail along the river and a loop in the west end of the park. Also, come to the visitor center and learn about the history and wildlife of the park through numerous exhibits and displays.

STRICKLER PLANETARIUM

One University Avenue (I-57 S to exit 315, Bradley/Bourbonnais. Rte 50 S to right on Armour Road. Left onto Convent Street to Main Street, follow signs to Olivet Nazarene Univ.) **Bourbonnais** 60914

- Phone: (815) 939-5308 **http://strickler.olivet.edu/**
- Shows: Generally late afternoon or early evening performances - especially near holidays and Saturdays.
- Admission charge is $3.00 per person/per show. There are no advanced ticket sales. Doors open 10-15 minutes prior to show time.

Named after Dr. Dwight Strickler, a former biology professor at Olivet, the planetarium features a dome presentation screen with specially designed seating. Each year, approximately 8,000 people view astronomy shows in the planetarium, one of only a few planetariums located on private university campuses nationwide and the only planetarium located on a Christian campus. Explore the universe, and learn about the stars, comets and asteroids - even poetry. Special shows take place during holiday seasons.

BYRON FOREST PRESERVE/ JARRETT PRAIRIE

7993 North River Road **Byron** 61010

Phone: (815) 234-8535 www.byronforestpreserve.com
Hours: Center- Monday-Friday 8:00am-4:30pm, Saturday 9:00am-4:00pm,
Sunday 1:00-4:00pm. Tuesday & Thursday open until 8:00pm.

NATURAL HISTORY MUSEUM - The Jarrett Prairie Center's focal point
with its prairie, woodlands, and wetland exhibition areas. The museum depicts
how the area appeared before the arrival of the European settlers. Kids like
climbing through the wolf den. The center has large diorama aquariums -
home to the native turtles and snakes you would find in the nearby Rock
River area and its tributaries. A glass-sided beehive gives visitors a close-but
safe-encounter with honey bees at work making honey, caring for their queen
and her un-ending brood, and protecting their home.

HERITAGE FARM MUSEUM - Also located in the Byron Forest Preserve
District, this house includes five rooms: a bedroom, a living room, a kitchen,
a summer kitchen, and a room showing a section of original grout house.
The rooms contain furniture representative of the time period 1843 - 1869.
Currently the outbuildings, which include the big barn, the corncrib, the hog
barn, and the milk house, are being restored.

THE PUMPKIN PATCH

Caledonia - *Fiorello's Farm, 3178 Hwy 173. www.thegreatpumpkinpatch.com. Two
miles of trails and turns in the corn maze, pick your own pumpkins, pony/wagon rides,
cornstalk maze. Pumpkin Launching and Artists House for Free Personalization
of Your Painted Pumpkin, face painting; Expanded Free Petting Zoo. Free to the
grounds, petting zoo and barn; Admission to attractions and activities by tickets or
wristbands. (daily, September and October)*

CHANNAHON STATE PARK & I&M CANAL TRAILHEAD

2 West Story Street (I-55: take the Rte. 6/ Channahon exit; one mile south of US 6 and Canal Street) **Channahon** 60410

Phone: (815) 467-4271
http://dnr.state.il.us/lands/landmgt/parks/I&M/EAST/CHANNAHO/Park.htm
Admission: FREE

This state park serves as the trailhead for the 61-mile I&M Canal State Trail. Channahon is an Indian word meaning "the meeting of the waters" and signifies the joining of the DuPage, Des Plaines and Kankakee Rivers. Historic structures include a canal locktender's house and canal locks 6 and 7. Anglers of all ages will enjoy fishing in either the Illinois & Michigan Canal or the DuPage River. Primitive tent camping only.

JOHNNY APPLESEED FESTIVAL

Crystal Lake - *Downtown. Bushels of fun for everyone, with music, entertainment, pony rides, petting zoo, pumpkin train, pumpkin bowling, apple bobbing, apple pie baking contest, clowns, children's games, square dancing, face painting, story telling, temporary tattoos, wagon rides, farmer's market, ball race and an appearance by Johnny Appleseed himself! (815) 479-0835 or www.downtowncl.org. FREE (last Saturday in September)*

GLIDDEN HOMESTEAD AND HISTORICAL CENTER

921 West Lincoln Highway (I-88 to Annie Glidden Road exit, to Lincoln Highway east) **Dekalb** 60115

- Phone: (815) 756-7904 **www.gliddenhomestead.org**
- Hours: Second & Fourth Sundays from Noon-4:00pm (May-first week of December).
- Admission: $1.00-$2.00.

The Glidden Homestead & Historical Center is restoring and developing the site where in the 1870s, Joseph F. Glidden invented "The Winner," one of the most widely-used types of barbed wire. It is still a work in progress. Built in 1861, the house and brick barn were constructed for local farmer and barbed wire inventor, Joseph Glidden. It is considered the birthplace of barbed wire, one of several important inventions to encourage homesteading on the prairie.

STAGE COACH THEATRE

126 South 5th Street **Dekalb** 60115

- Phone: (815) 758-1940 **www.stagecoachers.com**
- Shows: Thursday-Saturday evenings, Sunday matinees.
- Admission: Tickets run $9.00-$15.00 depending on venue.

Attend a drama, comedy or musical in one of the oldest community theaters in Illinois. Productions include family friendly shows like Huck Finn and a Christmas Carol. Children under 5 are recommended to attend matinees.

OLD SYCAMORE FARM PUMPKIN PATCH

Dekalb (Sycamore) - *15326 Quigley Road (one mile south of IL 64) Pumpkins, apples and cider and such at the market. Hayride, maze of corn, Giant Pumpkin Patch, Charlotte's Web, barnyard animals and refreshments. Pumpkin Festival display of 1000s of decorated pumpkins, downtown, last week in October. Admission.* **www. facebook.com/pages/Kokomo-IN/Old-Sycamore-Farm-Pumpkin-Patch-Haunted-Barn/99615214793** *(daily, late September thru October)*

RONALD REAGAN BOYHOOD HOME

816 S. Hennepin (look for signs off IL 26 north) **Dixon** 61021

- Phone: (815) 288-5176 **www.reaganhome.org**
- Hours: Monday-Saturday 10:00am-4:00pm, Sunday 1:00-4:00pm (April - mid-November).
- Admission: $5.00 per person. FREE for children 12 and under with adult.
- Tour: Begin at the Visitors Center with a short video, then followed by a 15 minute house tour. Just the right amount of time for kids.

Reagan's parents, Jack and Nelle, moved to Dixon in 1920, when Reagan was 9 years old. The Ronald Reagan Boyhood Home is restored to its 1920 condition and decorated with furniture typical of the period. Family activity extended beyond the house to the barn where "Dutch" and his brother "Moon" raised rabbits. The boys also played football on the side yard with their friends. Listen and watch for the signed football and the secret hiding place for coins (hint: by the fireplace). What was their favorite evening snack? No, not jelly beans! Learn how diverse his interests were and some of his heroics (saving 77 lives as a lifeguard). This is a great way to study a modern-day President as a boy. Excellent presentation.

JOHN DEERE HISTORIC SITE

8334 S Clinton Street (take I-88 to IL-26. north on IL-26/IL-2) **Dixon (Grand Detour)** 61021

- Phone: (815) 652-4551

www.deere.com/en_US/corporate/our_company/fans_visitors/tours_attractions/historicalsite.page

Hours: Wednesday - Sunday 9:00am-5:00pm (May-October).

Admission: $5.00 (ages 12+).

Vermont native, John Deere, with a few tools and very little money, struck out on his own towards Illinois. He promised his wife Demarius and their children that he would be back to get them after he made a good start. It didn't take long, Grand Detour was in need of a blacksmith and John Deere was just the man needed. Shortly after arriving in town, Deere learned that the commonly used cast-iron plows of the day performed poorly in the sticky soil of the Midwest. Convinced that a plow with a highly polished surface would clean, or self-scour as it moved through the field, John Deere fashioned just such an implement in 1837, using steel from a broken saw blade. It wasn't long before manufacturing plows, not blacksmithing, became the main focus of Deere's livelihood. Visit the Center's exhibits and film, then go onsite through the Deere home and the re-created blacksmith shop where it all began. See the original floor of the actual workshop where he invented the "singing" plow. They present an interesting description and demonstration of how Deere ran his shop. How does a blacksmith put a muffler on his anvil? What does the term "beat the daylight out of it" mean? In the home, hear a simulated conversation, John and Demarius Deere talking of daily events. A wonderful place to explore the history of a famous man and his invention.

NATIONAL MISSISSIPPI RIVER MUSEUM & AQUARIUM

350 E. 3rd Street (follow the signs off Rte. 20 west, just over the bridge from IL) **Dubuque (IOWA)** 52001

Phone: (563) 557-9545 or (800) 226-3369 **www.rivermuseum.com**

Hours: Daily 10:00am-5:00pm. Opens one hour earlier Summer and Fall seasons.

Admission: $15.00 adult, $13.00 senior (65+), $10.00 youth (3-17).

Note: Boat & Breakfast - stay overnight in bunks on a steam ship dredger. Have a hearty sailors' breakfast. Depot Café for lunch. Educators: click on the icon: EDUCATION & GROUPS for Lesson Plans (about a dozen) and complete conservation-themed curriculum.

Take an historic and natural journey on the Mighty Mississippi. Begin with the Mississippi Journey - a sight, sound and motion short film that grabs you into the river "scene". Chart a course as you pass floor-to-ceiling glass panels framing gators, otters (so playful), ancient sturgeon and paddlefish. Walk on working riverboats, go into cargo holds in the Barge theatre, touch fish or "Noodle" a catfish (ewe!). If you're not squirmy yet, let their educators introduce you to freshwater mussels, snails, and crawfish in the touch tank. Kids can also roll on logs like lumberjacks, pilot a boat or walk through a lead mine (actually, almost crawl). Outside, tour the Logsdon towboat, see huge steamboat artifacts, and watch as a boat is launched into the Mississippi. The floating dock features houseboats, scientific vessels, and the traveling Audubon Ark. A recreated Indian village and nature boardwalk follows the outside historic trail. Finally, watch craftsmen carve a boat in the wood shop. Look for "Sippi" the river otter mascot, too. A lot of money and time has produced an excellent site to feel the mighty Mississippi from on, and in, the water. Well worth the trip over to the Iowa shores.

APPLE RIVER FORT STATE HISTORIC SITE

311 E Myrtle **Elizabeth** 61028

- Phone: (815) 858-2028 **www.appleriverfort.org**
- Hours: Wednesday-Sunday 9:00am-5:00pm (April-October); 9:00am-4:00pm (November-March).
- Admission: Suggested donation of $4.00 adult, $2.00 youth (under 18) or $10.00 family.
- Note: Living History Weekends are held almost every weekend (May-October). Chat with the townsfolk and find out what their chores were and what they feared.

Apple River Fort State Historic Site is the site of one of the battles fought during the Black Hawk War. The discovery of lead in the Galena area during the 1820's brought many miners to the area. Black Hawk, a Sauk warrior who had fought with the British against the United States in the War of 1812, was determined to return to the land he believed belonged to his people. Black Hawk and his warriors attacked the hastily erected fort on June 24, 1832. The Sauk had over 200 warriors, the settlers only 25 men. How did settler womens' bravery during the fighting help them win and earn the town's name? Located a short walk from the fort, the Interpretive Center relates the story of the Black Hawk War and the Apple River Fort. A series of illustrated panels tells the story of Sauk and Fox, the early miners, and the conflict between the two cultures that led to the Black Hawk War. Other exhibits at the two-story Interpretive Center include a 15-minute video of the Black Hawk War (pull up a tree stump chair) and archaeology exhibits telling how the fort was located and displaying some of the artifacts uncovered at the site. Exhibits along the trail to the fort explore the role of Abraham Lincoln and other notables in the Black Hawk War.

INDEPENDENCE DAY CELEBRATION

Elizabeth - *Apple River Fort State Historic Site. Costumed interpreters portray the Apple River Fort settlers as they bravely celebrate Independence Day in the year 1832. Despite the ongoing war, neighbors gather to commemorate the day. Military speeches, demonstrations, a reading of the Declaration of Independence, and 1830s version of baseball, games and more. FREE. (July 4th)*

KEEPING CHRISTMAS

Elizabeth - *Apple River Fort. Experience the sights, sounds and smells of an 1830s Christmas. Costumed interpreters demonstrate winter activities such as candle dipping, sausage making and target shooting. Interpreters will demonstrate customs of Christmas and discuss sometimes-controversial ideas regarding the celebration of Christmas as a holiday. Hot cider will be served around warming fires. FREE (second weekend in December)*

FRANKLIN CREEK STATE NATURAL AREA & GRIST MILL

1872 Twist Rd (one mile NW of town, 8 miles east of Dixon, just north of IL 38)
Franklin 61031

  Phone: (815) 456-2878 or (815) 456-2718 (mill)
  http://dnr.state.il.us/lands/landmgt/parks/R1/FRANKLIN.HTM
  Hours: Gristmill: Weekends Noon-4:00pm (April-October).

The beautiful Franklin Creek flows throughout the 664-acre park and serves to offer fishing, horseback riding, hiking and cross-country skiing sites. The Mill Springs Trail is a unique, concrete-surfaced trail suitable for people of all mobility levels. The easy trail leads to the beautiful Mill Spring. Pioneer Pass is highly recommended to see the park's unique, natural beauty. The original early American corn meal and wheat flour producing mill, constructed in 1847, was the "largest and most complete" grist mill in Lee County.

The newly reconstructed Franklin Creek Grist Mill became operational in 1999. Along with milling demonstrations, the building serves as a visitors center for the natural area. All four levels of the Grist Mill are handicapped accessible.

CHAPLIN CREEK HISTORIC VILLAGE HARVEST FESTIVAL

Franklin Grove - *Whitney Road. Celebrate the harvest in this 19th-century Midwestern prairie village featuring buildings from the region. Scenes and demonstrations are set in the mid-to-late 1800s time period. (first weekend in August)*

SILVER CREEK AND STEPHENSON RAILROAD ANTIQUE STEAM TRAIN RIDES

2954 S. Walnut (IL 20 west of Rockford, Walnut and Lamm Roads)
Freeport 61032

- Phone: (815) 235-7329 or (815) 232-2306 **www.thefreeportshow.com**
- Hours: Typically weekends beginning in May thru October. 11:00am-4:00pm.
- Admission: $3.00-7.00 per person for railroad or shows, $4.00 adults for museum.

All aboard as a 36-ton 1912 Heisler steam locomotive pulls three cabooses, including an antique red caboose reported to be the oldest in the state, and two passenger flatcars for a four mile ride through farmlands and across a bridge 30' above Yellow Creek. Purchase your ticket at the Silver Creek Depot, a turn-of-the-century replica filled with railroad artifacts. Browse for novelties in the Freight House. Visit the 25-room Silvercreek Museum filled with early Americana and enjoy homemade food served for lunch.

CHRISTMAS TEA

Freeport - *Silvercreek Museum and Stephenson County Historical Museum. Tour these mansions decorated for the Christmas season with holiday lights and oil lamps. Tea and cookies served. Small admission or donation accepted. (first weekend in December)*

CHRISTMAS IN THE CANYON

Fulton - *Heritage Canyon, North Fourth Street. (815) 589-2838. At these events, the Early American Crafters, the Civil War reenactors, and other historical groups take us back in time as they recreate history in the mid-1800's. The setting is a 12-acre quarry settlement. Paths through wooded hillsides lead you to a church, schoolhouse, covered bridge, swinging bridge and more. Donation. (first weekend in December)*

CHESTNUT MOUNTAIN RESORT ACTIVITIES
8700 W. Chestnut Road **Galena** 61036

- Phone: (815) 777-1320 or (800) 397-1320 **www.chestnutmtn.com**
- Hours: Slide Weekends and Holidays 10:00am-8:00pm (dusk). Weekdays generally 3:00pm-8:00pm.
- Admission: $4.00-$8.00 per slide or mini-golf. Unlimited passes available, too. Note: once you go down the Alpine Slide once, you'll want to go again.
- Tours: Cruise: Several times each weekend during season (Please arrive 1/2 hour early for departure time. Tickets can be purchased at Alpine Slide) - $20.00-$30.00 per person (age 3+).
- Note: Skiing, of course, is their specialty with many chairlifts and slopes to choose from. Lodging rooms are available year-round and chalet atmosphere dining, too. The resort is modest and caters towards skiers and simple accommodations.

- <u>ALPINE SLIDE</u> - Fun for all ages. No special skills needed — you control your own speed. Ride your own sled down the 2,050 ft. of terrain-tailored track to the banks of the Mississippi. What a thrill - go slow the first ride - then, challenge yourself with speed! Travel back up on the scenic chair lift and enjoy a three-state view. Opens Memorial Day Weekend-Labor Day. Spring and Fall hours are weekends only. Children six and under must ride with an adult.

- <u>MISSISSIPPI EXPLORER CRUISES</u> - Jump aboard the Mississippi Explorer's newest cruise and experience all the nature the Upper Mississippi River National Wildlife & Fish Refuge has to offer. This 1½ hour expedition cruise offers explorers an in-depth exploration of the Mississippi River's ecosystem, navigation, and history. It's a slow and lazy tour - good for relaxation but not terribly exciting for active kids. Binoculars are provided. Summer weekends only. *All cruises include Alpine Slide/Scenic Chair Ride to and from departure area.

DESOTO HOUSE HOTEL

Galena - *230 S. Main Street 61036. (815) 777-0090 or www.desotohouse.com. Guest accommodations in one of 55 graciously decorated Victorian style rooms. Courtyard Restaurant - A lovely four-story atrium serving breakfast and lunch daily. Sunday breakfast buffet and weekday lunch buffet.*

EAGLE RIDGE INN RESORT

(US 20 west, just a few miles east of town) **Galena** 61036

Phone: (815) 777-2444 or (800) 892-2269 **www.eagleridge.com**

Spending the week or just a weekend, Eagle Ridge offers a variety of lodging options that will meet the needs of everyone from a well-appointed guest room at the Inn ($149-$199) to the spaciousness of a fully furnished private villa or home (the best way to spend a few overnights). They have a stocked General Store and wonderful food at the restaurants and cafes (or, cook your own meal at your home rental). Lake Galena dominates the setting below the Inn with its 7 miles of shoreline and picturesque marina. In addition to the 80 guest rooms and suites, the main Inn complex houses a spacious common area with a double-sided fireplace and comfortable conversation areas.

Golf not your game? Not to worry, the resort also offers the best in outdoor recreational facilities that include fishing, gorgeous hiking trails, horseback riding and kids programs. Often, they have special festivals, hayrides, campfires, crafting, scavenger hunts and movies in tubies. Enjoy cross-country skiing, sledding, skating, and horse-drawn sleigh rides throughout the winter. The resort is friendly, not stuffy and a destination to work from as you explore this adorable town. The Camp Eagle Program is available in half-day and full day (both including lunch), providing children ages 4-12 with a wide variety of supervised Arts and crafts, swimming, pool games, and nature trail hikes. The Kids Night Out Program is every Friday and Saturday nights from 7:00-10:00pm for children ages 4-12. Pizza, movies, games, boat rides and crafts will fill up their evening while Mom and Dad have a quiet evening alone or out with friends. (3 children minimum, reservations required by 2:00pm the day of).

• <u>HOT AIR BALLOON RIDES</u> - Escape to a tranquil world that is sure to give you a new perspective. What a way to see the Territory. Come for a peaceful journey above the treetops and a celebration upon landing. Flights offered daily at dawn and dusk. $150 per person. For additional information or to reserve your flight, contact the Recreation Department at (815) 776-5035.

GREAT GALENA BALLOON RACE

Galena - *Eagle Ridge Resort. Friday night balloon glow. Weekend hot air balloon launch for Hare and Hound races, bicycle race, kite flying and a skydiving show. (third weekend in June)*

GALENA HISTORY MUSEUM

211 S. Bench Street (downtown) **Galena** 61036

- Phone: (815) 777-9129 **www.galenahistorymuseum.org**
- Hours: Daily 9:00am-4:30pm.
- Admission: $5.00-$7.00 (ages 10+). Family $18.00.

Exhibits include Civil War, mining, steamboating, clothing, geology, dolls, and toys. Shown hourly, watch the 15 minute slide show detailing Galena's history. Learn how early mining, smelting and steamboating made Galena a lead mine boom town. They recently found (during renovations) an opening to a real mine shaft. Now, you can lean over the clear-covered opening and look down. Kids really like this and the hands-on area where kids can pretend to make a pie or weigh lead. Incredibly, nine of Galena's citizens became Union Generals for service rendered during the Civil War, including the most famous of all - Ulysses S. Grant. Keep a watchful eye over the gallery for the famous Thomas Nast painting "Peace in the Union" depicting Lee's surrender to Grant at Appomattox in 1865.

DID YOU KNOW ? The *Field of Dreams* Movie Site is just one hour away in Iowa? Go to www.fodmoviesite.com to get directions to the site in Dyersville, Iowa. Open daily 9:00am-6:00pm (April-November). FREE.

GALENA TROLLEYS

314 S. Main Street **Galena** 61036

- Phone: (815) 777-1248 **www.galenatrolleys.com**
- Admission: $11.00 adult, $6.00 child (under 12) - one hour non-stop.
- Tours: Leaving every hour, except weekends every 1/2hr. April-November/ daily (seasonal hours February to March).

Did you know that 85% of the world's lead ore was extruded from this territory by the 1870's (a Lead Rush vs. a Gold Rush)? Galena is Latin for lead. Galena is the most historically preserved 19th century town in the United States and 85% of the buildings are on the National Historic Registry.

The lead mining and river boating era left behind evidence of tremendous wealth and prosperity. The trolley tours travel up and down the hills and valleys, passing by the beautifully restored mansions (the biggest and the oldest) and U.S. Grant's pre and post civil war homes. Drive through the flood gates - make sure you're on the right side. See and hear about the first candlemaker; the train depot; a boot company; riverboat captains; a garden with a tin man and a dinosaur; a high school turned into condos; and the oldest continually running Post Office in the U.S. End the tour passing shops and restaurants lining Main Street, which is bustling with pedestrians, horse carriages and adorable window storefronts tempting you to enter. Now that you're armed with information, we recommend walking Main Street, reading many of the historic plaques, trying to find the spot filmed as Chisholm, Minnesota in *Field of Dreams* (ask about stories from townsfolk), or purchasing treats from Chocolat' or American Popcorn Company. This town is too fun!

NIGHT OF THE LUMINARIA

Galena - *Riverfront & Trolley Depot. More than 5,000 luminaria trace the riverfront levee, steps, hillsides and parks. Cookie Walk. Trolley rides viewing the luminaria, hot cider and caroling. FREE to walk around, Fee for trolley rides & Cookie Walk. (third Saturday in December)*

ULYSSES S. GRANT HOME & OLD MARKET HOUSE STATE HISTORIC SITES

500 Bouthillier Street/ 123 North Commerce Street **Galena** 61036

- Phone: (815) 777-3310 **www.granthome.com**
- Hours: Wednesday-Sunday 9:00am-5:00pm (April-October). Museums close at 4:00pm (winters). Both sites are closed on Monday & Tuesday. The sites are also closed on all winter holidays.
- Admission: $3.00-$5.00.

GRANT HOME: In March 1864, Grant was appointed lieutenant general and commanded the Union army to war's end. On April 9, 1865, Confederate General Robert E. Lee surrendered his troops to Grant at Appomattox Court House, and Grant's image as a war hero was complete. On August 18, 1865, Galena celebrated the return of its Civil War hero. Following a jubilant procession with much flag waving and speeches, a group of Galena citizens presented the General with a handsome furnished house on Bouthillier Street.

The 1860s brick home is furnished and decorated as it was in 1868. With many masculine touches, you'll see the "presence" of Grant in every room. You'll learn something of his personal life, too.

OLD MARKET HOUSE: The Old Market House, constructed in 1845-1846, was the focal point of community life during Galena's heyday. The Greek revival Old Market House sheltered vendors and shoppers, who gathered in the heart of the river city's business district until 1910. Buyers and sellers would congregate there, wrote Galena's semi-weekly newspaper, The Jeffersonian, and the competition would lower prices. Galenians would no longer be compelled to "traverse half the city to make some paltry purchase." The House is connected to Grant through a special exhibit. In it, look for a "Get Well" letter written by a little girl.

ROYAL OAK FARM ORCHARD

Harvard - *15908 Hebron Road. Pick your own or chose already picked apples, pumpkins, gourds, squash, fall raspberries. Farm store, restaurant, apple donuts, caramel apples, cider, cider slushes, petting zoo, train, carousel, orchard tours and more.* **www.royaloakfarmorchard.com**. *Small fees. (daily except Sunday in September/October)*

TOMS FARM MARKET FALL FESTIVAL

Huntley - *10214 Algonquin Road. Enjoy the giant inflated caterpillar, animal land, play land, 4-acre corn maze, straw mounds, goat walk, straw maze. Weekends: pony rides, pick-your-own pumpkins, barrel rides, face painting, tons of pumpkins, gourds and cornstalks. Homemade apple cider donuts and fudge, cafe and bakery. Educational tours for children grades pre-school thru second grade. Antique Tractors, Costume Parade October.* **www.tomsfarmmarket.com**. *Entrance fees. (October)*

LAKE LE-AQUA-NA STATE PARK

8542 North Lake Rd (IL 73 north and to 2 miles into the town of Lena. Turn left onto Lena Street. 3 miles north of town) **Lena** 61048

Phone: (815) 369-4282
http://dnr.state.il.us/lands/landmgt/parks/R1/LEAQUANA.HTM

Lake Le-Aqua-Na takes its name from a combination of the words Lena and aqua, the Latin name for water. The family oriented park surrounds a 40-

acre, man-made lake offering fishing and boating. Bring your own, or rent a rowboat, canoe or paddleboat at the park concession stand (only electric motors are allowed on the lake). Food and picnic snacks are also available (seasonally). There's a small beach especially for children (open daily 8:00am-8:00pm, Memorial Day-Labor Day (no lifeguards). Campers will find RV, tent, equestrian and youth group campgrounds. Deer are common at Lake-Le-Aqua-Na, and wild turkeys are sometimes seen. Migrating waterfowl frequent the lake in the spring and autumn. The park's 7 miles of wooded trails are rated easy to moderate. Cross-country skiing, sledding and ice fishing are popular in the winter months.

TORKELSON CHEESE COMPANY

9453 W Louisa Road **Lena** 61048

Phone: (815) 369-4265 **www.torkelsoncheese.com**

Duane and Cheryl Torkelson have been involved in the cheese industry for over 30 years. Torkelson Cheese Company manufactures Brick, Muenster, Quesadilla, and Asadero. Torkelson Cheese purchases quality milk from local farmers, helping to produce more than 30,000 pounds of cheese per day. See cheese made, then stock up on award-winning cheese at Factory prices. Generally, weekday mornings are best for viewing. Call ahead for tours or best viewing times.

JONAMAC ORCHARD

Malta - *19412 Shabbona Road. www.jonamacorchard.com. Fresh apples, pumpkins and other fall produce at the market daily. Kids activity area, wagon rides, 10 acre corn maze, hayrides, apples train and apple launcher. Admission. (weekends in September and October)*

BETHLEHEM WALK

Manteno - *Christian Church of Manteno. As a patron of the Bethlehem Walk, you will enter the marketplace as a shopper and be alternately greeted, wooed and accosted by costumed Roman and Jewish characters in the streets and vendor's booths. FREE. http://ccmanteno.org/index.php/bethlehem-walk/ (second weekend in December)*

ILLINI STATE PARK

2660 East 2350th Road (on the southern bank of the Illinois River south
of town) **Marseilles** 61341

Phone: (815) 795-2448

http://dnr.state.il.us/lands/landmgt/parks/I&M/EAST/ILLINI/PARK.HTM

The 500-acre park is a haven for songbirds, waterfowl and other wildlife.
Many of the shelters were constructed by CCC in the 1930s. Birders mention
this trail as one of the best sites in the county for viewing migrating vereos,
warblers, thrushes, and other songbirds in Fall. Illini State Park is the perfect
place for winter fun. An ice skating pool and hills ideal for sledding provide
hardy outdoor enjoyment. A shelter offers a comfortable setting for warming
fingers and toes after a winter workout. They also have ball fields, fishing,
hiking, biking, cross-country, and skiing trails. The LaSalle Lake area features
rocky shorelines, a wildlife refuge and power boating.

MORAINE HILLS STATE PARK

1510 South River Road (IL Rt. 12 south to Rt. 176. West to River Road.
North on River Road approx. 2 miles to entrance) **McHenry** 60051

Phone: (815) 385-1624

http://dnr.state.il.us/lands/landmgt/parks/R2/MORHILLS.HTM

From angling to hiking, from viewing rare plants to observing migratory
waterfowl, more than 10 miles of one-way trails make Moraine Hills popular
for hikers and bicyclists. Deriving its name from the accumulation of boulders,
stones and other debris left by glaciers, the park also includes marsh areas.
Pike Marsh, a 115-acre area in the southeast corner of the park, is home to
many rare plants. Its outer fen area (a very rare marsh wetland) includes one
of the state's largest known colonies of pitcher plants, which attract, trap,
and digest insects. McHenry Dam, on the Fox River, is on the park's western
border. Boat rentals and concessions are available.

HARMS FARM

McHenry - *4727 W Crystal Lake Rd. Pick your own or chose already picked apples,
pumpkins, gourds, squash, fall raspberries. Farm store, restaurant, apple donuts,
caramel apples, cider, cider slushes, petting zoo, train, carousel, orchard tours and
more.* ***Http://harmsfarmandgarden.com****. (October)*

SHADES OF AUTUMN FALL FESTIVAL

McHenry - *Stade's Farm and Market. Bring the whole family for a full day of fun on the farm. Home cooked food at great prices, pumpkin picking, hayrides, mazes, crafts, crafters, pony rides, petting zoo, pumpkin cannon demonstrations, produce, music and "The Dark," haunted house. FREE. Some attractions, including haunted house, have fees. Information: (815) 675-6396 or www.shadesofautumn.net. (October)*

SWEET CORN FESTIVAL

Mendota - *www.sweetcornfestival.com. Free, hot, buttered Del Monte sweet corn will be the highlight of this annual festival with over 60,000 visitors consuming nearly fifty tons of corn during the weekend. Downtown area provides entertainment, a parade and carnival. Enjoy one of the Midwest's oldest and largest festivals. FREE. (second weekend in August)*

GEBHARD WOODS STATE PARK
401 Ottawa Street **Morris** 60450

Phone: (815) 942-0796
http://dnr.state.il.us/lands/landmgt/parks/I&M/EAST/GEBHARD/Park.htm

Dotted with shade trees, the park stretches along the I&M Canal. Today, hikers, campers, picnickers, and canoeists frequent this 30-acre site, making it one of the state's most popular state parks. Gebhard Woods is only a footbridge away from the historic Illinois & Michigan Canal State Trail. This 61 mile trail on the old canal towpath is easy walking and gives access to unparalleled scenic and historic sights. Bicyclists can also take advantage of the groomed towpath to enjoy the natural and man-made wonders. The trail is marked and has various wayside exhibits that describe features of the canal era encountered along the way. Due to the trail's composition, horseback riding isn't allowed, however, winter snow brings out registered snowmobilers.

GOOSE LAKE PRAIRIE STATE NATURAL AREA
5010 North Jugtown Road (southeast of town, midway between Hwy 47 and I-55) **Morris** 60450

Phone: (815) 942-2899
http://dnr.state.il.us/lands/landmgt/parks/I&M/EAST/GOOSE/HOME.HTM

Visiting Goose Lake Prairie State Natural Area today is much like seeing

Illinois as it was 150 years ago, when prairie covered nearly 60 percent of the state. Looking much like prairie you've see on TV shows, you'll see big bluestem, Indian grass and switchgrass plus broad-leafed flowering plants known as forbs. One of the best ways to experience Goose Lake Prairie is to hit the trails. With 7 miles of hiking trails including a floating bridge, you'll have ample opportunity for viewing the plants and animals that make the area unique.

• PRAIRIE VIEW TRAIL, with 3.5 miles of moderate hiking, goes through prairie and farmland. Visible are strip mine reclamation areas, low-lying marshes and farmland.

• TALL GRASS NATURE TRAIL is a self-guiding trek that winds through the prairie and the trail's trademark grasses of big bluestem and Indian grass, which can grow to 8 feet in height.

Depending on the route you decide to take, the trail can be 1 or 3½ miles long. One loop offers a hard-packed, wheelchair-accessible surface. Trails are available for cross-country skiing in the winter.

MORRISON-ROCKWOOD STATE PARK

18750 Lake Road (I-88 to IL 78 exit north thru town to Damen Road. Turn left on Crosby Road, follow signs about 1.5 miles) **Morrison** 61270

Phone: (815) 772-4708
http://dnr.state.il.us/lands/landmgt/parks/R1/MORRISON.HTM

Boasting an abundant animal population, this State Park offers woodland and water to coyotes, deer, foxes and large birds. The site includes Lake Carlton and offers camping, fishing, horseback riding, hiking trails, and boating. Take the large, two-span Covered Bridge on part of the road to the park. At 148 feet long, it has 32 windows on each side, letting light in and adding to its antique look. Plan a family outing at the Lakeview picnic area, or just do some bird watching among the hickory, ash, oak and walnut trees.

WHITE PINES FOREST STATE PARK

6712 West Pines Road (southwest of town, US 20 west to Rte. 2 south) **Mt. Morris** 61054

Phone: (815) 946-3717 or (815) 946-3817 lodge
www.dnr.illinois.gov/Parks/Pages/WhitePinesForest.aspx

The park features the southernmost strand of native white pines in Illinois. It is also noted for its vine-covered limestone bluffs. You can drive through Pine Creek's flowing stream via the concrete fords. History tells us that this was for years the principal route east and west across the northern part of the state. Today, there are plenty of outdoor recreation activities, such as hiking, fishing, camping and picnicking. Whether you choose an easy walking trail or a more difficult path, three of the seven marked trails are less than a mile long. Amidst the serene setting, modern lodge facilities, log cabins and camping allow for overnighting. Each cabin sleeps four people and is complete with shower, gas log fireplace, one queen bed and one trundle bed. All cabins are air-conditioned and heated, and have telephones and televisions. The historic lounge area, which is part of the main lodge, is filled with crafts and artwork, including a gift shop.

- **WHITE PINES DINNER THEATRE**: Afternoon matinees (evening performances in December only) are for those who enjoy nostalgic musicals, charming entertainers, lots of laughter, and delicious food served in a log cabin lodge. www.whitepinesinn.com. Best of all, it's reasonably priced and you can be home before dark (April through mid-December).

CASTLE ROCK STATE PARK

1365 W. Castle Rd. (4 miles south of town on IL Hwy 2) **Oregon** 61061

Phone: (815) 732-7329
http://dnr.state.il.us/lands/landmgt/parks/R1/CASTLE.HTM

This 2,000-acre, day-use-only park (no camping) is named for a large sandstone wall along the Rock River. Picnic tables are scattered along the river. There's a boat-launching ramp opposite the park entrance. Castle Rock has 6 miles of easy to moderate hiking trails, including three trails near the south edge of the park. Hikers may spot white-tailed deer or wild turkey. Beaver, great blue herons, indigo buntings and kingfishers are common park residents. The park's namesake lies about one-half mile south of the entrance. It's a healthy hike up the wooden steps to the top of Castle Rock, but the bird's-eye view of the Rock River is worth it. Winter activities include cross-country skiing and tobogganing.

LOWDEN STATE PARK

1411 N. River Road (I-39, exit #104 on Rt 64 west 16 miles) **Oregon** 61061
Phone: (815) 732-6828
http://dnr.state.il.us/lands/landmgt/parks/R1/LOWDENSP.HTM

Set on high bluffs, the park is best known as the home of Chicago sculptor Lorado Taft's huge concrete statue of an American Indian. Taft named his 50 foot-high, 100-ton creation "Eternal Indian." But, it's universally called "Black Hawk," after the famed 19th Century Sauk warrior. Legend has it that Chief Black Hawk, as he left the area after the Black Hawk War, talked of the beauty of the area and admonished his captors to care for the land as he and his people had. The 207-acre park offers splendid views of the Rock River and Oregon. There are several picnic areas with tables, drinking water and park stoves. Individual and group camping sites include limited electricity and a shower building; reservations are not accepted. Four miles of hiking trails rated moderately difficult wander through scenic woods and along the bluff tops. White-tailed deer and many species of birds, including the brilliant red-headed woodpecker, are park residents.

WHITE PINES RANCH

3581 Pines Road (I-90 West to Rockford, West on 20 (towards Freeport), South on IL Route 2) **Oregon** 61061
Phone: (815) 732-7923 **www.whitepinesranch.com**
Note: The dormitories are complete with bunk beds, carpeting, electrical heating and adjoining bathrooms with showers, flush toilets, and vanities with mirrors. The main lodge has a large dining hall where home-cooked meals are served buffet style. A game room and gift shop are on the premises.

A dude ranch just for kids! White Pines Ranch covers 200 acres of beautiful woods, pastures and horse trails. The buildings are modern structures built with an old west theme. This ranch offers horseback riding, swimming (in season), hiking through a beautiful sandstone canyon, horse studies with grooming, scavenger hunts, mapping, orienteering, outdoor games, fossil hunts, and studying wildlife. Evening activities may include hayrides, bingo, country line dancing and campfire songs. Winter activities include cross country skiing, sledding and lots of hot chocolate. Hours and admission are per package or program offered/scheduled.

BUFFALO ROCK STATE PARK & EFFIGY TUMULI

Dee Bennett Road, 1300 North 27th Road (banks of Illinois River, two miles west of town) **Ottawa** 61350

> Phone: (815) 433-2220
> http://dnr.state.il.us/lands/landmgt/parks/I&M/EAST/BUFFALO/Home.htm

On the bluffs of the River, stand five earthen sculptures molded from Illinois clay. Called Effigy Tumuli, this unique "earth art" is one of the most prominent displays of outdoor sculpture around. All five subjects - snake, catfish, turtle, frog and insect are native to the area. The park has ball diamonds, picnic areas, biking, canoeing, hiking, snow-mobiling and cross-country skiing trails, too.

ILLINOIS WATERWAY VISITORS CENTER

950 North 27th Road, Dee Bennett Road (I-80 to Utica and exit south on rt. 178, across from Starved Rock State Park) **Ottawa** 61350

> Phone: (815) 667-4054
> https://dnr.state.il.us/Lands/Landmgt/parks/I&M/EAST/WATERWAY/
> **Home.htm**
> Hours: Daily, daylight hours.
> Admission: FREE

Water is still the least expensive way to transport heavy bulk goods like grain, coal, sand and gravel. In 1933, the US Army Corps of Engineers replaced the I&M Canal with the Illinois River to create a waterway from Chicago to the Mississippi River. Today, one barge can carry 1500 tons - the same freight it would have taken 10 canal boats to carry. One tugboat can push 15 barges at a time. Explore the observation area and visitors center where you can see huge barges going through a lock. Interpretive programs discuss the lock and dam system of the Illinois River and the national waterway system.

PROPHETSTOWN STATE RECREATION AREA

Riverside Drive and Park Avenue (south side of Rock River, northeast edge of town) **Prophetstown** 61277

> Phone: (815) 537-2926
> http://dnr.state.il.us/lands/landmgt/parks/R1/PROPHET.HTM

Once the site of an American Indian village, the 53-acre park derives its name from the Native American prophet Wa-bo-kie-shiek. This park offers camping, fishing, a boat ramp, canoe access, and hiking. Wa-bo-kie-shiek nature trail follows along the edge of Coon Creek for approximately 1/3 of a mile. It offers access for anglers while also providing a scenic walk for hikers.

BEEF-A-ROO

Rockford - Various locations. Another Rockford original with 7 stores specializing in sandwiches, burgers, salads and seasonal soups and shakes. Love the special flavor shakes. www.beefaroo.com.

MARY'S MARKET

Rockford - Various locations especially near malls. www.marysmarket.com. Yet another Rockford original with stores decorated in modern tones and serving freshly made breads sided or filled with soup (try cream of Broccoli) of the day and chicken salads. All the ingredients are wafting in the air as you dive into your food. Modern comfort food.

KLEHM ARBORETUM & BOTANIC GARDEN

2701 Clifton Avenue **Rockford** 61102

- Phone: (815) 965-8146 **www.klehm.org**
- Hours: Daily 9:00am-4:00pm (April-October). Closed Sunday and Monday (November-March).
- Admission: $3.00-$6.00 (age 3+)

Planted initially as a nursery, today, the site showcases spring blossoms, summer flowers, fall foliage and winter evergreens, plus themed gardens (like the Butterfly Garden), sculptures and fountains. All ages can enjoy the maze and interactive sundial in the Children's Garden. Look for the mascot, Klehmantine, as you take in whimsical sights, sounds and scents. Enjoy the paved figure-eight and many other wood-chipped paths.

BURPEE MUSEUM OF NATURAL HISTORY

737 North Main Street (downtown) **Rockford** 61103

- Phone: (815) 985-3433 **www.burpee.org**
- Hours: Daily 10:00am-5:00pm.
- Admission: $8.00 general admission (age 13+). $7.00 child (age 3-12) Wednesdays FREE to all. Free Parking.

The Natural History Museum is housed in three buildings on the west bank of the Rock River. The big attraction: JANE! This young dinosaur died in the Montana Badlands. In 2001, a group from Burpee discovered her bones. Experts have called this find "one of the ten most important dinosaur discoveries in the past 100 years." Upon entering the exhibit, visitors encounter a flat-screen television that shows the barren Badlands landscape of today. One by one, the dinosaurs appear on the scene. Next to the TV is a display of fossils that were found near Jane's bones. What did a housewife and professor find first? Tucked in a corner of the exhibit hall is a recreation of a paleontologist rustic cabin camp. Visitors can watch "home movies" that show what camp life was like and tell stories of how the team excavated Jane. Turning a corner, you finally come face-to-face with the fully restored REAL skeleton of Jane! What a great story! It's like solving a mystery along with the team of pros and amateurs. And, the area has easy, hands-on displays (for example: tap on the shoulder of a scientist to learn about his experiments). Other wonderful exhibits include: Walking through a Coal Forest - watch out for the thunderstorm; Native American recreated wigwam, tipi and pueblo (even sit a spell listening to storytellers or watch a PowWow); walk into the Woodlands in spring where you hear, touch and smell nature in the noisy season; and an interesting Viewing Lab where you can watch scientists at work as they prepare specimens.

PALEOFEST

Rockford - *Burpee Museum of Natural History. The annual celebration of fossils and dinosaurs bringing world-famous dino experts together for workshops, childrens activities, fossil ID and Jane. FREE. (first weekend in March)*

DISCOVERY CENTER MUSEUM

711 North Main Street (adjacent to the Burpee Museum) **Rockford** 61103

- ☐ Phone: (815) 963-6769 **www.discoverycentermuseum.org**
- ☐ Hours: Daily 10:00am-5:00pm.
- ☐ Admission: $8.00 general (age 2+).
- ☐ Note: Theatre has live science shows during peak times using theatrics. Fun, playful Family Fridays each summer are popular.

Discovery Center is a children's museum with 200+ hands-on arts and science exhibits and an outdoor science park (the play of a Kinetic ball maze, friction slides, pendulum swings, water play and digging for dinos like Jane). There's a Planetarium where kids can pretend they're astronauts; a TV Studio with live broadcasts on a local museum station (be an anchor, cameraman, producer or disappearing weatherman); Team Up where you explore science in sports choosing proper equipment, position and play; a Tot Spot with a huge dollhouse 5-feet high and pretend play; and the special Spiral staircase with a giant mouse-hole maze between the museum's two levels. Ag-Zibit is the new space that explores how agriculture affects our everyday lives. Drive a combine, climb aboard the tractor, study live bees, gather the eggs, milk the cows and more.

OLYMPIC TAVERN

*Rockford - 2327 N Main Street. 61103. (815) 962-8758 or **www.theolympictavern.com**. A Rockford Original that's 60 years old and an easy drive from the Museums. They offer a big menu and kids menu (that even features steak). Baked potato soup, house dressings on salad, giant one-pound burgers, wonderful daily special pasta dishes, chicken and fish. $$.*

TROLLEY STATION & FOREST CITY QUEEN RIDES

324 N. Madison Street (Riverview Park, south end) **Rockford** 61103

- Phone: (815) 987-8894 **www.rockfordparkdistrict.org/index.php/ facilities/recreation/trolley-car36**
- Admission: $7.00-$8.00 per seat. $2.00 discount for residents.
- Tours: Trolley: Thursday, Saturday, Sunday afternoons. Queen: Daily except Tuesday afternoons. Tours depart on the hour, hourly (early June - late August).
- Note: Family Fun Nights are offered Wednesdays with pizza and the best seat on the river for Ski Broncs water ski shows. This fun-filled 2 hour cruise is packed with excitement for kids of all ages. Order whole pizzas or by the slice.

All aboard! Departing from downtown Rockford, by rail or by sail, you will discover interesting tidbits about the early history of the community by enjoying a ride on the Track Trolley or the Forest City Queen Riverboat.

- <u>TROLLEY CAR 36</u>: Makes its way from the Trolley Station beside the scenic Rock River Recreation Path, makes a stop for a brief visit to the Sinnissippi Greenhouse, then turns around at Symbol and returns to the station.

- <u>FOREST CITY QUEEN</u>: The Forest City Queen gives you an up close and personal glimpse of some of the most stately homes on the banks of the Rock River. You'll hear lighthearted stories about Rockford's humble beginnings on the River and its constant influence today. A variety of cruise options are available, from hourly narration tours, family-style picnics, Ski Broncs performances, to elegant dining.

MIDWAY VILLAGE

6799 Guilford Road (I-90 to BR20 west. North on Bell School Rd, west on Guilford Rd.) **Rockford** 61107

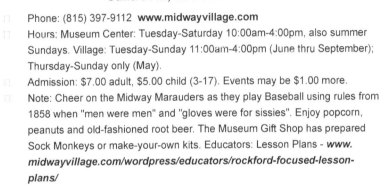

- Phone: (815) 397-9112 **www.midwayvillage.com**
- Hours: Museum Center: Tuesday-Saturday 10:00am-4:00pm, also summer Sundays. Village: Tuesday-Sunday 11:00am-4:00pm (June thru September); Thursday-Sunday only (May).
- Admission: $7.00 adult, $5.00 child (3-17). Events may be $1.00 more.
- Note: Cheer on the Midway Marauders as they play Baseball using rules from 1858 when "men were men" and "gloves were for sissies". Enjoy popcorn, peanuts and old-fashioned root beer. The Museum Gift Shop has prepared Sock Monkeys or make-your-own kits. Educators: Lesson Plans - *www. midwayvillage.com/wordpress/educators/rockford-focused-lesson-plans/*

Explore stories of ancestors in the Museum Center galleries: Swedish Singers, Rockford Peaches, Industry, and Aviation. Walk the route of soldiers on the floor map. Discover the invention of the sock knitting machine and the famous red-heeled sock - now, the tube sock and the endearing Sock Monkey toy! Now, wander overseas as stories are told in the world of miniatures in the Old Dolls House Museum where the cultures of countries around the world are represented in miniature homes. Kids love this doll museum (even boys) because every house is completely different and everything is much more adorable in miniature. Visit the Millhouse located on Lake Severin featuring an exhibition, video presentation, and functioning waterwheel. Finally, experience stories of the Victorian age as you stroll through Midway Village, featuring 26 historic structures including a hardware store, general store, print shop, one-room schoolhouse, fire station, police station, hospital, bank, and homes. Be sure to allow time for a guided tour.

WORLD WAR II DAYS

Rockford - *Midway Village. Watch as more than 300 members of the Historical Re-enactment Society transform Midway Village into a European village with reenactments and pyrotechnics. Then, learn period dances and dance with soldiers. Admission. (September)*

SCARECROW FESTIVAL

Rockford -*Midway Village. Costumed interpreters help re-create the atmosphere of an old-fashioned harvest fest within the living history village. Fun fall activities include period games and crafts, live music and wagon rides around the village. Plus, you'll be able to make your own scarecrow to take home. Old time baseball on Saturday. Admission. (second weekend in October)*

COCO KEY WATER RESORT

Best Western Clock Tower Resort, 7801 E. State Street **Rockford** 61108

Phone: (866) 754-6958 **www.cocokeyrockford.com**

Coco is the mascot parrot who makes his home in the Key West-inspired tropical environ that contains looping slides, an interactive playhouse with dump buckets, hoses, a dropping raft ride, tube rides and whirlpools. Also an arcade, snack shop and poolside cabanas. Day Passes: ~$20. Overnight lodging family package starts around $180, specials start at $99.00. Waterpark hours vary by season and day. Check ahead on website to be sure waterpark is open during your prospective visit.

ILLINOIS SNOW SCULPTING COMPETITION

Rockford - *Sinnissippi Park. **www.snowsculpting.org**. Watch snow-sculpting teams form stunning figures from giant blocks of snow. Giant dragons, abstract shapes and whimsical figures take shape under the skilled hands of 30 top competitors. FREE. (third full week of January)*

MAGIC WATERS WATERPARK

7820 CherryVale North Blvd. (I-90 exit BR 20west, Bell School Rd. south, across from Cherryvale Mall) **Rockford (Cherry Valley)** 61016

- Phone: (815) 332-3260 or (800) 373-1679 **www.magicwaterswaterpark.com**
- Hours: Summers opening at 10:00am until 7:00 or 9:00pm.
- Admission: $17-$20. $4.00 (age 2 and under). Residents and youngsters under 48" save $5.00 off. Save more after 3:00pm. $12 buck Wednesdays.

"Totally Splashtacular Family Fun". Start in the darkness of the Abyss or the light of the water bucket Island. Daring? Try Splashblaster - the Midwest's largest Water Coaster thrill ride. This is really a thrill as it's a combination of the "big hill" to start a coaster ride, combined with the twists and falls being cushioned by water. Tsunami Bay wavepool is 650,000 gallons of heated water, alternating between ocean waves and calm. Kick back and tube up, because you'll be set in motion on the 1200-foot floating River. Body slides splash, twist and careen at speeds up to 30 mph. Pipeline tube rides send you on wet, winding fun adventures down a wave of water. Little ones have their own Little Lagoon waterplay area. Clean and nice park for families.

SKI BRONCS WATER SKI SHOW

Shorewood Park on the Rock River (Forest Grove Street between Junius and McKinley Streets) **Rockford (Loves Park)** 61103

- Phone: (815) 378-3000 **www.skibroncs.com**
- Shows: Wednesdays and Fridays 7:00pm (late June-Labor Day weekend)
- Admission: FREE, donations collected at intermission.

The Ski Broncs Water-Ski Show Team performs summer shows with a humorous "Around the World in 80 Days" theme or some sort of variation of a sitcom theme. Support local, competitive skiers who are honing their presentation skills.

ROCKFORD SPEEDWAY

9572 Forest Hills Rd (just two miles west of Interstate 90 at the intersection of Forest Hills Road and Highway 173) **Rockford (Loves Park)** 61105

- Phone: (815) 633-1500 **www.rockfordspeedway.com**

Exciting NASCAR stock car races and novelty races take place April - October. They host the Natl Short Track Championships. Tickets $5.00-$10.00.

ROCK CUT STATE PARK

7318 Harlem Road (Go North on Perryville to Hwy. 173, Go East on Hwy.
173 about 1-1/2 miles) **Rockford (Loves Park)** 61111

- Phone: (815) 885-3311
  http://dnr.state.il.us/lands/landmgt/parks/R1/ROCKCUT.HTM
- Hours: Summer hours (April - October) 6:00am-10:00pm.
- Winter hours (November - March) 8:00am - 5:00pm.
- Admission: Beach swimming $1.00.

Two lakes set off the park's 3,092 acres. Pierce Lake, with 162 acres, is a retreat
for people wanting to fish, ice fish or ice skate. A second 50-acre Olson Lake
is for swimmers. Recreational options are camping, hiking, horseback trails
and cross-country skiing. The trail system at Rock Cut offers opportunities
for hiking (40 miles), mountain biking (23 miles), and equestrian (14 miles).
Trail users will find updated trail head/information signs at picnic areas and
trail access points for trail information and regulations.

HISTORIC AUTO ATTRACTIONS

13825 Metric Drive (I-90 exit 3 west to Metric. Turn right)
Rockford (Roscoe) 61073

- Phone: (815) 389-7917 **www.historicautoattractions.com**
- Hours: Tuesday-Saturday 10:00am-5:00pm, Sunday 11:00am-5:00pm
  (summers). Weekends only (September-November)
- Admission: $13.00 adult, $11.00 senior (65+), $8.00 student (6-15).

More than just a display of historic automobiles - ten huge rooms where
history meets entertainment. See several Presidential Limos from Grant to
Eisenhower. The Kennedy Day in Dallas presentation represents cars present
in the motorcade the fateful day of his death. Or, see Abraham Lincoln's
chair from his presidential rail car. On the lighter side, view Cars of the
Stars - including Elvis Presley. Movieland has Batmobiles, Ghostbusters and
Superman mobiles. TV Land is where you revisit Andy Griffith or Sanford
and Son vehicles. There's even a Money Car covered with 120,000 coins. Not
just a display of cars, each exhibit area displays era artifacts that are often just
as interesting. And, because they are constantly adding to, and changing, the
space - it's a new visual experience each visit. Trust us when we say this is a
special find - one of those "treats" we discover in our travels that awes us!

MISSISSIPPI PALISADES STATE PARK

16327A Illinois Highway 84 (3 miles north of town) **Savanna** 61074

Phone: (815) 273-2731
http://dnr.state.il.us/lands/landmgt/parks/R1/PALISADE.HTM

On first impression, this park has but two directions - up and down. The rugged, 2,500-acre park sits atop a line of towering bluffs overlooking the Mississippi River. Four developed overlooks provide views of the Mississippi; Oak Point Overlook is accessible by visitors with limited mobility. Mississippi Palisades' 13 miles of trails are rated moderate to strenuous. Trails in the northern part of the park are less strenuous than those in the southern part. The Native American pathfinders along the rock palisades of the Mississippi River did as present-day hikers do - in coursing the bluffs, they took the paths of least resistance. The trails at the Mississippi Palisades, especially the park's southern routes, puts you in touch with the past. Walk them and you'll trace the footsteps of all those natives thousands of years ago. Pileated woodpeckers, wild turkeys, deer, fox and other small animals make their home here. The park has numerous scenic picnic areas and a campground with 241 RV campsites (105 with electrical hookups), showers and a convenience store; reservations are accepted. You can go fishing or boating on the Mississippi River and enjoy cross-country skiing, sledding and ice fishing in winter months.

SHABBONA LAKE STATE PARK

4201 Shabbona Grove Road (off US 30, midway between DeKalb and Peru) **Shabbona** 60550

Phone: (815) 824-2106
http://dnr.state.il.us/lands/landmgt/parks/R1/SHABBONA.HTM

Named for the Potawatomi chief who briefly held a small parcel of this land 10 years after the 1832 Black Hawk War, this park offers boating, camping, picnicking, fishing and some neat trails. Just over eight miles of scenic hiking and cross-country skiing trails weave through the wooded areas of the park. A trail brochure is available at the office. A specially developed cassette tape can guide you along on the "Touch the Earth" trail. The tape and a special brochure is available at the park office.

For updates & travel games visit: **www.KidsLoveTravel.com**

CHAIN O'LAKES STATE PARK

8916 Wilmot Road **Spring Grove** 60081

Phone: (847) 587-5512
http://dnr.state.il.us/lands/landmgt/parks/R2/CHAINO.HTM

Explore 6,500 acres of water, woods, fields and twisting shoreline. Try cross-country skiing and ice fishing in winter. Enjoy hiking, horseback riding, camping, fishing, and boating the rest of the year. Bike and boat rentals are available. Chain O Lakes has four trail systems. The Nature's Way hiking trail starts at Oak Grove Picnic Area and is 2 ¼ miles in length. The Pike Marsh North Picnic Area has a trail especially designed for disabled users that is ¼ mile long. The park also contains an equestrian trail with three loops and a total length of 8 miles. A biking/hiking trail, 6 miles in length can be accessed at any picnic area between the concession stand and the park office. In the winter all trails can be used by cross-country skiers with the park office doubling as a warming house on weekends with 3" of snow; hours are 10:00am-3:00pm.

RICHARDSON ADVENTURE FARM & CORN MAZE

Spring Grove - *9407 Richardson Road. World's largest (28-acre) corn maze, wooded picnic area, free campfires, 50' tall observation tower, giant slide, pumpkins, pedal cars, concessions. Admission.* ***www.richardsonadventurefarm.com*** *(Wednesday-Sunday in October)*

RONALD REAGAN BIRTHPLACE

111 South Main Street (Reagan Apartment and Museum) **Tampico** 61283

(815)438-2130 or **www.facebook.com/RonaldReaganBirthplace?ref=br_tf**
Hours: Monday-Saturday 10:00am-4:00pm, Sunday 1:00-4:00pm.(April-October)
Admission: Donations accepted.

Today, visitors will enjoy a step back in time as they tour the birthplace of President Reagan (40th President). The apartment is decorated as it had been when the Reagans lived there in the early 1900s. Memorabilia of Reagans childhood, acting career, and terms in office can be viewed at the Visitor Center below the apartment. A visit to Tampico would not be complete without a piece of homemade pie at the Dutch Diner located just a few doors down from the birthplace. Also of interest is the Hennepin Feeder Canal where the Reagan boys learned to swim.

PRESIDENT RONALD REAGAN BIRTHDAY CELEBRATION

Tampico- *Celebrate the 40th President's birthday in the town where he was born. Enjoy cake, punch, Reagan videos, movies and tours. FREE. (February 6th)*

DONLEY'S WILD WEST TOWN

8512 South Union Road (I-90 exit US 20 Hampshire / Marengo. Turn left (west), go 4.5 miles to South Union Rd) **Union** 60180

- Phone: (815) 923-9000 **www.wildwesttown.com**
- Hours: Daily 10:00am-6:00pm (Memorial Day-4th weekend in August) Weekends only (September & October).
- Admission: $17.00 per person (age 3+).

Visit a Wild West town complete with mock gunfights, a blacksmith shop, and pony rides. Try your hand at panning for gold (pyrite); or the shooting range or bow & arrow target practice. Union Jail has original jail cells that once held the local desperados. The Marshal even deputizes upstanding young citizens for special posses. Want to be a miner - try the Hand car rides - see how fast you can ride the line. Visit and play or slide in the playhouse Cowboy's Place. Catch the Magic Show at the Saloon. Board a scale model of a locomotive with special surprises along the way. Visit the Toy Store, Gunshop, Tobacco Shop, Telegraph Office, the Lamp Store, and a collection of toy trains in the Museum. Stop by the Ice Cream Parlor or Steakhouse for supper or sweets. Many shops have personalized souvenirs (like Indian face painting or names engraved on a lucky horseshoe) to purchase. However, most all activities are included in admission making this town a good value. A wonderful, easy to manage family outing awaits you here - too cute!

ILLINOIS RAILWAY MUSEUM

7000 Olson Road (I-90 to US 20 northwest, follow signs) **Union** 60180

- Phone: (815) 923-4000 or (800) BIG-RAIL **www.irm.org**
- Hours: Weekend operations: 10:30am-5:00pm, grounds 9:00am-6:00pm (usually May-October on Saturdays and most Sundays). Weekday operations: 11:00am - 4:00pm, grounds 10:00am - 5:00pm. (daily, summer)
- Admission: $10.00-$14.00 adult, $7.00-$10.00 child
- Note: 1934 Diner serves food in the museum.

The Illinois Railway Museum is a Museum in Motion. Watch now, as a little red streetcar clangs across Depot Street on the car line, or as the thundering steam train whistles past on the mainline, or perhaps as the gleaming streamliner simply whispers by. These artifacts don't just sit there, they move! Electric cars operate on weekdays, and the Museum grounds and barns are open to visitors on weekdays. Weekend operations during the season feature a steam or diesel train that departs from the Museum's East Union depot on a posted schedule. During the forty minute round trip to Kishwaukee Grove, the trains roll past a small farmstead, a bit of Illinois prairie and a rural grade crossing before dropping into the Kishwaukee Valley. The demonstration railroad includes a one-mile trolley loop around the property and a five-mile mainline. Your admission ticket entitles you to an unlimited number of train rides, as well as several barns with over two miles of indoor track, and their collection of over 375 pieces of railroad rolling stock.

FOURTH OF JULY WEEKEND

Union - *A red, white and blue weekend at the Illinois Rail Museum. On July 4th, view the annual trolley pageant – the largest display of trolleys in the Midwest. Admission. (July 4th weekend)*

HAPPY HOLIDAY RAILWAY

Union - *Illinois Rail Museum. Embark on a magical train ride through the winter countryside on your way to visit with Santa Claus. Warm treats served and gifts given to "good list". Admission. (weekends in December)*

STARVED ROCK STATE PARK

P.O. Box 509 (I-80 Eastbound and Westbound: Get off at exit #81 (Rt.178, Utica). **Utica** 61373

Phone: (815) 667-4906 or (800) 868-ROCK

http://dnr.state.il.us/lands/landmgt/parks/I&M/EAST/STARVE/PARK.HTM

Hours: Trail Parking Lots 8:00am to sunset. Visitors Center 9:30am-3:30 or 4:30pm.

LODGE: The lodge has been refurbished, but still reflects the peaceful atmosphere of yesteryear. The Lodge features an indoor swimming pool, children's pool, whirlpool, saunas and an outdoor sunning patio. The lodge offers 72 luxury hotel rooms and 22 comfortable cabin rooms. The original Great Room is furnished with decorative rugs and art and is centered around a massive stone fireplace. The restaurant is open seven days a week and offers many house specialties. A tour boat company also offers seasonal cruises departing near the Visitors Center.

Starved Rock State Park derives its name from a Native American legend about an Indian Chief who sought refuge on the rock and eventually starved to death versus being slain by enemies below. The backdrop for your activities are 18 canyons formed by glacial meltwater and stream erosion. They slice dramatically through tree-covered, sandstone bluffs for four miles through the park with overlooks at opportune points along the south side of the Illinois River. The park has 13 miles of hiking trails. Evidence of beavers and muskrats can be seen as you walk along the River Trail. During early spring, when the end of winter thaw is occurring and rains are frequent, sparkling waterfalls are found at the heads of all 18 canyons. The Visitors' Center offers displays and information about the area's geology, French and Native American history, flora, and fauna. Orient yourself first watching short videos. Now, you're ready to grab your backpack, water bottle, and maybe a hiking stick (all can be purchased at the gift shop/café) and hit the trails. Boating, fishing, camping, horseback riding, picnicking, and winter sports can all add to your Starved Rock experience. Rental of canoes, boats, horseback rides, and skis are available. No swimming or rock climbing - however, they allow ice climbing!

INTERTRIBAL POW WOW

Utica - *Starved Rock State Park. The beat of native drums, the colorful rituals and clothing. Native American wares, dances and rituals with vendors selling food and crafts. Admission. (third weekend in July)*

CHALLENGER LEARNING CENTER
222 Church Street, downtown **Woodstock** 60098

☐   Phone: (815) 338-7722 **www.challengerillinois.org**
☐   Admission: $25.00-$75.00 per student. First come, first serve, by deposit
       reservation only. Family Nights are $12.00 per person (includes pizza and pop).

Join a crew for a week-long adventure full of interactive activities. Summer 1 to 5-day camps spotlight flight, rocketry, robotics and space travel. Participants have the opportunity to visit the new interactive exhibit area, build rockets and gliders, fly in the Boeing 737 cockpit simulator and experience a simulated space mission. During the school year, school groups (best grade 5+) or organized civic or home-school groups can arrange similar experiences. The Family Science Night Series focuses on a different theme with activities about rockets or mission assignments.

GROUNDHOG DAYS

Woodstock - *Downtown. It's Groundhog Days in Woodstock Illinois, home of America's best town square and film location for the movie <u>Groundhog Day</u> starring Bill Murray. Come to Woodstock, to get in the spirit and witness the prediction of the end of winter. Festivities kick off Feb. 1, with the lighting of the Groundhog at the Woodstock Opera House. Join Woodstock Willie, Woodstock's resident groundhog, in the historic Woodstock Square and be the first to know if he sees his shadow at the annual prognostication set for 7:07am, Feb. 2. Afterwards celebrate Willie's prediction with a hearty breakfast served immediately after the prognostication. Seating for breakfast is limited. Tickets may be purchased for $14 each. There are plenty of activities for everyone to enjoy the rest of the day including walking tours of the filming sights, free showing of Groundhog Day the Movie at the Classic Cinema theater, a chili cook off, a woodcarving demonstration and movie symposium at the Stage Left café, next to the Opera House where Bill Murray took his fateful dive from the belfry. Fee for organized tours/meals.* **www.woodstockil.gov/** *(February 1 & 2)*

ALL SEASONS ORCHARD

Woodstock - *14510 Route 176. Pick your own apples, or choose from 12 varieties of already picked ones. Enjoy freshly pressed apple cider and apple donuts. Farm market has baskets, jams, honey and more. Relax at the Patio Grille. Hayrides, petting zoo, pick your own pumpkins too!* **www.allseasonfarm.com**. *Admission. (Wednesday-Sunday September & October)*

OLD FASHIONED HARVEST FEST

Woodstock - *Woodstock Square. A day long celebration, the annual Harvest Fest features a farmer's market; old-time craftspeople including weavers, spinners and quilters; vintage farm equipment; blacksmithing; woodworking; wagon rides; children's activities; and a fiddlers contest for youth and adults. Also, the Fair in The Square craft show featuring Midwest crafters. (815) 338-2436. FREE. (September Saturday)*

RED BARN FARM FALL FESTIVAL

Woodstock - *3500 S IL Route 47. Activities every day during October at the Red Barn include: A Corn Maze, A Corn Walk, A Spooky House, A Hay Stack, Many Farm Animals to pet & feed! Also Scarecrow Characters, Fall Produce, Pumpkins of all kinds.* **www.redbarn.us**. *(October)*

Travel Journal & Notes:

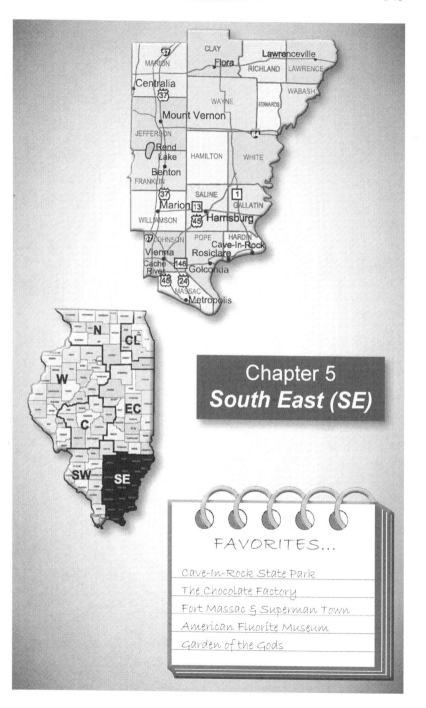

Chapter 5
South East (SE)

FAVORITES...

Cave-In-Rock State Park

The Chocolate Factory

Fort Massac & Superman Town

American Fluorite Museum

Garden of the Gods

Belknap
- Cache River Natural Area

Cave-in-Rock
- Cave-In-Rock State Park

Eddyville
- Millstone Bluff

Elizabethtown
- Illinois Iron Furnace

Flora
- Little Toot Railroad

Golconda
- Chocolate Factory, The
- Dixon Springs State Park
- War Bluff Valley Wildlife Sanctuary

Goreville
- Ferne Clyffe State Park

Grand Tower
- Devil's Backbone Park, Devil's Bake Oven, Tower Rock

Harrisburg
- Saline Creek Pioneer Village And Museum

Johnsonville
- Sam Dale Lake

Johnston City
- Bandy's Pumpkin Patch

Kinmundy
- Stephen A. Forbes State Recreation Area
- Fall Festival At Ingrams' Pioneer Village

Marion
- Crab Orchard National Wildlife Refuge

Metropolis
- Fort Massac State Park
- Super Museum (Superman)

Mt. Carmel
- Beall Woods State Park

Mt. Vernon
- Mitchell Museum At Cedarhurst

Rosiclare
- American Fluorite Museum

Salem
- William Jennings Bryan Birthplace Museum

Sumner
- Red Hills State Park

Vienna
- Garden Of The Gods Recreation Area
- Pounds Hollow/ Rim Rock Recreational Area
- Tunnel Hill State Trail

Whittington
- Rend Lake/ Wayne Fitzgerrell State Park
- Southern Illinois Artisans Shop & Visitors Center

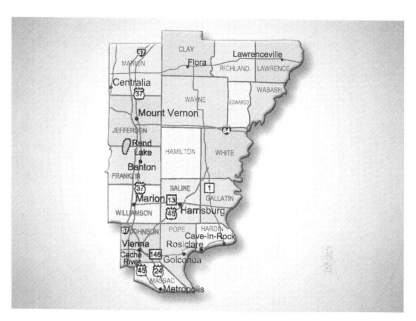

Garden of the Gods - Superman must live around here somewhere...

Sites and attractions are listed in order by City, Zip Code, and Name. Symbols indicated represent: 🍽 Restaurants 🛏 Lodging

---

CACHE RIVER STATE NATURAL AREA

930 Sunflower Lane (south on Rte. 45 thru Vienna, then west on Belknap. Right on Main, right on Sunflower - Headquarters) **Belknap** 62908

- Phone: (618) 634-9678
  http://dnr.state.il.us/lands/landmgt/parks/R5/CACHERVR.HTM
- Hours: Visitors Center: Fridays and Saturdays from 8:30am - 4:30pm. Park open daylight hours.
- Admission: FREE
- Note: The Tunnel Hill State bicycle trail travels through eight miles of the Cache River State Natural Area terminating at the Wetlands Visitor Center.

Among the outstanding natural features found within the area today are massive cypress trees whose flared bases exceed 40 feet circumference. They're surrounded by ancient blackwater swamp. A boardwalk winds its way into the relatively undisturbed depths of this forested swamp, providing visitors a chance to step back in time and observe wetland and aquatic ecosystems (best moderate trail: Lower Cache River Swamp Trail (2.5 miles) or Section 8 Boardwalk (accessible and only 500 ft). Look for the award-winning giant Tupelo tree at the end of the trail. Visitors can experience this lost world while paddling a canoe through 6 miles of trails that meander through rivers, swamps and ponds in a portion of the Lower Cache River known as Buttonland Swamp. Maybe you'll catch a glimpse of a bird-voiced tree frog or a soaring eagle. Heron Pond Trail crosses the Cache River on a new truss bridge. Walk on a floating boardwalk into the middle of Heron Pond.

Located south of Whitehill on Illinois Route 37, the Wetlands Center helps visitors gain a better understanding of the area and learn the importance of wetlands through exhibits, displays, audio-visual presentations and viewing decks. Among the features at the center are a sound amplification system, bird feeders, birdhouses and shrub and tree landscaping to attract wildlife. The sound being amplified allows visitors the chance to hear outdoor wildlife sounds, while standing or sitting inside the wildlife viewing area.

CAVE-IN-ROCK STATE PARK
#1 New State Park Rd. (I-57 exit Hwy 13 east to SR 1 south for 22 miles)
Cave-in-Rock 62919

Phone: (618) 289-4325 or (618) 289-4545 lodge
http://dnr.state.il.us/lands/landmgt/parks/R5/CAVEROCK.HTM
Note: Boating, camping, fishing, marina and 2 marked hiking trails. Fees for camping.

The heavily wooded park is named for the 55-foot-wide cave that was carved out of the limestone rock by water thousands of years ago. Cave in Rock was a landmark on the maps of the early 1800's. Lewis and Clark knew of the Cave and its reputation for housing pirates and other rogues. Today, you can see the cave by taking a short walk from the ferry landing at Cave in Rock. Trails winding along the riverbank offer views of riverboats, barges and other river scenes. The deep, dark recesses engage images of adventure, mystery, terror, robbers and pirates. The cave served as a backdrop for a scene in the movie "_How The West Was Won_." The scene was a portrayal of how ruthless bandits used the cave to lure unsuspecting travelers in to rob them. Enjoy the walk down Pirates Bluff into the cave and take in the outstanding view of the river.

Cave-In-Rock Restaurant and Lodging features four duplex guest houses with eight suites, each accommodating up to four people comfortably. The suites contain deluxe baths, a dining area and wet bar, a large bedroom/living room, and a private patio deck overlooking the Ohio River. The Lodge operates on a seasonal basis. Southern-style cooking is presented at the restaurant (8:00am-9:00pm).

MILLSTONE BLUFF
(Hwy 147, 1/2 east of Robbs, Shawnee National Forest) **Eddyville 62928**

Phone: (618) 658-2111
Note: In the same town, within the Shawnee National Forest, walk through Bell Smith Springs (8 miles west of IL 145 south - 800-699-6637) has coldwater springs and a large natural stone bridge. Indian Kitchen Cave and the 80 to 100 foot sheer bluffs is the remains of an ancient native American stone wall. They were built by prehistoric hunters to stampede the woodland buffalo over the cliffs that intersect the walls at right angles. Lusk Creek & Indian Kitchen (618) 658-2111. (1 mile east of Eddyville on Hwy. 145)

The site has remained relatively undisturbed because it is perched in a high hill surrounded by an 80-foot high bluff. The Mississippian period village is thought to have been active for 500 years, ending about 500 years ago. The paved trail leads to a Native American Cemetery, the remains of a stone wall, and the depressions excavated for buildings in the small town. There were probably two to six individuals per household living here. But the highlights of the site are the petroglyphs (carvings in rock) of a thunder bird, rattle snake, corn stalk on bloom, etc. The figures are actually "pecked" into the stone, and not carved.

ILLINOIS IRON FURNACE

(along Big Creek, north of town above Tecumseh Lake)
Elizabethtown 62931

  Phone: (618) 287-2201
  **www.fs.usda.gov/recarea/shawnee/recreation/fishing/
  recarea/?recid=10687&actid=42**
  Hours: Daylight
  Admission: FREE

While hiking, you can see the remains of huge 1837 stone furnaces. During the Civil War pig iron was smelted here, then shipped down the river to make the Union iron clad boats. Explore some of the easy hiking trails and you may see coyotes, gray and fox squirrels, little brown and red bats, and many songbirds and woodland flowers in a forest of towering beech and maple trees. The Furnace Trail is a .9-mile trail leading from the back of the picnic area. The trail winds along Big Creek and offers 2 or 3 deep old-fashioned fishing holes. Fishing, hiking and picnicking opportunities are nearby.

LITTLE TOOT RAILROAD

Old US 50 (County Road 425) **Flora** 62839

  Phone: (618) 662-8313 or (866) 836-8668 (railroad) **www.littletootrailroad.com**
  Hours: Weekends morning and afternoon (mid-May - mid-December).
  Admission: $5.00 per person per trip.

This 100-acre park features a swimming pool, playground, a golf course, fishing, camping, and steam engine rides. Little Toot Railroad is a 15-inch-gauge locomotive that runs through the park. Visitors can ride the rails and wave to passers-by. The depot has a gift shop and party room.

For updates & travel games visit: **www.KidsLoveTravel.com**

CHOCOLATE FACTORY, THE

Rt. 2 Box 164 (on Hwy 146 east, right across from Dixon Springs State Park)
Golconda 62938

- Phone: (877) 949-3829 **www.thechocolatefactory.net**
- Hours: Monday-Saturday 9:00am-5:00pm.
- Admission: FREE. Samples a plenty. Reasonable prices for theme chocolates to fit any hobby or interest.

Follow your sweet tooth west on Hwy 146 to the Chocolate Factory which is right across the highway from Dixon Springs State Park. There's over 50 kinds of chocolates, in a wide variety of shapes, hand painted novelties, plus ice cream and the best chocolate turtles! Ask them, they would love to give you a demonstration! We watched them paint a tractor and mint chocolate chip ice cream cone chocolates. The trick is the temperature of the white chocolate "paint" and the artist using brushes working from front to back, layering the color for the right effect. Their ice cream is only $1.00 a scoop, too.

DIXON SPRINGS STATE PARK

RR #2, Box 178, Route 146 (I-24 traveling East, take exit #16 to Rt. 146. At the stop sign turn left and the park is 13 miles on the left - near Rte. 145)
Golconda 62938

- Phone: (618) 949-3394
  http://dnr.state.il.us/lands/landmgt/parks/R5/DIXON.HTM
- Note: The Chocolate Factory is across from the entrance.

Dixon Springs takes its name from William Dixon, one of the first white settlers to build a home in this section, who obtained a school land warrant in 1848. At one time, a great hotel and spa were here with promises that the mineral water could cure anything from alcoholism to rheumatism. The park offers hiking trails, picnic spots, camping areas, and an outdoor swimming pool (seasonal). Just north of here is Lake Glendale Recreation Area (618-949-3807) where visitors can fish, swim, camp and horseback ride. This park is super popular with camping families.

WAR BLUFF VALLEY WILDLIFE SANCTUARY

(north on IL 146 from town. West on Bushwack Road (gravel road) for a
couple miles) **Golconda** 62938

- Phone: (618) 457-6367 **www.shawneeaudubon.org/?page_id=73**
- Hours: Dawn to dusk.
- Admission: FREE

This wildlife sanctuary is nestled in the uplands of the Shawnee National
Forest and supports many ancient oak-hickory woods, river bottom forests,
young forests and old field habitats. Simmons Creek and several ponds
provide the water needed to support a diverse natural community. Look for
more than 300 types of plants, including a rich variety of wildflowers and
nine types of ferns. Other features include 7 ponds, historic homestead sites,
and interesting geology. There are 10 walking trails or tractor paths allowing
access to all areas of the sanctuary.

FERNE CLYFFE STATE PARK

Illinois Route 37, PO Box 10 (one mile south of town, between I-57 and I-24)
Goreville 62939

- Phone: (618) 995-2411
  http://dnr.state.il.us/lands/landmgt/parks/R5/FERNE.HTM

Ferne Clyffe has been known as an outstanding natural scenic spot for nearly
100 years. An abundance of ferns, unique geological features and unusual
plant communities create an atmosphere that enhances the many recreational
facilities offered at the park. Trails wind through the woods, allowing visitors
to view unusual rock formations and an intermittent waterfall (Big Rocky
Hollow Trail). Ferne Clyffe Lake is open to bank fishing, but boating and
swimming are prohibited. Camping, horseback riding and picnicking are
available, too.

DEVIL'S BACKBONE PARK, DEVIL'S BAKE OVEN, TOWER ROCK

(Grand Tower and Brunkhorst Roads, IL 3 & Great River Road)
Grand Tower 62942

- Phone: (618) 565-8380 or (618) 565-2454 campground
  www.prairieghosts.com/devil1.html

When early explorers journeyed down the Mississippi River in 1673, they recorded in their journals a large rock that is known as Tower Rock today. The name was given to the landmark after three French missionaries erected a large wooden cross on the rock's crest in 1678. During the heyday of river travel and exploration, a number of people were killed in the rapids that sometimes run at the base of the rock. Thanks to this, the Native Americans were convinced that evil spirits lurked here, waiting to claim the lives of unwitting victims.

Devil's Backbone is an unusual rock ridge that runs along the Mississippi River. Another unusual rock formation called Devil's Bake Oven is at the north end of the park. Pitted with caves, the Oven once harbored river pirates until a U.S. cavalry troop drove them away in 1803. The park also was the site of an Indian massacre in the early 1800s. The foundation walls of an old house still stand atop Devil's Bake Oven. According to legend, the ghost of a young girl who died of a broken heart lingers among the ruins and is sometimes seen on quiet, moonlit nights.

SALINE CREEK PIONEER VILLAGE AND MUSEUM

1600 Feazel Street (east on Rte. 13, southwest part of town)
Harrisburg 62946

Phone: (618) 253-7342
Admission: $3.00
Tours: Tuesday-Sunday 2:00-5:00pm.

The village represents a pioneer settlement of the era 1800 to 1840. Here you'll go back in time when you walk through this log cabin village with its school, old Moravian church, general store and post office. Venture through the 1877 Victorian era museum which once served as the county poor house and farm. Today each room is filled with unique collections. Also, are several log family cabins, a threshing barn filled with tools and other antique items.

SAM DALE LAKE

Illinois Route 161 (I-57, take exit #109, turn East on Rt 161, travel approx. 22 miles) **Johnsonville 62850**

Phone: (618) 835-2292
http://dnr.state.il.us/lands/landmgt/parks/R5/SAMDALE.HTM

The highlight of a visit here will be Sam Dale Lake, a beautiful 194 acre lake with eight and a half miles of shoreline to hike around, swim in, or just sit beside and enjoy. The tall, shady trees and plentiful flowers and greenery beckon picnickers at Sam Dale Lake. One of the picnic areas has shelter. Several picnic areas are available with tables, drinking fountains, and outdoor stoves. Playground equipment, concession stand. In addition, several smaller ponds are home to fish and wildlife.

BANDY'S PUMPKIN PATCH

Johnston City - *(half mile west of Johnston City on Pumpkin Patch Road just off the Herrin/Johnston City Road). Explore a large maze – different shape each year, petting zoo, little kids straw maze, barn activities, hayrides and pumpkin carving contests. Admission.* **www.bandyspumpkinpatch.com** *(September and October)*

STEPHEN A. FORBES STATE RECREATION AREA

6924 Omega Road (15 miles northeast of Salem, off I-57) **Kinmundy** 62854

Phone: (618) 547-3381
http://dnr.state.il.us/lands/landmgt/parks/R5/STEPHEN.HTM

As the sun comes up, take a swim at sandy Rocky Point Beach. The rest of the day offers many options, from hiking on the nature trails, softball , volleyball, water skiing and boating. Or, you may want to spend the night at the Oak Ridge Campground.

FALL FESTIVAL AT INGRAMS' PIONEER VILLAGE

Kinmundy - *Ingrams Pioneer Log Cabin Village (I-57 exit 127).* **www.facebook. com/pages/Ingrams-Pioneer-Log-Cabin-Village/146249100495**. *Leisurely walk the streets of the Log Cabin Village and be transported back in time to a pre-Civil War era. Visit log cabin homes, a general store, doctor and apothecary, preacher's cabin, cobbler shop, cooper, and carpenter shop. Visit Jacob's Well, which was frequented by Abraham Lincoln. The festival brings the village to life with demonstrators. Admission. (last two weekends in September and first weekend in October)*

CRAB ORCHARD NATIONAL WILDLIFE REFUGE

8588 Route 148 (IL 148, south of Rte. 13, west of town) **Marion** 62959

Phone: (618) 997-3344 **www.fws.gov/midwest/craborchard/**

Admission: FREE

Crab Orchard is well-known for hunting, fishing, camping and boating opportunities. This 4,000-acre refuge is especially beautiful in the fall when the geese return for the winter. Every Sunday in October, wildlife enthusiasts drive through sections of the refuge normally closed to traffic, watching for wild turkeys, coyotes, foxes and bobcats. Little Grassy, Devil's Kitchen and Crab Orchard lakes are well-known for fishing opportunities and six small ponds that are open to the public. Crab Orchard Lake is popular for water skiing, swimming and sailboating. The refuge also has about 30 eagles.

FORT MASSAC STATE PARK

1308 E. 5th Street (I-24 exit 37, follow signs) **Metropolis** 62960

Phone: (618) 524-4712
http://dnr.state.il.us/lands/landmgt/parks/R5/frmindex.htm
Hours: Daily 8:30am-4:00pm (Winter), Daily 10:00am-5:30pm (April-November)
Note: Picnicking, camping, hiking, and boating. The 2.5-mile Hickory Nut Ridge Trail is one not to miss, as it takes hikers along the scenic Ohio River.

Native Americans, early Spanish DeSoto crews and even the French used this point overlooking the Ohio River as a lookout and fortress. It was rebuilt after the Revolutionary War as George Washington thought it to be a strategic location. Lewis and Clark with their party arrived here on November 11, 1803 and stayed here 2 days. While here, Lewis and Clark recruited several enlisted men and they also hired George Drouillard to act as an interpreter and hunter for the party. It was again re-fortified for part of the War of 1812 and the Civil War. Edward Everett Hale used the setting of Fort Massac and the Burr-Wilkinson plot as basis for his classic historical novel, "*The Man Without a Country*."

Today, Fort Massac is an excursion through the entire course of American history. The historic site is a replica of the 1802 American fort that was on site. The fort area contains 2 barracks, 3 block houses, officer quarters, well, stockade along with a fraise fence. There is also a visitors center and museum with a short video and some artifacts. The site is best to visit during monthly or bi-weekly weekend re-enactments to relive history. If you come during the week, let the kids just play "fort" while parents sit nearby with a nice breezy view of the Ohio River.

FORT MASSAC ENCAMPMENT

Metropolis - *Fort Massac. Both days begin with posting of colours, continue with entertainment, river activities, and children's games. Military and civilian craft activities and demonstrations. FREE. (third weekend in October)*

OLDE TYME CHRISTMAS

Metropolis - *Fort Massac. Different rooms in the replica of the 1802 American Fort will represent the Christmas traditions form the 1750 to 1865. Reenactors will welcome visitors to the fort and tell of the Christmas traditions from the historical period they represent. The Visitors center will be decorated and period music and refreshments will be served. FREE. (second Saturday in December)*

SUPER MUSEUM (SUPERMAN)

611 Market Street (Superman Square) **Metropolis** 62960

- Phone: (618) 524-5518 **www.supermuseum.com**
- Hours: Daily 9:00am-5:00pm.
- Admission: $5.00 per person (ages 6+). Includes admission to The Americana Hollywood Museum is next to Harrah's at 100 West 3rd Street. Hollywood icons (Elvis, NASCAR, Finding Nemo & John Wayne cowboys).

View a collection of Superman memorabilia including the original costume worn by George Reeves, the first Superman in the 1950s and every Superman toy ever made. Browse through movie props, rare toys and comic books. The museum is filled with a $2.5 million collection spanning 60 years, honoring the most famous hero of all time. See Lex Luther's Scientific Lab as the mysterious theme music plays and you walk the colorful isles. Get energy from the Krypton - beware of Kryptonite! The gift shop has hundreds of items to buy. The famous Superman Statue is a 15-foot bronze figure that overlooks the uptown area of the city (Market St. & 5th Street). Visitors enjoy having photos made with this famed "Man of Steel." After a while roaming the town, you'll feel like your family is in a superhero movie!

SUPERMAN CELEBRATION

Metropolis - *Downtown. (800) 949-5740. The Man of Steel gets a hero's welcome in his hometown with a museum and statue to visit, a DC Comics costume contest, carnival rides and games. Superboy and Supergirl contests. Man of Steel timberjack contest. Often, celebrities from Superman films make appearances. FREE (second long weekend in June)*

For updates & travel games visit: **www.KidsLoveTravel.com**

BEALL WOODS STATE PARK
9258 Beall Woods Avenue (six miles south of town on Rte. 1)
Mt. Carmel 62863

Phone: (618) 298-2442

http://dnr.state.il.us/lands/landmgt/parks/R5/BEALL.HTM#Visitor

Hours: Beall Woods is open year-round from sunrise to 10:00pm. The park is closed on Christmas Day and New Year's Day.

The forest contains trees over 120 feet tall and as much as 3 feet in diameter. The five established trails offer the hiker an excellent view of this old-growth forest. From the easy 1-mile Tuliptree trail which features a self-guided trail brochure to the 1¼-mile moderately easy White oak trail, the nature enthusiast can get a sense of what the settlers saw when they arrived at the banks of the Wabash River. Besides hiking, Beall Woods also offers camping, picnicking, and fishing.

MITCHELL MUSEUM AT CEDARHURST
2400 Richview Road **Mt. Vernon** 62864

Phone: (618) 242-1236 **www.cedarhurst.org**

Hours: Tuesday - Saturday 10:00am-5:00pm, Sunday 1:00-5:00pm.

Admission: FREE

Explore rolling meadows and woods, home to Cedarhurst Sculpture Park, the museum's outdoor gallery with over 60 large-scale sculptures. Visit the Mitchell Museum with contemporary art exhibitions in two galleries, including the Children's Gallery. The hands-on Children's area features Art History and making art like the masters.

AMERICAN FLUORITE MUSEUM
Main Street (across from City Hall) **Rosiclare** 62982

Phone: (618) 285-3513

Hours: Thursday, Friday & Sunday 1:00-4:00pm, Saturday 10:00-4:00pm (March-December).

Admission: $3.00 adult, $1.00 child (6-12).

Note: Although the mines are now closed (China mines most fluorspar now), you can still mine for your own minerals. Search through heaps of rock piles outside the museum digging for fluorite crystals (pay $1.00 per pound of rock to dig through). This isn't gem panning - it's hand-panning.

The American Fluorite Museum is located in the former office building of the Rosiclare Lead and Fluorspar Mining Company. Once the largest fluorspar mining area in the United States, the specimens were collected from this region. A good many of these are well over a foot across. "Butterball, floating, peppered or oil slicks" are descriptions of some of the unusual formations. Of the colored crystals, purple, blue and yellow are prevalent. One display includes a scale model of one of the mines and shows the workings of everyday mining operations in the district. Fluorspar was mined no where else in the United States. Fluorspar is made from super - saturated minerals at great temperatures and pressures deep in the earth. When driven through faults they congeal into the mineral rich deposits of fluorspar, the state mineral of Illinois. Do you use fluoride toothpaste? It comes from fluorite.

WILLIAM JENNINGS BRYAN BIRTHPLACE MUSEUM

408 South Broadway (I-57 exit 116) **Salem** 62881

☐   Phone: (618) 548-7791
     www.salemil.us/Pages/SalemIL_About/S008FEDDB?Close=-1
☐   Hours: Monday, Wednesday and Saturday from Noon-4:30pm. Closed holidays.

"Billy," as his friends knew him, was born at this address in 1860. William Jennings Bryan was the son of Judge Silas M. and Maria E. (Jennings) Bryan. Silas was a teacher, lawyer, school superintendent, state senator and circuit court judge. As a devout Presbyterian, he would pray to God for assistance before he made a decision. He had an active political career during his entire life, from a young lawyer entering the House of Representatives to the seasoned prosecuting attorney at the Scopes Trial, where the issue of whether evolution should be taught in school was argued in 1925. William was known as "The Great Commoner" and "The Silver-Tongued Orator" and he ran for president of the United States in three campaigns (never won, though). He became famous at the 1896 Chicago Democratic Party convention when he uttered words which lived on in history - "You shall not crucify the working man upon a cross of gold!" This building is on the National Register of Historical Places.

RED HILLS STATE PARK

1100 N. & 400 E. (midway between Olney and Lawrenceville
northeast of Sumner) **Sumner** 62466

- Phone: (618) 936-2469
  http://dnr.state.il.us/lands/landmgt/parks/r5/redhls.htm
- Note: The Trace Inn is named for the Cahokia Trace. The restaurant provides
  seating for 100, and is open year-round. A beautiful canopied deck for warm
  weather dining is a popular attraction. It also offers a scenic overlook of
  Red Hills Lake. Visitors to the Trace Inn will also enjoy a unique craft and
  collectibles shop. For more information call (618) 936-2351.

Red Hills is a carefully preserved and maintained 948-acres of high wooded
hills, deep ravines, meadows and year-round springs. Pause to enjoy the
spectacular scenic view from atop Red Hills - the highest point of land
between St. Louis and Cincinnati - and the 120-foot tower and cross rising
from its summit. The sparkling 40-acre lake is ideal for fishing and boating.
An open-air tabernacle at the base of the tower (financed and constructed
by area residents cooperating with an inter-denominational council) holds
services on Sunday evening during the summer. A popular activity since 1943
has been the annual Easter sunrise services.

GARDEN OF THE GODS RECREATION AREA

Hidden Springs Ranger District / Shawnee National Forest (Rte. 45 north)
(I-24 exit 16, Rte. 146 east, north on SR 34 to intersection with Rte. 1)
Vienna 62995

- Phone: (618) 658-2111 or (800) MY-WOODS
  www.fs.fed.us/r9/forests/shawnee/recreation/trails/gog/
- Hours: Daylight
- Admission: FREE

As you arrive, you will be in the surrounding 3,300 acre wilderness of the
Shawnee National Forest. Garden of the Gods Observation Trail is a .3-mile
flagstone moderate loop walk that contains interpretive signs explaining the
geological history. A great uplift, and then erosion, formed the unusual shapes
of rock peaks. Wooden and rock steps occur at midpoint. Taking one of the
many marked paved trails, you'll find yourself standing on sandstone bluffs
that are over 400 feet above the forest floor.

Rock formations have been given names such as Camel Rock, Devil's Smokestack and Noah's Ark because of their unique shape and size. We named some smaller formations - turtle, frog, lizard and table rock. It's fun to find some new shape around every corner. Many side-views of formations look like faces. Bring your camera to capture the views of the plant and wildlife in this panoramic setting.

POUNDS HOLLOW / RIM ROCK REC AREA

Hidden Springs Ranger District / Shawnee National Forest (Rte. 45 north)
(Garden of the Gods, continue east on Karber's Ridge Road to route 1)
Vienna 62995

Phone: (618) 658-2111 or (800) MY-WOODS
www.fs.fed.us/r9/forests/shawnee/recreation/trails/
Note: Also offered in this quadrant of the Shawnee National Forest are camping, picnicking, fishing, boat rentals, and a swimming beach.

At Pounds Hollow / Rim Rock Recreational Area you will view walls almost a ¼ mile long and originally 8 to 10 feet high, believed to have been Indian forts. Several enclosures were thought to have been used to entrap animals and thus the name Pounds. Even after the Indians, the early logger pioneers kept their oxen and horses within the fenced in walls. Rim Rock Trail is a .4-mile difficult trail that leads the hiker around the top rim of the "Pounds," which is a circular 40-acre tract of land isolated from the surrounding terrain by steep sandstone bluffs. Interpretive signs along the trail explain the history of the much-used "Pounds." The trail meanders past an old Indian Wall, the Ox-Lot Cave and Fat Man's Misery, a narrow passage through massive cliffs and boulders.

TUNNEL HILL STATE TRAIL

Illinois Route 146 **Vienna** 62995

Phone: (618) 658-2168
http://dnr.state.il.us/lands/Landmgt/PARKS/R5/tunnel.htm
Hours: Dawn to dusk daily.
Note: Bicycles can be rented from Peddles and Paddles @ (618) 658-3641.

Tunnel Hill State Trail stretches for 45 miles from Harrisburg to Karnak, with 2.5 mikes being managed by the city of Harrisburg. The trail is so named for a 10-mile stretch from Tunnel Hill to Vienna. It passes through a 540-

foot railroad tunnel that was built in the 1870s. Several high trestles pass over deep-narrow valleys in the hilly southern Illinois countryside. The trail continues on a trails spur for 2.5 miles from Karnak to Cache River State Natural Area - Henry Barkhausen Wetlands Center on the old Chicago and Eastern Illinois railroad bed. The 9.3-mile section between Tunnel Hill and Vienna crosses trails already known to outdoor recreationists, including the Trail of Tears, the primary route the Cherokee Indian tribe took in the winter of 1838-39 during their forced move from the Great Smokies to Oklahoma. A Visitors Center in Vienna features a reception and interpretive area highlighting features of the region's communities. Most of the landscape is flat farm country or wetlands (no more than 2% grade). Each trailhead has parking areas from which hikers, runners and cyclists can access the trail.

REND LAKE / WAYNE FITZGERRELL STATE PARK
11094 Ranger Road and Fitzgerrell Drive **Whittington** 62897
Phone: (618) 629-2320
http://dnr.state.il.us/lands/Landmgt/PARKS/R5/WAYNE.HTM

Make a splash in this huge lake, the second largest man-made lake in the state. Build a sand castle, play beach volleyball, take a swim or just kick back and relax at one of two public beaches. Rend Lake offers many recreation opportunities. Begin your adventure by exploring nature on foot, bicycle or horseback. A 4-mile bike trail runs the length of the park and connects Rend Lake Resort and Rend Lake College. Trails and hiking areas are outlined in a free watchable Wildlife Guide, available at the Rend Lake Visitor Center and the Rend Lake Visitor Center and the Rend Lake Project Office. Enjoy fishing, bird watching (blue herons and bald eagles), and power boating. Overnight visitors can stay at the Wayne Fitzgerrell State Park which has primitive and developed camp sites, or at the Corps of Engineers campgrounds on Rend Lake. For those who prefer not to camp, the Rend Lake Resort has waterside rooms, sport courts, playground, stables, horse and carriage rides, bicycle rentals, indoor (Rend Lake College) & outdoor swimming pool, and marina facilities.

SOUTHERN ILLINOIS ARTISANS SHOP & VISITORS CENTER

14967 Gun Creek Trail (6 miles north of town on I-57, just west of exit 77, Rend Lake) **Whittington** 62897

☐   Phone: (618) 629-2220 **www.museum.state.il.us/ismsites/so-il**
☐   Hours: Daily 9:00am-5:00pm except major winter holidays.
☐   Admission: FREE

Fine artwork is displayed here, but families gravitate towards traditional craft products made by Illinois artists and sold at their marketplace. Ask for the daily schedule of crafters on-site, demonstrating their art. See work in metals, wearables, jewelry, painting, ceramics, glass and textiles - all made in Illinois.

RIVER FERRIES OF THE MIDDLE MISSISSIPPI RIVER VALLEY

☐   Phone: (800) 373-7007
   www.greatriverroad.com/SecondaryPages/ferries.htm
☐   Note: If you are planning a visit to any of the ferries in the Middle Mississippi Valley and believe the ferries might not be operating due to flood conditions or ice please call the number above or go on the website.

Early American ferries consisted of rafts, rowboats and horse boats that could cross rivers where demand for transportation existed but where there weren't any easy crossings. The advent of railroads and bridges put most ferries out of business and motorized vessels replaced the earlier forms of transportation of those that survived. For modern travelers, the remaining ferries in operation can save time as well as providing scenic river views.

• **GOLDEN EAGLE FERRY** - (618) 396-2535. This ferry takes vehicles across the Mississippi River between the small town of Golden Eagle in Calhoun County in Illinois and St. Charles County in Missouri. To reach the Golden Eagle Ferry from Pere Marquette State Park or Grafton, cross the Brussels Ferry and continue on County Road 1 until you see the signs directing you to the ferry. From the Missouri side of the Mississippi River take MO-94 to County Road B north of St. Charles. Take CR-B west to Golden Eagle Ferry Road. Take Golden Eagle Ferry Road to the ferry. Daily from 8:00am-9:00pm. Toll fees: Car or pickup truck $8.00 one-way

---

or $15.00 round trip. Motorcycles $5.00, bicycles or pedestrians $4.00.

- **GRAFTON FERRY** - The Grafton Ferry is located on the Illinois side at the foot of Illinois Route 3, just upriver of the Grafton public boat ramp. On the Missouri side, it terminates just off of Grafton Ferry Road alongside the St. Charles County Airport. From there it is a short ride to highway 94 and about 10 miles to the St. Charles city line. Toll Fees: $8.00 one way, $5.00 for motorcycles, $4.00 for bicycles, & $3.00 for pedestrians) with reduced rates for round trips. Daily except major winter holidays.

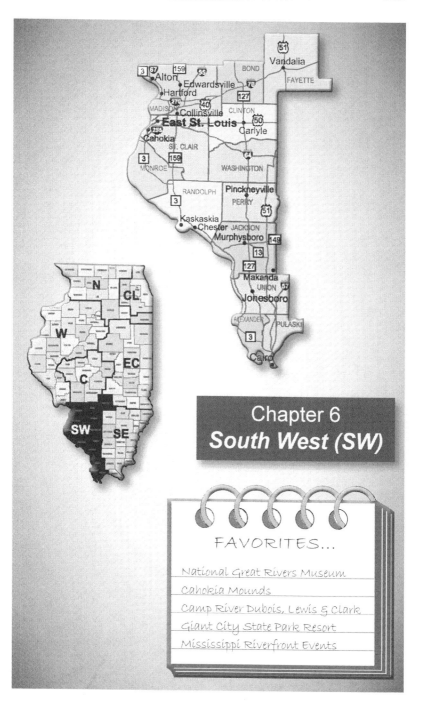

Chapter 6
South West (SW)

FAVORITES...

National Great Rivers Museum

Cahokia Mounds

Camp River Dubois, Lewis & Clark

Giant City State Park Resort

Mississippi Riverfront Events

Alto Pass
- Easter Sunrise Service

Alton
- Alton Museum Of History And Art
- National Great Rivers Museum
- Christmas Wonderland

Belleville
- Eckerts Country Store & Farm
- Way Of Lights

Cahokia
- Cahokia Courthouse State Historic Site
- Greater St. Louis Air And Space Museum

Carlyle
- Carlyle Lake/ Eldon Hazlet State Park/ South Shore State Park

Centralia
- National Outboard Hydro Plane Boat Races
- Balloon Fest

Chester
- Popeye Statue And Park
- Randolph County Conservation Area

Collinsville
- Brooks Catsup Bottle
- Cahokia Mounds State Historic Site
- Drury Hotel
- Splash City Family Waterpark
- Italian Festival

East St. Louis
- Gateway Geyser

East St. Louis (Sauget)
- Gateway Grizzlies

Edwardsville
- Bilbrey Farms Bed & Breakfast & Animal Zoo
- Children's Museum Of Edwardsville
- Watershed Nature Center

Ellis Grove
- Fort Kaskaskia & Kaskaskia Bell State Historic Site
- Pierre Menard Home State Historic Site

Godfrey
- Great Godfrey Maze

Granite City
- Horseshoe Lake State Fish & Wildlife Area

Hartford
- Camp River Dubois, Lewis & Clark St. Historic Site

Highland
- Homestead Harvest Days

Jonesboro
- Trail Of Tears State Forest

Makanda
- Giant City State Park
- Giant City State Park Resort
- Little Grassy Fish Hatchery

Marine
- Mills Apple Farm

Murphysboro
- Lake Murphysboro State Park And Kinkaid Lake State Fish And Wildlife Area
- Shawnee Saltpetre Cave

Nashville
- Rainbow Ranch Petting Zoo

Pinckneyville
- Pyramid State Park

Pomona

- Pomona Natural Bridge

Prairie Du Rocher

- Fort De Chartres'

St. Louis, MO

- Gateway Arch
- Old Chain Of Rocks Bridge

Vandalia

- Vandalia Statehouse Site

"New Members" of the Lewis & Clark Expedition...

Sites and attractions are listed in order by City, Zip Code, and Name. Symbols indicated represent: 🍽 Restaurants   🛏 Lodging

EASTER SUNRISE SERVICE

Alto Pass - *Bald Knob Cross (IL 127). www.baldknobcross.com. One of the most visible and most famous of Southern Illinois' attractions, the 111-foot cross tops Bald Knob Mountain. When illuminated at night, it can be seen for miles. The road winding up to the cross is an adventure in itself, and the view from the top of Bald Knob is spectacular year-round. Thousands attend the Easter sunrise services that have been conducted annually since 1937. In 1951, the Bald Knob Christian Foundation Inc. began efforts to place a permanent shrine on Bald Knob Mountain, the highest point in Southern Illinois. Ground was broken in 1959 and the cross finished in 1963. FREE. (Easter morning)*

ALTON MUSEUM OF HISTORY AND ART

2809 College Avenue/ Loomis Hall **Alton** 62002

- Phone: (618) 462-2763 or (800) 258-6645 **www.altonmuseum.com**
- Hours: Wednesday-Saturday 10:00am-4:00pm, Sunday 1-4pm.
- Admission: $1.00-$2.50 per person.
- Note: Around downtown squares visit the Lincoln / Douglas Debate spot where Abraham Lincoln and Stephen A. Douglas held their last debate while campaigning for U.S. Senate in 1858. At Monument & Fifth Streets, The Lovejoy Monument honors Elijah P. Lovejoy, an abolitionist editor who was murdered because of his support for freedom of the press.

The museum does pay particular tribute to one of its cherished citizens... Robert Pershing Wadlow. Robert is world renowned as the tallest man on record (who grew to 8-feet-11½ inches). His gentle demeanor and cheerful disposition lead to his being called Alton's Gentleman Giant. A life-size cardboard cutout serves as an interactive "measure" up to show proportions of a visitor to this tall man. There is also a video that gives a glimpse of Roberts' life and times. The Transportation room looks back to Alton's legacy as a hub of commerce and travel. The Pioneer Room describes the exploits of Lewis & Clark, The Wood River Massacre, The Lincoln & Shields Duel, the Confederate Prison at Alton, and the Black Pioneers.

NATIONAL GREAT RIVERS MUSEUM

#2 Lock and Dam Way, Melvin Price Lock & Dam (Illinois Route 3 intersects I- 270 approximately two miles east of the Mississippi River. Take IL Route 3 North to Hwy 143 west 2 miles) **Alton** 62002

- Phone: (877) 462-6979 **www.mvs.usace.army.mil/Missions/Recreation/ RiversProjectOffice/NGRM.aspx**
- Hours: Daily 9:00am-5:00pm except major winter holidays.
- Admission: FREE
- Tours: Free tours of the Melvin Price Locks and Dam are conducted daily at 10:00am, 1:00pm and 3:00pm. Also explained are what causes floods, with emphasis on the Great Flood of 1993 and how the Corps of Engineers fights these destructive acts of nature, and what future strategies are being developed to limit their impact.
- Educators: They have a in-house link (http://education.wes.army.mil/ navigation/navigate.html) to an amazing array of simple and in-depth lessons, games and projects related to navigation and water science of great rivers-all presented on a very teachable level.

NATIONAL GREAT RIVERS MUSEUM (cont.)

The Museum features state of the art interactive displays and exhibits that help visitors understand the many aspects of the Mississippi River and how humans interact with it. A large model of the bluffs of the region is in the center of the museum and provides info on the various wildlife from prairie plants and trees to birds and other animals. An aquarium displays the various species of fish that inhabit the Mississippi River. Stir river sediment banks; make a stairway of water; or make your own map. One display explains how the Mississippi has been used as a highway, not only by humans but by migrating waterfowl, and chronicles the different types of vessels used from canoes to steamboats to modern day barges. The Pilot House simulator allows visitors to see what it's like to guide a 1,000 foot tow of barges under a bridge or through a lock. We took on the challenge (harder than it seems) of steering a barge as a parent/child team and finally successfully made it through. This activity, and the dam tour, are the kids' favorites. It sure is eventful when a big barge comes through during the 45-minute lock tour!

CHRISTMAS WONDERLAND

Alton - *Rock Springs Park. Drive through Rock Springs Park to see more than 2.5 million lights adorning trees and lighting displays throughout the park. Admission per car. www.christmaswonderlandofaltonil.net/ (weekend after Thanksgiving through end of December)*

ECKERTS COUNTRY STORE & FARM

901 South Green Mount Road **Belleville** 62220

- ☐ Phone: (618) 233-0513 **www.eckerts.com**
- ☐ Hours: Daily 8:00am-8:00pm. Closed in January.
- ☐ Note: Strawberry festival in mid-May. Memorial Day festival with pony and carnival rides. Barnyard Olympics Labor Day.

- PEACH PICKING TOURS: Peach picking tours are available at the Belleville farm only, and are available on Thursdays and Fridays (late July thru mid-August). Reservations required. The cost is $6.00 per child, and includes a tractor ride to the orchard to pick a small bag of peaches.
- FALL CLASSIC TOURS: Monday-Friday (mid-September thru October). Reservations. Cost $8.00 per child. Kid Corral Play Area   and petting farm. Show. Tractor ride. Apple picking or pumpkin picking. Cup of apple cider.

EASTER EGG-CITEMENT & BREAKFAST WITH THE BUNNY

Belleville - *Eckert's. Did you know the Easter Bunny's favorite meal is scrambled Easter eggs with a side of pancakes? Join the Bunny for breakfast at the Restaurant for a hearty country meal to start this fun-filled day! No registration required. Eckert's Annual Egg Hunt, baby chicks & bunnies, face painting, a photo with the Easter Bunny, plant a seed and savor a yummy Easter treat. This is the largest Egg Hunt in Southwestern Illinois. Fee for breakfast, separate fee for Egg Hunt. (weekend before and of Easter)*

APPLE FEST

Belleville - *Eckert's Country Store and Farm. Wagon rides, music, live entertainment, great festival foods, children's activities. Whether riding a pony or feeding a goat, your young 'uns will enjoy getting acquainted with common farm animals. Children's carnival and/or activities at all three farms. Funnel cakes, roasted sweet corn, caramel apples. And, of course, there are plenty of apples to pick. The last weekend of the month, hear the story of Johnny Appleseed, sing "Happy Birthday" and enjoy a piece of birthday cake. You'll even meet ol' Johnny himself. School group educational tours offered. Fee for some activities. (weekends in September)*

JUMPIN' PUMPKIN JAMBOREE

Belleville - *Eckert's Country Store and Farms. Ride the wagons out to the pumpkin patch to search for your great pumpkin. Their pumpkins range from a couple of pounds to more than 150 pounds. Wagon rides, country music, live entertainment, pony rides, make-a-scarecrow, funnel cakes and festival foods make this a fun-filled weekend for everyone. School group educational tours offered. Children's activities. Petting farm. Fee for some activities. (weekends in October)*

BRUNCH WITH SANTA

Belleville - *Eckert's Country Store and Farm. Join them for a meal with Santa on the farm. Children can show their holiday spirit by singing Christmas carols and telling Santa their Christmas wishes. Santa has a special gift for each child. They will capture the moment in a photo of your child with Santa. Reservations are suggested. While there, pick your own Christmas tree (either pre-cut or head out to the tree farm and cut one yourself). Admission for visit and brunch. (first three Saturdays in December)*

WAY OF LIGHTS

Belleville - *Shrine of Our Lady of Snows.* ***www.snows.org.*** *This 1.5 mile drive-through Christmas display is lined with more than a million lights and leads to a life-size straw-lined manger cradling the baby Jesus. Indoors you'll find seasonal displays, a restaurant and gift shop. FREE. (nightly, mid-November thru New Years week)*

CAHOKIA COURTHOUSE STATE HISTORIC SITE

First and Elm Streets (I-55/70, exit State Route 3 South, 3 miles to State Route 157) **Cahokia** 62206

-     Phone: (618) 332-1782 **www.illinois.gov/ihpa/Experience/Sites/ Southwest/Pages/Cahokia-Courthouse.aspx**
-     Hours: Tuesday-Saturday 9:00am-5:00pm. Winter hours closes at 4:00pm. Closed: Thanksgiving, Christmas, and New Year's Day

Constructed as a dwelling about 1730, the building became a courthouse in 1793, and for twenty years it served as a center of political activity in the Old Northwest Territory. The Cahokia Courthouse is an excellent example of early French log construction known as poteaux-sur-solle (post-on-sill foundation). Inside are four rooms that originally functioned as a courtroom, a schoolroom, and offices for attorneys and clerks. Nearby (east First & Church Streets) is the Holy Family Log Church. It is the oldest church structure west of the Allegheny Mountains and one of the oldest continuously operating parishes in the U.S. (since 1699). Both buildings originate from the Lewis and Clark era.

LEWIS & CLARK'S ARRIVAL IN CAHOKIA

Cahokia - *Courthouse State Historical Site. The anniversary celebration of the explorers' arrival in Cahokia will feature updates on the progress of the Corps of Discovery through exhibits. FREE. (December 7th)*

GREATER ST. LOUIS AIR AND SPACE MUSEUM

2300 Vector Drive (Hanger 2, St.Louis Downtown Airport, 5 miles from the Arch) **Cahokia** 62206

-     Phone: (618) 332-3664 or (877) 332-3664 **www.airandspacemuseum.org**
-     Hours: Friday-Sunday 10:00am-4:00pm.
-     Admission:

Devoted to accomplishments throughout the St. Louis region in all facets of aerospace, including lighter-than-air vehicles, airplanes, and spacecraft. Indoors and out, check out war planes, cut-a-ways of engines, space suits and bi-planes. Stop in at Oliver's Restaurant for lunch or dinner and watch the planes through a bank of windows. Also look at the photos on the wall to see which celebrities have landed at this airport. Air traffic includes private planes, helicopters and St. Louis TV station weather copters.

CARLYLE LAKE / ELDON HAZLET STATE PARK / SOUTH SHORE STATE PARK

20100 Hazlet Park Road **Carlyle** 62231

Phone: (618) 594-2484 **www.carlylelake.com or http://dnr.state.il.us/ lands/landmgt/parks/r4/eldon.htm**

Note: In town, the original suspension bridge crossing the Kaskaskia River now serves as a pedestrian bridge and historical attraction. www.carlyle.il.us/bridge.htm.

Carlyle Lake is the largest man-made lake in Illinois and a great source of outdoor recreation. A challenge for sailboats, many less-avid sailors choose jet skis, houseboats, and pontoon boats rented from the marina. Over 200 species of migratory birds, including eagles and blue heron, stop here in the fall and winter. Visitors can also fish, swim and beach, camp or cabin. The Lakefront Cottages at Eldon Hazlet State Park offer a great view of the Lake shoreline. The rustic-style cottages have a living room, kitchenette, wet bar, bath, bedroom and upstairs loft.

NATIONAL OUTBOARD HYDRO PLANE BOAT RACES

Centralia - *Raccoon Lake. www.centraliail.com/powerboatraces/index.htm Come see the National Championship Outboard Hydro Plane Boat Races competition heats on Friday and Finals over the weekend. Food available. Small admission for 12 years and older. (first weekend in August)*

BALLOON FEST

Centralia - *Foundation Park. Over 40 hot air balloons grace the summer sky during this three-day family festival. Balloon races, balloon glows, cardboard boat races, free children's activity area, car show, pop/rock performances, and parades. Small admission. www.balloon-fest.com (third weekend in August)*

POPEYE STATUE AND PARK

(off IL 3, Great River Road) **Chester** 62233

Phone: (618) 826-2326 **www.chesterill.com/character-trail/**

The towering Popeye Statue in the Elzie C. Segar Memorial Park is found by crossing the Mississippi River, the Chester Bridge. The monument honors Elzie Segar, creator of Popeye who was born in Chester. There's more Popeye than spinach at Spinach Can Collectibles inside Chester's historic 1875 Opera House building. Popeye merchandise and a mini Popeye museum fill the space and headquarters of the Popeye Fan Club.

POPEYE PICNIC

Chester - Segar Memorial Park & Spinach Can Collectibles. www.chesterill.com. For over 75 years, Popeye has been a popular cartoon. One of his cartoons airs somewhere in the world nearly every minute of every day. Popeye's creator, Elzie C. Segal, was born in Chester and many of his comic strip characters were modeled after town residents. FREE. (weekend after Labor Day)

RANDOLPH COUNTY CONSERVATION AREA

4301 S. Lake Drive (northeast of town a few miles, off Palestine Road) **Chester** 62233

Phone: (618) 826-2706
http://dnr.state.il.us/lands/Landmgt/PARKS/R4/RAND.HTM

Note: Hiking, horseback riding trails, camping.

PINEY CREEK RAVINE STATE NATURAL AREA - This scenic spot has steep rock formations and views of Native-American pictographs high on a rock wall. Pecked designs (petroglyphs) that can be seen within Piney Creek Ravine include human figures, deer, serpents and crosses. Painted designs (pictographs) within the ravine include human figures, deer, birds, human hands and a canoe. A hiking trail that winds along the top of a bluff overlooking the creek crosses scenic Piney Creek. The trail is especially beautiful in the autumn when fall colors abound, and also in the winter, when the leafless trees allow unrestricted viewing into the ravine below.

FULTS HILL PRAIRIE - Located a few miles north of Prairie du Rocher and offers a spectacular view from the bluff overlooking the Mississippi flood plain. Prairie flowers, soaring eagles and hawks provide a breathtaking experience.

BROOKS CATSUP BOTTLE

800 South Morrison Avenue (Hwy 159, just south of downtown)
Collinsville 62234

Phone: (618) 345-5598 **www.catsupbottle.com**

The "World's Largest Catsup Bottle" is the now empty, steel water tank and tower measuring 170 feet. This unique water tower was built by the W.E. Caldwell Company for the G.S. Suppiger catsup bottling plant - bottlers of Brooks old original rich & tangy catsup. The landmark, representing "Roadside Architecture at its Best," was constructed in 1949 and was restored in the Spring of 1995.

CAHOKIA MOUNDS STATE HISTORIC SITE

30 Ramey St (I-255 to the Collinsville Road exit 24. Go 2 miles west on Collinsville Road, Hwy. 40 and Ramey Street) **Collinsville** 62234

Phone: (618) 346-5160 **http://cahokiamounds.org**
Hours: Wednesday-Sunday 9am-5pm. Closed wintertime holidays.
Admission: Donations suggested: $2.00-$4.00 per person/$10.00 family.
Note: Today Cahokia is within sight of the famed Gateway Arch in St. Louis.

On this site are the remains of an ancient city where a Mississippian culture flourished from 700-1400 AD and then mysteriously vanished. Mississippians developed an agricultural system with corn, squash, and several seed bearing plants as the principal crops. The stable food base, combined with hunting, fishing, and gathering of wild food plants, enabled them to develop a very complex community with a highly specialized social, political, and religious organization. Cahokia became a regional center for the Mississippian culture after A.D. 900. It features 65 man-made earthen mounds, including 100 ft. Monks Mound, a wooden calendar and a 33,000 foot modern interpretive center near the Mound. After the short (15 minute) video, the screen glides up and one of the best indoor diorama museums is revealed. Feeling sick? - go to the "Sweat House". The Monks Mound is the largest prehistoric earthen mound in the New World. Are you ready to go outside and climb it? This is our favorite Indian Mound site - well worth the trip with intriguing dioramas inside and fun climbs outside!

DRURY HOTEL

*Collinsville - 602 N Bluff (I-55/70 exit 11, IL 157). 62234. (618) 345-7700 or **wwws. druryhotels.com/PropertyOverview.aspx?Property=0051**. Enjoy free long distance - one hour, every room, every night. Free high-speed internet. Evenings they serve complimentary snacks and beverages, mornings they offer free hot Quikstart breakfast. Also a nice indoor pool and spacious lobby/food sit-down area. Just minutes from IL attractions, 10 miles from the Gateway Arch, Lewis & Clark or Great Rivers.*

SPLASH CITY FAMILY WATERPARK

10 Gateway Drive (I-55/70 to Hwy 157 exit north) **Collinsville** 62234

- Phone: (618) 346-4571 **www.splashcity.org**
- Hours: Daily 11:00am-8:00pm (late May-Labor Day week). Closed Monday-Wednesday, mid-August to Labor Day weekend.
- Admission: $14.00-$18.00 (age 3+). $4.00 discount for residents/military.

Southern Illinois' newest water entertainment park features: water slides, a "lazy river", sand volleyball courts, a zero depth-entry pool, a child spray area, grass tanning areas and a wet sand play area. The best part, the Monsoon Mountain is a fifty-foot fortress of multi-slides and climbing and a bucket dump every few minutes.

ITALIAN FESTIVAL

*Collinsville - Main Street, downtown. **www.italianfest.net**. Parade, entertainment, Fest Olympics, cooking contest, Bocce Ball, Grape stomp, and Italian fare. Children's Area. FREE. (third weekend in September)*

GATEWAY GEYSER

Front Street and Trendley Avenue **East St. Louis** 62201

- Phone: (800) 853-0017 **www.hydrodramatics.com/gateway_geyser.htm** or **www.meprd.org/MMMP.htm**
- Hours: The Geyser Fountain runs from April thru October. It usually runs twice a day at Noon, 3:00pm, 6:00pm, 9:00pm daily, but only for 15 minutes. Schedule subject to change. The FAA has placed time restrictions on the Geyser.

Currently the tallest fountain in the world, the Gateway Geyser rises as a testimonial to the engineering expertise and 16-year effort of Hydro Dramatics. Soaring to nearly 630-feet, the geyser's height mirrors that of St. Louis' famed Gateway Arch, located directly across the Mississippi River. The center fountain is complemented by four auxiliary fountains, which represent the four rivers that converge in the St. Louis area. The "park" setting around the geyser is FREE of charge to wander through.

GATEWAY GRIZZLIES

GCS Stadium (just off I-255, exit 15) **East St. Louis (Sauget)** 62206

Phone: (618) 337-3000 **www.gatewaygrizzlies.com**

The Gateway Grizzlies minor league baseball team plays in the outdoor GCS Stadium. The 6,000 seat stadium includes reserved box seats, picnic table seats (for families/groups), general and lawn seats. This stadium is the area's own "field of dreams," It's minor league baseball at its finest in a small venue and for a small price. Game tickets run $5.00-$9.00. There's a kids zone area where children can climb and play ball on their "turf." They get the kids involved on the field and every week there are theme nights (ex. Hat night, bobbleheads, etc.).

BILBREY FARMS BED & BREAKFAST & *ANIMAL ZOO*

8724 Pin Oak Road (I-55 south to Rte. 143 east) **Edwardsville** 62025

Phone: (618) 692-1950 **www.bilbreyfarms.com**

Hours: Animal Farm only open on Fridays & Saturdays. Check in after 3:00pm, Checkout by 11:00am.

Admission: By reservation only. Rooms range $106.00 to $122.00 per night (based on double occupancy). No longer accept credit cards.

Bed and Breakfast accommodations include a country breakfast and rooms with themes from rainforest to castle to garden. Guests have access to the hot tub and on-site movie theatre. The Animal Farm hosts more than 40 animals including a zebra, an emu, a llama, pygmy goats, miniature horses and donkeys, and colorful macaws.

CHILDREN'S MUSEUM OF EDWARDSVILLE

722 Holyoake Road (Hwy 159 and Park Place. Next to LeClaire baseball field) **Edwardsville** 62025

- Phone: (618) 692-2094 **www.edwardsvillechildrensmuseum.org**
- Hours: Tuesday, Friday, Saturday 10:00am-4:00pm.
- Admission: $4.00 per person (age 1+).

The Museum has several rooms with innovative exhibits and programs that stimulate curiosity and learning for children up to age 12. The kids favorite place is the Fix-It Station where kids can take apart small appliances to see how they work. Learn from magnets and Legos, Star City pretend shops, Puppets, or fun Dress-up.

WATERSHED NATURE CENTER

1591 Tower Road **Edwardsville** 62025

- Phone: (618) 692-7578 **www.watershednaturecenter.com**

The Watershed Nature Center features two large lakes and wetland areas, tallgrass prairies and an upland forest. Visitors may walk on the 3,000 ft. wheelchair-accessible pathway at lake level or hike wood-chipped trails through the forested areas. An elevated walkway spans the wetlands and two observation towers, a wildlife viewing blind, and an outdoor amphitheater.

FORT KASKASKIA & KASKASKIA BELL STATE HISTORIC SITE

4372 Park Road (6 miles North of Chester, Illinois, via Route 3. Turn West on Fort Kaskaskia Road and go approximately 2 miles) **Ellis Grove** 62241

- Phone: (618) 859-3741 **www.illinois.gov/ihpa/Experience/Sites/ Southwest/Pages/Fort-Kaskaskia.aspx**
- Hours: Daily 8:00am-4:00pm.
- Admission: FREE

Fort Kaskaskia State Historic Site preserves what's left of the old fort - one of the first built on the Mississippi River. The fort was built to protect Kaskaskia from British attack during the American Revolution. Lewis and Clark's boats landed here, establishing a recruitment base and post office. All that remains today are the earth works around the perimeter. A scenic overlook offers views of the Mississippi and Kaskaskia Rivers and of Old Kaskaskia.

PIERRE MENARD HOME STATE HISTORIC SITE

4230 Kaskaskia Street, R.R.1 Box 58 (off Illinois Rte 3, located near Fort
Kaskaskia) **Ellis Grove** 62241

  Phone: (618) 859-3031 **www.illinois.gov/ihpa/Experience/Sites/
Southwest/Pages/Pierre-Menard.aspx**

  Hours: Wednesday-Sunday 9:00am-5:00pm. (May-October)

  Admission: Suggested donation: $2.00 adult, $1.00 child.

The Pierre Menard Home is the finest example of French Colonial architecture
in the Central Mississippi River Valley. Built in the early 1800's for Illinois'
first lieutenant governor, this elegant residence depicts the upper class
French-American lifestyle of the early 19th century. The home is furnished
with many of the Menard family's personal possessions and other period
pieces. The surrounding grounds and outbuildings include an herb garden,
smokehouse, springhouse, and adjoining kitchen.

GREAT GODFREY MAZE

Godfrey - *Glazebrook Community Park.* ***http://godfreyil.org/index.cfm?page=2549.***
Popular 2 ½ mile maze open extended weekends. (September/October long wkends)

HORSESHOE LAKE STATE FISH & WILDLIFE

3321 Highway 111 (nearby Cahokia Mounds) **Granite City** 62040

  Phone: (618) 931-0270

  http://dnr.state.il.us/lands/landmgt/parks/r4/horsesp.htm

This state park has the ancient oxbow lake, wetlands and low floodplain
environments. The Walker Island bird walk is popular. Evidence shows Native-
American tribes were here around 800 BC. Fishing, boating, picnicking and
camping are available. Four miles of hiking trails wander through the natural
area on the island.

CAMP RIVER DUBOIS, LEWIS & CLARK ST. HISTORIC SITE

Illinois Rte. 3 & New Poag Road (Take 1-270 West to IL-3 North to Poag
Road just south of Hartford) **Hartford** 62048

  Phone: (618) 251-5811 or (800) 258-6645 **www.campdubois.com**

  Hours: Wednesday-Sunday 9:00am-5:00pm.

☐ Admission: FREE, donations accepted.
☐ Educators: Lesson Plans about the Lewis & Clark expedition are found on links on the For Teachers page of the website.

On May 14, 1804, Captain Meriwether Lewis wrote, "The mouth of the River Dubois is to be considered the point of departure." Visit the Lewis and Clark Interpretive Center, a replica of the 1803-04 winter encampment, and the Lewis and Clark Monument at this facility. The space tells the story of how the Corps of Discovery assembled equipment, supplies and men at Camp River Dubois. In the Convergence Theater an original 15-minute, high definition film, "At Journey's Edge," is shown every 20 minutes. Highlighting the tour is the "Cutaway Keelboat," a 55-foot long replica of the keelboat Lewis had built in Ohio. The boat has been cut in half revealing how it was filled with "tools of every description." This is the room where kids can really explore! Be sure to ask the front desk for the scavenger/stamp hunt sheet. As you explore and log your provisions and usefulness, try to determine whether you would be able to pack and organize as well as these folks. Try it.

Finished packing? Now venture outside towards the reconstruction of the camp. The volunteers act as guides to the fort where visitors can view the sleeping quarters of the men and the main building that served as guardhouse, storehouse, and the Captain's quarters. Be sure to behave so you don't get 100 lashings. The Camp often had visitors, many who provided information about the west. Today you are invited to visit and share as many may have done before. We promise, this historic site sparks a kids' sense of adventure.

WOOD RIVER RENDEZVOUS

Hartford - *Camp Dubois Historic Site area (Route 143 and Route 3). www. greatriverroad.com/Cities/Wood/duBois.htm. Celebrate the fur trapping era that lasted from 1700 to 1840 at the historic Camp DuPois site. Come and commemorate the departure of the Lewis and Clark Expedition. This encampment of living history uses re-enactors portraying pre-1840 historical characters including French & Indian War soldiers, Colonial militia, fur trappers, and Native Americans. Historical crafts and skills demos along with children's activities. FREE, donations encouraged. (first weekend in May)*

ARRIVAL AT CAMP RIVER DUBOIS

Hartford - *Lewis & Clark State Historic Site. Witness the arrival of the Lewis and Clark expedition as reenactors arrive at the mouth of the River DuBois to establish* *their 1803-04 winter encampment. Join the members of the Corps in a military demonstration of the 1803 US Army Expedition and much more. FREE. (second weekend in December)*

HOMESTEAD HARVEST DAYS

Highland - *1464 Old Trenton Road. A farming history show with threshing, plowing and grinding, plus tours of the Latzer 13-room Victorian home and mini-Pet Milk Factory, children's tractor pull, entertainment and food. Admission. (second long weekend in September)*

TRAIL OF TEARS STATE FOREST

3240 State Forest Road (access from SR 127 or SR 3 from the west
Jonesboro 62952

    Phone: (618) 833-4910

    http://dnr.state.il.us/lands/landmgt/parks/r5/trltears.htm

    Note: Hiking trails, picnicking, horseback riding and camping (fee).

TRAIL OF TEARS STATE FOREST is a multiple-use site managed for timber, wildlife, ecosystem preservation, watershed protection and recreation. The forest lies within the southern section of the Ozark Hills, one of the most rugged landscapes in Illinois. The hills are composed of chert (a weathered limestone residue). Chert was mined (for making tools) at Iron Mountain, east of the Forest.

TRAIL OF TEARS: The disposed Cherokee along with Creek, Choctaw and other tribes were forced from their homes in the east and south and forced to migrate to Oklahoma in 1839. The trail of Tears as it came to be known entered Illinois at Golconda and then divided near Anna-Jonesboro before entering Missouri. The worst winter was at the encampment near Vienna in which almost 5000 people died. Many Southern Illinois families proudly trace ancestry to Cherokee people who left the trail during that time and became absorbed into the pioneer culture.

GIANT CITY STATE PARK

235 Giant City Road (off IL 13 east of Carbondale, head south on Giant City;
I-57 exit 45, SR 148 NW, follow signs) **Makanda** 62958

- ☐ Phone: (618) 457-4836 or (618) 457-4921 lodge
  http://dnr.state.il.us/lands/Landmgt/PARKS/R5/GC.HTM
- ☐ Hours: Visitor Center open 8:00am-4:00pm.
- ☐ Note: Boating, fishing and camping are also offered in the park.

From camping and horseback riding to fishing and rappelling, it's an outdoor lover's paradise. The park was named for the massive rock structures nature formed that resembles a primitive city. Visitors will love walking the many wilderness trails, especially hiking the Giant City Nature Trail, home of the "Giant City Streets" formed 12,000 years ago by huge bluffs of sandstone. The trail actually takes you through the "city" streets vs. just hiking overlooks. It's spectacular to stand against the tall rock "buildings". Trails range from 1/3 mile to 12 miles, so take your pick! Be sure to get an interpretive trail guide at the Visitors Center. The park features a 50-foot observation deck that provides panoramic views of large expanses of the area. The Visitor Center facility houses exhibits on the natural and cultural history of the park, as well as a gift shop, audio-visual room, and a discovery corner for children.

GIANT CITY STATE PARK RESORT

Makanda - *62958. (618) 457-4921 or* **www.giantcitylodge.com** *The multi-hued sandstone and the white oak timber Giant City Lodge (closed winters) has rustic beauty and holds many restored original furnishings. Three types of cabins offering forest views are available to accommodate overnight guests. Twelve historic cabins are one-room units; 18 prairie cabins are two-room units; and four bluff cabins, the largest and most scenic, can conveniently house a family of six. Each cabin has full baths, TV's, telephones and mini-fridge (no cooking appliances or cooking is allowed in the cabins). The Lodge also features an outdoor pool and a kiddie pool. The Bald Knob dining room serves breakfast, lunch and dinner daily and has a reputation for good food at a reasonable price. It is especially well known for its family-style, home-fried chicken (closed from mid-December thru January).*

LITTLE GRASSY FISH HATCHERY

1258 Hatchery Lane (seven miles south of Carbondale) **Makanda** 62958

    Phone: (618) 529-4100
    http://dnr.state.il.us/education/interprt/LITGRAS.HTM
    Hours: Daily 8:00am-3:30pm.
    Tours: Offered year-round during both production and non-production season.
    Walk-ins and Scheduled are welcome.

Little Grassy is known primarily for production of warm-water species such as channel catfish, largemouth bass, red-ear sunfish, and bluegill. However, cool-water species (walleye, muskellunge) may be produced depending upon water temperature and egg availability. Little Grassy currently produces 15 million fish annually. During the non-production season, visitors may view the state-of-the-art facility. Various mechanical operations and fish production techniques and procedures are explained with aid of photo storyboards. During production season, visitors may view broodfish in spawning cubicles, eggs incubating in artificial hatching jars, and various sizes of fish in indoor rearing tanks. Young catfish in outdoor raceways may be fed by visitors. Can you believe how much pampering goes into these fish? With this many fish "growing up" here, there are plenty to look at.

MILLS APPLE FARM

11477 Pocahontas Road **Marine**

www.millsapplefarm.com

Primarily a family run pick-your-own apple and peach orchard with chose and cut Christmas trees. On-farm bakery produces made-from-scratch pies, cookies and other products. Apple and Pumpkin educational tours. Kids play area. Farm animals. Wagon rides in season. Apples to pick from August through October. PYO Pumpkins in October. FREE to wander, pay to pick. www.millsapplefarm.com (daily, September & October)

- APPLE TOURS: Fun, interactive way to learn how apples grow, how to pick them, and how they make them into fresh apple cider. And of course, the taste of a tree-ripened apple can't be beat! Educational Tours are available Tuesday through Thursday, at 9:30am, 11:00am, and 12:30pm. (September & October)

LAKE MURPHYSBORO STATE PARK AND KINKAID LAKE STATE FISH AND WILDLIFE AREA

52 Cinder Hill Drive (about one mile west of Murphysboro off Route 149)
Murphysboro 62966

Phone: (618) 684-2867 or (618) 687-4914 (marina)
http://dnr.state.il.us/lands/Landmgt/PARKS/R5/MURPHYSB.HTM

Kinkaid Lake has hiking trails around the lake, camping facilities, and a 300-slip marina on the east end. The spillway is a beautiful natural rock waterfall, quite popular for sunning and swimming, and the pool formed by the runoff from the spillway has produced some record size bass and catfish. Lake Murphysboro State Park sits adjacent to the east end of Kinkaid Lake and offers hiking, fishing, and camping.

RAINBOW RANCH PETTING ZOO

9906 State Route 15 **Nashville** 62263

Phone: (618) 424-7979 **www.rainbowranchzoo.com**
Hours: Open Wednesday-Saturday 9:00am-5:00pm, Sunday Noon-5:00pm (April - October). By appointment, rest of year.
Admission: $5.00 per person, kids under 1 year free.

Wear old shoes to Rainbow Ranch Petting Farm near Nashville. On this farm you get to know donkeys, sheep, goats, cows, horses, fallow deer, pigs, chickens, ducks, geese, rabbits, llamas and even a camel by name. As you tramp through the paddocks, deer, sheep and even a yak come up to be petted.

PYRAMID STATE PARK

1562 Pyramid Park Rd. **Pinckneyville** 62274

Phone: (618) 357-2574
http://dnr.state.il.us/lands/Landmgt/PARKS/R5/PYRAMID.HTM

Pyramid State Park is the largest State Recreation Area in Illinois and gets its name from a coal mine that once existed here. There are 16.5 miles of foot and horse trails and this includes mountain bike riding. Since many of the lakes can be reached only by foot, Pyramid affords an opportunity for the angler to get away from crowds. The park offers picnic sites and campgrounds, as well.

POMONA NATURAL BRIDGE

(c/o Murphysboro Ranger District. Off IL 127, north of town) **Pomona** 62975

  Phone: (618) 529-4451 or (800) 526-1500
www.shawneeforest.com/Hiking/PomonaNaturalBridge.aspx

This stone arch or "natural bridge", was formed by the forces of erosion over thousands of years. This natural bridge and other rock outcrops in the area consist of sandstone, which is a fairly soft, erodible bedrock. Water erosion had a powerful effect here, as it gradually washed away softer, less resistant sandstone leaving a natural rock bridge, spanning 90 feet. Located 25 feet above a trickling stream, this bridge is one of a few natural stone bridges in the country (see "*Kids Love Kentucky*" or "*Kids Love Virginia*" for others). Short loop trails lead through a mature forest. As the trail descends to the creek bottom an overlook reveals a view of the natural bridge from above. There is a great photo spot at the base of the rock bridge where a semicircle of trees and rock outcroppings serve as a beautiful backdrop for this natural wonder. Picnic areas are available.

FORT DE CHARTRES'

1350 State Route 155, RR 2 (four miles west of town on SR 155)
Prairie Du Rocher 62277

  Phone: (618) 284-7230 **www.illinois.gov/ihpa/Experience/Sites/
Southwest/Pages/Fort-de-Chartres.aspx**
  Hours: Wednesday - Sunday 9:00am-5:00pm.
  Admission: FREE. Donations accepted.

This great stone fort, formerly one of the strongest forts in North America, was built in 1753 as the seat of government for the French colony in America. Fort de Chartres' limestone gateway, guardhouse, and some of the outer walls have been rebuilt atop original stone foundations. The chapel, priest's room, commander's office and ammunition storage room (complete with cannon balls and weaponry) have been restored. The storehouse is home to the Piethman Museum, which uses discovered artifacts to interpret life in Illinois during the colonial period. What your kids like best? Climbing around the fort walls.

FORT DE CHARTRES TRAPPERS AND TRADERS RENDEZVOUS

Prairie Du Rocher - *Hundreds of military and civilian reenactors set up camp and present authentic cooking, crafts, dancing, and other activities from the French Colonial period. (first weekend in June)*

GATEWAY ARCH

(St. Louis Riverfront) **St. Louis (MISSOURI)** 63102

- Phone: (877) 982-1410 **www.gatewayarch.com**
- Hours: Generally 8:00am-9:00pm. Shorter hours in winter season.
- Admission: $10.00 adult, $5.00 child (3-15) for tram to the top. Arch Entry only is $3.00 for adults. Museum of Westward Expansion is FREE. Visiting the Gateway Arch in the summer? That's peak season for visits to the nation's tallest monument and "Journey to the Top" tram tickets sell out fast. Guarantee your ride for the day and time you want by ordering tickets in advance via online or phone number above.
- Security Checks: At one or more points before entering an exhibit space, you must allow some extra time to pass thru a security checkpoint. Note: Be sure to purchase tickets to ride to the observation deck at the top of the arch when you arrive. They sell timed tickets. You can visit the museum while waiting for your tram time.

The imposing Gateway Arch, America's tallest monument, is a must see attraction. The Arch and Old Courthouse sit on riverfront land where the original Route 66 passed by - forging a trail to the American West. Take a ride to the top of the Arch - 630 feet high over the Mississippi - which was built as a monument to President Thomas Jefferson's dream of a continental United States. Journey to the Top is a two-part multi-media exhibit where riders board trams to the top. The south leg has *When Riverboats Ruled*, which offers a tour of St. Louis during the 1800s with sights and sounds of the era - including Mark Twain. The north leg has *Fitting the Final Piece*, which explains the history of the arch and gives you recreated echoed voices of construction workers creating the masterpiece. The ride feels like a somewhat slower version of a carnival ferris wheel. Although the "pods" you ride on are painted soothing robin egg blue, the "ride" is like a futuristic adventure in the dark (except for you lighted pod). You'll catch the frontiersmen's sense of adventure, for sure! (Note: visitors with claustrophobia or "fear of heights" may have trouble with this ride. If in doubt, ask an attendant to let you try a pod first). From the top of the monument, you'll get a 30-mile panoramic view of the river and St. Louis far below.

As you're waiting for your timed ticket tram tour to the top, why not meander around the base of the museum - the Museum of Westward Expansion. You'll step back in time to see buffalo, covered wagons, Native American teepees, Lewis & Clark expedition dioramas and many other artifacts from America's western beginnings in St. Louis. To keep it interesting for the youngins, look for these animatronic figures - Thomas Jefferson; William Clark; a buffalo soldier; and a 1846 Overlander woman preparing to head west. If you have more time, purchase a movie ticket to be submerged in high tech movies about westward expansion or the building of the arch.

Since this is possibly a once-in-a-lifetime family experience, be sure to bring your camera. We took pictures of everything - even the funky pods you ride to the top. At times, you'll get butterflies and feel so proud of America!

OLD CHAIN OF ROCKS BRIDGE

10950 Riverview Drive **St. Louis, MO** 63137

- www.nps.gov/nr/travel/route66/chain_of_rocks_bridge_illinois_missouri.html
- Hours: Daily 9:00am-dusk.
- Note: Follow the city's Riverfront Trail, a hiking and biking path, from the Old Chain of Rocks Bridge to the Gateway Arch.

The Old Chain of Rocks Bridge, at 5,353 feet long, is one of the world's longest bicycle and pedestrian bridges. The Bridge spans the Mississippi River and provides a vital link in the bi-state trail system, connecting to the St. Louis Riverfront Trail in Missouri and the MCT Confluence Trail in Illinois. The Bridge, once part of the beloved Route 66, has a rich history and is on the National Register of Historic Places. Located north of downtown, the bridge was Route 66's original crossing over the Mississippi River at St. Louis. The span, which is one of the longest pedestrian and biking bridges in the world, is open to visitors every day. From the bridge, you'll see stunning views of downtown St. Louis and the city's whimsical castle-like water intake towers from high over the Mississippi. Route 66 themed bump-out, full-span pedestrian lighting, Missouri-side restrooms, benches, bike racks and interpretive plaques. Parking available on either side.

EAGLE DAYS AT THE OLD CHAIN OF ROCKS BRIDGE

St. Louis, MO - *Old Chain Of Rocks Bridge. This FREE public program gives visitors the opportunity to view wintering bald eagles in a natural habitat. Educational eagle program repeated every 20 minutes; Viewing scopes on the Bridge permit close-ups of eagles Lewis & Clark re-enactors interact with the public and acquaint visitors with aspects of their 1804-06 expedition, the Corps of Discovery; View St. Louis area birds through hands-on exhibits by St. Louis Audubon volunteers; Get your photo taken in the replica of an eagle's nest. Bring your binoculars and dress to stay warm. Note: Programming is at both Bridge entrances and in the middle of the Bridge. It is about a 1/2-mile walk to the middle of the Bridge for assisted eagle viewing and programming in the warming tent.*

VANDALIA STATEHOUSE STATE HISTORIC SITE

315 West Gallatin Street **Vandalia** 62471

- Phone: (618) 283-1161
  www.illinois.gov/ihpa/Experience/Sites/Southwest/Pages/Vandalia-StateHouse.aspx
- Hours: Wednesday-Saturday 9:00am-4:00pm, extended summers-open Tuesdays. It is closed on major holidays.

Vandalia, the second capitol of Illinois, is steeped in history. The 1836 Statehouse Historic Site is the oldest Illinois State Capitol building. The Federal-style white building is impressive with its high ceilings, tall windows and vintage furnishings. At the top of the broad, curving staircase are the Senate and House of Representatives chambers, where Abraham Lincoln began his political career for the grand sum of $4.00 a day. The Courtroom is an imposing room - full of rich woods that make it very dark and serious. Visitors walk on the same floorboards where the future President made his early arguments against slavery.

HOLIDAY OPEN HOUSE

Vandalia - *Vandalia Statehouse State Historic Site. Candlelight tour of Illinois' oldest existing capitol building and period music. FREE. (second Saturday in December)*

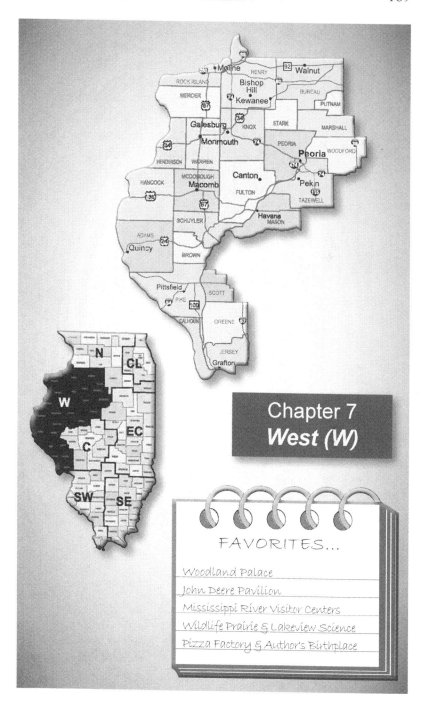

Chapter 7
West (W)

FAVORITES...

Woodland Palace

John Deere Pavilion

Mississippi River Visitor Centers

Wildlife Prairie & Lakeview Science

Pizza Factory & Author's Birthplace

Bishop Hill
- Bishop Hill State Historic Site

Brimfield
- Jubilee College Historic Site

Clayton
- Siloam Springs State Park

Coal Valley
- Niabi Zoo

Colchester
- Argyle Lake State Park

Forest City
- Sand Ridge State Forest

Fulton Countywide
- Spoon River Valley Fall Festival

Galesburg
- Carl Sandburg Birthplace
- Discovery Depot Museum
- Railroad Days
- Heritage Days

Grafton
- Pere Marquette State Park And Visitors Center
- Raging Rivers Waterpark
- Great Rivers Towboat Festival
- Gathering Of The Waters Rendezvous

Jacksonville
- General Grierson Days Civil War Reenactment
- Steam Engine Show & Fall Festival

Kampsville
- Center For American Archeology Museum
- Old Settlers Days

Keithsburg
- Big River State Forest

Kewanee
- Johnson-Sauk Trail State Park
- Woodland Palace
- Hog Days
- Dickson Mounds Museum

Moline
- Celebration Belle Paddlewheel Boat Cruises
- Channel Cat Water Taxi
- John Deere Pavilion & Collectors Center
- Lagomarcino's
- Radisson On John Deere Commons
- Riverway Parks And Trails
- Christmas At Historic Deere-Wiman House And Butterworth Center

Moline (East)
- Greek Cultural Festival

Moline (Rock Island)
- Backwater Gamblers Water Ski Shows
- Black Hawk State Historic Site
- Circa 21 Dinner Playhouse
- Quad City Botanical Garden
- Rock Island Arsenal/ Mississippi River Visitor Center
- Bald Eagle Days
- World's Largest Kart Race
- Season Of Light – Star Of Bethlehem

Monmouth
- Wyatt Earp Birthplace

Nauvoo
- Nauvoo State Park

Oquawka
- Delabar State Park

Peoria
- Peoria History Trolley

- Spirit Of Peoria Riverboat
- Glen Oak Park, Zoo & Garden
- Wheels O' Time Museum
- Lakeview Museum Of Arts And Sciences
- Wildlife Prairie State Park
- Wildlife Prairie State Park Lodging
- Erin Feis

Peoria (East Peoria)

- Splashdown Waterpark
- Stoney Creek Inn

Peoria (Morton)

- Morton Pumpkin Festival

Peoria Heights

- Tower Park

Peoria, East

- Festival Of Lights

Princeton

- Historic Owen Lovejoy Homestead And Colton Schoolhouse

Quad Cities

- Great River Tub Fest

Quincy

- Avenue Of Lights

Sheffield

- Hennepin Canal State Trail

Speer

- Tanners Orchard

Taylor Ridge (Andalusia)

- Ski Snowstar

Walnut

- Avanti Foods

Wyoming

- Rock Island Trail State Park

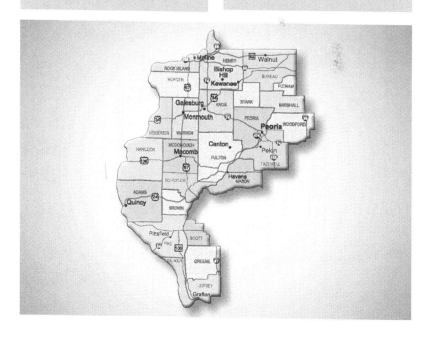

Learning the past and future of farming - John Deere Pavillion

Sites and attractions are listed in order by City, Zip Code, and Name. Symbols indicated represent: 🍽 Restaurants   🛏 Lodging

BISHOP HILL STATE HISTORIC SITE

PO Box 104 (17 miles east of I-74, SR 17/US 34 east, follow signs)
Bishop Hill 61419

☐ Phone: (309) 927-3345 **www.bishophill.com**
☐ Hours: Wednesday-Sunday 9:00am-5:00pm. Closes at 4:00pm winters.
    Closed most major government holidays.
☐ Admission: FREE. Donations accepted.
☐ Note: Because Eric Janson would be considered somewhat of a cult leader
    in contemporary times, it is best to focus on the villagers and their craft and
    food, rather than the focus be on Janson, his leadership, and death.

It has been called "the most valuable Swedish monument outside Scandinavia...". In 1846, a Swedish religious leader named Eric Janson brought his followers to a new land where they could practice religious freedom in a settlement they named Bishop Hill. Many of the original colony buildings remain today and descendants of the original colonists have restored the area. Take a tour of historic buildings (Church, Hotel - modern by mid-1800 standards), eat at their wonderful Swedish eateries, do some shopping, and see full-time demonstrators in the shops. A new hobby might be spawned by watching the craftspeople so closely. Our kids got easy beginner weaving kits (and started weaving as soon as we got back in the van!) The Heritage Museum has some exhibits, a video and internationally recognized folk art paintings of Olof Krans. The Henry County Museum has a scavenger hunt plus a working windmill outside. As you wander the village, be sure to stop by the Colony Store for treats and Swedish sodas (plus, a lot of cute gifts). We really liked P.L. Johnson (try Swedish meatballs, fresh breads, soups, salad dressings or pies) for lunch. Everything Miss Ann and company prepared was fresh and so yummy!

JORDBRUKSDAGARNA (AGRICULTURE DAYS)

Bishop Hill - *Bishop Hill State Historic Site, Celebrate with 19th-century Swedish harvest activities and demonstrations, hands-on activities, children's games, farm produce and Colony stew and live music. (last weekend in September)*

JULMARKNAD

Bishop Hill - *Bishop Hill, Christmas market with special music, Swedish folk characters, Swedish food, handmade wares, Make and Take Holiday workshops, Cookie Walk and Chocolate Walk. (Thanksgiving weekend and first weekend in December)*

LUCIA NIGHTS

Bishop Hill - *Bishop Hill will be illuminated by candlelight. "Lucias" serve coffee and sweets in museums and shops. Special music and singing at various locations. FREE. (second weekend in December)*

JUBILEE COLLEGE STATE HISTORIC SITE PARK

13921 West Hwy 150 (I-74 exit 82 north to Kickapoo. Turn west on US 150)
Brimfield 61517

☐ Phone: (309) 446-3758
http://dnr.state.il.us/lands/landmgt/parks/r1/jubilee.htm
☐ Admission: Fee for some activities.

JUBILEE COLLEGE STATE PARK is a facility situated in the Illinoisan drift-plan, complete with rolling hills and a meandering Jubilee Creek. Along the creek, you may see glimpses of mink, muskrat and beaver or one of over 160 species of birds. The park has campgrounds, horseback riding and bike trails (25 miles long). In winter, the park also offers cross-country skiing and snowmobiling.

JUBILEE COLLEGE HISTORIC SITE was founded as a seminary in 1840 by the first Episcopal Bishop of Illinois. Jubilee College was the first American boarding college established in Illinois.

SILOAM SPRINGS STATE PARK

938 East 3003rd Lane (nine miles north of Route 104, off Route 24)
Clayton 62324

☐ Phone: (217) 894-6205
http://dnr.state.il.us/lands/Landmgt/PARKS/R4/SILOAMSP.HTM

Its forested terrain, dotted with wildflowers and accented with a sparkling lake, make this park an ideal setting for outdoor visits, whether your interest is hunting, fishing, camping, boating, picnicking, hiking or bird watching.

NIABI ZOO

13010 Niabi Zoo Road (off US 6) **Coal Valley 61240**

☐ Phone: (309) 799-5107 **www.niabizoo.com**
☐ Hours: Generally 9:30am-5:00pm (spring & summer). Weekends only until 4:30pm (winter). Weekday reduced hours (fall). Open April - mid-December.
☐ Admission: $6.25-$8.25 per person (age 3+).
☐ Note: Playgrounds, picnic areas and free stroller and wheelchair rentals.

Niabi Zoo is home to more than 900 animals on 40 acres. Large cats, monkeys, Asian elephants, birds, a petting zoo, Koi pond, and reptiles are some of the favorites. Ride the Express replica train and Endangered Species Carrousel.

The Discovery Center features interactive habitats to explore computer stations, an aquarium and live creatures.

ARGYLE LAKE STATE PARK

640 Argyle Park Road (Interstate 74 South to Route 34. Take Route 34 West to Route 67. Take Route 67 South to Route 136. Take Route 136 West)
Colchester 62326

Phone: (309) 776-3422
http://dnr.state.il.us/lands/Landmgt/PARKS/R1/ARGYLE.HTM

Located along an old stagecoach route between Galena and Beardstown, Argyle is home to rough terrain, beaver dams and more than 200 bird species. The heavily wooded park has a 93-acre lake for boating and fishing, 5 miles of rugged foot trails through luxuriant virgin forests, and full-service campgrounds. There are 12 trails and most are classified as difficult to very difficult, but Blackberry and Pitch Pine trails are rated as moderate. Be sure to look for the beaver dams along Shore Trail. They host an antique gas engine show each Labor Day weekend. You'll see demonstrations of wheat threshing, hay baling, sawmilling, sorghum making and blacksmithing. You can also watch crafts persons make quilts, whittle and make rugs. In addition, hundreds of antique tractors, cars and gas engines are on display.

SAND RIDGE STATE FOREST

25799 East County Road 2300 N (Follow IL Rt 136 to Mason County Road 2800E) **Forest City** 61532

Phone: (309) 597-2212 or (309) 968-7531 (Hatchery)
http://dnr.state.il.us/lands/Landmgt/PARKS/R4/sand.htm

For those who think central Illinois is one big corn field, Sand Ridge State Forest will come as a very pleasant surprise. The forest is an island in a sea of agriculture. Just minutes southwest of Peoria, this 7,200-acre, the largest of Illinois' State Forests, boasts sweeping expanses of native oak-hickory, extensive plantations of pine, sprawling open fields, grasslands, and completely unique sand prairies. Forty-four miles of marked trails, ranging from 1.6 to 17 miles each, and 120 miles of fire lanes offer unequaled opportunities to the hiker, back packer, horseback rider or snowmobiler. While visiting the park, be sure to stop by the contemporary Jake Wolf Memorial Fish Hatchery, which has an excellent visitor center explaining how to manage a fishery.

SPOON RIVER VALLEY FALL FESTIVAL

Fulton Countywide - *Spoon River has been a lifeline of water for eons, with Indians harvesting fish and mussels from the waters. The mussel shells were used for utensils/ spoons, hence came the name: Amaquonsippi, or Spoon River. Along the scenic drive, apple pies are freshly make and applebutter is cooked in black kettles over open fires at Riverside Park, London Mills. Butterfly porkchops and steaks are favorites at Mt. Pisgah Park, Smithfield, Cuba, and Avon. Farmington is known for its baked potatoes "ala everything," apple dumplings, and elephant ears. Red Brick School, Smithfield is known for its chicken and noodle dinners. Bernadotte, Fairview, and Lewistown have funnel cakes. Duncan Mills is known for its baked goods and beef and noodles. Along with the food, sounds of music, dancing, clogging, playgrounds, and tours of historic homes and museums. www.spoonriverdrive.org (first two full weekends in October)*

CARL SANDBURG BIRTHPLACE

313 East Third Street (E. Main St., right on Seminary St., follow signs)
Galesburg 61401

- Phone: (309) 342-2361 **www.sandburg.org**
- Hours: Thursday-Sunday 9:00am-5:00pm (May-October); Saturday only, 10:00am-4:00pm (October-April) and special events.
- Admission: Donations accepted.

In this small frame cottage, Pulitzer Prize-winning poet and Lincoln biographer, Carl Sandburg, was born in 1878. Carl Sandburg worked from the time he was a young boy. He quit school following his graduation from eighth grade in 1891 and spent a decade working a variety of jobs. He delivered milk, harvested ice, laid bricks, and shined shoes in Galesburg's Union Hotel before traveling as a hobo in 1897. The home reflects the living conditions of a typical late-19th century working-class family and is furnished with many Sandburg family belongings. Located behind the home is Remembrance Rock, where Sandburg's ashes have been placed. A Visitor's Center is located next to the house which offers videos and museum exhibits. Great to start here to orient. What word did he detest most?..." "Exclusive" - to know him is to understand why. Children enjoy hearing Sandburg's folk tales, songs and poems composed in between major works about Lincoln. See one of his guitars and the typewriter he used to write part of the Lincoln volumes. Inspiring…

DID YOU KNOW? - If you come by car or have an FM radio with you, tune to 88.7 and listen to a brief presentation about Carl Sandburg and the Historic Site.

DISCOVERY DEPOT CHILDREN'S MUSEUM

128 South Chambers Street **Galesburg** 61401

Phone: (309) 344-8876 **www.discoverydepot.org**
Hours: Tuesday-Saturday 10:00am-5:00pm, Sunday Noon-5:00pm.
Admission: $6.00 per person.

Explore a kid-sized 2-story home, police car, and ambulance, and climb across a fire truck ladder in Safety City. Maybe play in a real caboose or a real combine. Shop at the Grocery and then prepare a meal at the Diner or sort, stamp and deliver mail at the Depot Post Office. Build with over 15,000 Legos in Legoland or visit the dentist at the Land of Ah-h-hs (which one sounds better?) Climb into and slide out of the Depot Tree House and identify leaf shapes or play with water or puppets. All interactive exhibits promote families to stimulate their curiosity.

RAILROAD DAYS

Galesburg - *Railroad Museum, 423 Mulberry Street. Street fair, food, carnival, railroad exhibits, city and rail yard tours, concerts, mud volleyball, car show and much more. See 1900s memorabilia hosed in a former Pullman parlor car, climb up into a caboose or postal car. Model Train show at nearby Sandburg College. **www. galesburgrailroaddays.org** (last weekend in June)*

HERITAGE DAYS

Galesburg - *Lake Storey Park. Pre-1840s rendezvous and Civil War reenactment, children's activities, period demonstrations, crafts, storyteller, petting zoo, music and food. **www.galesburgheritagedays.com** (third weekend in August)*

PERE MARQUETTE STATE PARK AND VISITORS CENTER

Illinois Route 100 (five miles west of town) **Grafton 62037**

- Phone: (618) 786-3323 or (618) 786-2331 (lodge)
  http://dnr.state.il.us/lands/Landmgt/PARKS/R4/Peremarq.htm
- Tours: The Sam Vadalabene Bike Trail runs from Pere Marquette State Park to the City of Alton, approximately 20 miles. The entire trail is paved, and a map is available showing the location of historic sites, restaurants, and other local attractions.
- Note: The Lodge consists of both new facilities as well as those constructed by the CCC. Native stone and rustic timbers of the original Lodge blend with the new to provide first class accommodations in an historical setting. The mammoth stone fireplace in the lobby soars to a roof height of 50 feet, and is said to weigh 700 tons. There are 50 spacious guest rooms and 22 stone guest cabin rooms. Among the facilities available are a restaurant, gift shop, indoor swimming pool, whirlpool, saunas, game room and tennis court.

Pere Marquette State Park is a nature lover's paradise. In addition to enjoying the spectacular views of the Illinois River and its backwaters from several points atop the bluffs, visitors can take advantage of a variety of year-round recreational opportunities, including horseback riding, camping, hiking, fishing, hunting and boating.

Pere Marquette's Visitor Center has a 3-D map of the park and wealth of other displays and exhibits concerning the Illinois River, wildlife habitat, local history and geology. A favorite there is the giant, climb in, eagle's nest.

RAGING RIVERS WATERPARK

100 Palisades Parkway (along Great River Road) **Grafton 62037**

- Phone: (618) 786-2345 **www.ragingrivers.com**
- Hours: Daily 10:30am-6:00pm (Memorial Day weekend thru Labor Day weekend). Open one hour later mid-summer.
- Admission: $20.95-$24.95 (age 3+). Save $5.00 after 3:00pm. Parking $5.00. Tubes Free except for Wave Pool which is $5.00-$7.00 per tube.
- Note: Locker rooms, Showers, concessions. No coolers.

Raging Rivers WaterPark is cool when it's hot! From the zoomin' Cascade Body Flumes, to the tube (or tubeless) wave pool, to a lazy Endless River, there's something for everyone. SwirlPool: It's a two-bowl attraction that's really three rides in one. Slide quickly down the tunnel flume, spin swiftly in the giant vortex, then drop into a deep pool of water. If you think that was fun in the daylight, try going down the enclosed Swirlpool in the dark for a double dare! The milder Runaway Rafts Ride: Take this 600-foot long journey down the hillside and experience the real-life adventures of swift water and wild rapids. Or, ride the tubed Shark Slide: This ride floats you right down 45 feet of flume, into a catch pool. Fountain Mountain and TreeHouse Harbor are for the younger set.

GREAT RIVERS TOWBOAT FESTIVAL

Grafton - *500 Front Street. Any visitor to the Grafton area will almost certainly see the giant towboats that travel up and down America's Great Rivers. Conditions permitting, there will be a tow boat docked on the riverfront that will be available for guided tours. Music and storytelling, food, exhibits, and deckhand and tow-rope throwing contests. Demonstrations of radio-controlled riverboat replicas. Small admission.***www.greatriverroad.com/cities/grafton/towfest.htm***(last weekend in July)*

GATHERING OF THE WATERS RENDEZVOUS

Grafton - *A Historical Re-enactment of the 1700-1840's Frontier Era.* ***www.greatriverroad.com/RV/waters.htm***. *Celebrates the French Fur Trading era which began after Louis Joliet and Jacques Marquette journeyed through the area in 1673 and ended around the time when Grafton was established in 1838. Teepees, tents, campfires, and costumed living history re-enactors adopt personas and carry on the day-to-day lifestyle as it would have been done 200 years ago. Hawk & Knife Throw, Primitive Bow Shoot, Canoe trip, Artisans/Traders, Authentic foods and music, and Children's Activities are also offered. FREE. (second or third weekend in October)*

GENERAL GRIERSON DAYS CIVIL WAR REENACTMENT

Jacksonville - *Community Park. The Midwest's largest Civil War reenactment gets better each year in the hometown of General Benjamin Grierson, a famous Civil War leader. Authentic battle reenactments, period vendors, lots of food and fun. FREE.* ***www.griersonsociety.com*** *(third weekend in June)*

STEAM ENGINE SHOW & FALL FESTIVAL

Jacksonville - *Prairieland Heritage Museum, 105 W Michigan Ave. Featuring antique steam engines and tractors, threshing demonstrations, hay bailing, a horse plow pull – all in the village with a vet's office, general store and blacksmith. Learn to drive a tractor and then have some grub for lunch. https://prairielandheritage. wordpress.com/about/ (last weekend in September)*

CENTER FOR AMERICAN ARCHEOLOGY MUSEUM

(IL 100, at Marquette and Broadway Streets) Kampsville 62053

- Phone: (618) 653-4316 www.caa-archeology.org
- Hours: Tuesday-Friday 10:00am-5:00pm, Saturday 10:00am-4:00pm (mid-April thru early November).
- Admission: FREE, donations accepted.
- Tours: Guided tours of facility, conducted by the CAA's staff of professional archeologists, are available by appointment and are available only to groups of 10 people or larger. A fee is charged for guided tours.

With more than 10,000 years of human occupation and thousands of recorded archeological sites in a 4,000 square mile area, the region surrounding the confluence of the Mississippi River and the Illinois River has often been referred to as the "Nile of North America". Ancient towns like Koster and South Koster opened the door for the average person to visit an archeological site, learn about the past, and participate in the ongoing research. With at least 26 separate living horizons defined, major villages were present at Koster ca. 3300, 5000, and 6600 BC. Burials and trade routes have been uncovered. The visitors center contains artifacts, exhibits and displays that explain the history of the lower Illinois River Valley and how archeologists learn about the past. The Gift Shop has many items of interest to children.

DID YOU KNOW? - Family Dig-It Weekends and Archeology Days are held throughout the summer.

OLD SETTLERS DAYS

Kampsville - *Riverside Park. www.greatriverroad.com/RV/kSettle.htm. Held on the banks of the Illinois River this event depicts the life and times of the early Calhoun settlers. Activities include: Mountain Man, Period demonstrations, fiddle contest, artisans/traders, Riverside encampment, food, children's activities, live entertainment* *and carriage rides. FREE. (second weekend in October)*

BIG RIVER STATE FOREST

Rural Route 1, Keithsburg Road (off Hwy 17 or Hwy 164, look for signs)
Keithsburg 61442

Phone: (309) 374-2496
http://dnr.state.il.us/lands/Landmgt/PARKS/R1/BIGRIVER.HTM

Big River State Forest is a remnant of a vast prairie woodland border area that once covered much of Illinois. Among its vegetation are two endangered plants - penstemon, commonly known as bearded tongue, and Patterson's bindweed, which N.H. Patterson documented in the forest in 1873 for the first time anywhere. Camp along the Mississippi waterfront or on the upper-level grounds. Launch your boat, walk on the sandy beach, cross-country ski or go snowmobiling on miles of trails. You can also hike the Lincoln Trail or the Pioneer Trail.

JOHNSON-SAUK TRAIL STATE PARK

27500 North 1200 Avenue, 28616 Sauk Trail Road (off IL 78, 6 miles south of I-80 and 5 miles north of town) **Kewanee** 61443

Phone: (309) 853-5589 or (309) 852-4262 (barn tour)
http://dnr.state.il.us/lands/Landmgt/PARKS/R1/JOHNSON.HTM

One of the largest round barns in the country can be seen here. Situated on a glacial moraine, the park is along a trail Sauk Indians used in their treks between Lake Michigan and the confluence of the Mississippi and Rock rivers. The park's centerpiece is a 58-acre lake that offers both fishing and boating, as well as nearly two and a half miles of shoreline to explore. Johnson-Sauk Trail has 10 to 15 miles of trails, ranging from ¼ mile to 1½ miles in length, from easy to moderate and taking hikers along the lake or through land ranging from rolling prairie to pine plantations and bottomland hardwood forests. The grounds are ideal for fishing, winter sports, and camping.

RYAN'S HISTORIC ROUND BARN: Take a guided tour of the round barn and visit the farm museum on the first floor. Tours are held May-October only.

WOODLAND PALACE

Francis Park, 401 E Third Street (Route 34, 3 miles east of town)
Kewanee 61443

- Phone: (309) 852-0511 **http://cityofkewanee.com/francis.php**
- Hours: Daily 1:00-5:00pm; (mid-April - mid-October).
- Admission: $1.00-$2.00.
- Tours: They'll give guided tours, last about 45 min.
- Note: The park also sports camping sites, shelter houses, picnic areas, playgrounds and a baseball diamond.

The unique home of Frederick Francis was built in 1890 out of brick, stone and native wood. The house features disappearing doors and windows (can you find them - even the hidden drawers?), an air cooling system (using tunnels!), radiant heat deflectors in the fireplace chimney and running water, all without the benefit of electricity. Other inventions were interesting including a rear view mirror for bicycles and multi-functional furniture. This place is so unusual and a little creepy - as you can guess, Fred was a bit eccentric. Don't ask too many questions about his odd ways or his death to keep it from being scary. If you're in the area, it's a quirky must-see.

HOG DAYS

Kewanee - *Downtown. Participate in the world's largest pork chop barbeque and the Hog Day Stampede, parade, carnival and market.* **http://kewaneehogdays.com/** *(long Labor Day weekend)*

DICKSON MOUNDS MUSEUM

10956 N. Dickson Mounds Road (between Lewistown and Havana, off
IL 97 and 78) **Lewistown** 61542

- Phone: (309) 547-3721 **www.museum.state.il.us/ismsites/dickson**
- Hours: Daily 8:30am-5:00pm. Closed major winter holidays and Easter.
- Admission: FREE
- Note: The front desk can give you maps to locate and see nearby Rockwell Mound (one of the largest burial mounds in the midwest).

Explore the world of the American Indian in a journey through 12,000 years of time in the Illinois River Valley - from the wild to the changes after the arrival of Europeans. Legacy, a large-screen video production, captures the past in a panoramic view of the valley. From the ice-age hunters to the tribal groups that left Illinois in the 19th century, Reflections of Three Worlds reveals the world of Mississippian people whose 800-year old sites surround the museum today. The end of the exhibit leads to a multimedia event of sights, sounds, symbols, music and voices of three worlds of Mississippian belief. Kids can apply what they've learned in the Discovery Center - a learning place with hands-on activities for visitors of all ages; discovery drawers, books, tapes, videos and a unique play scape area.

CELEBRATION BELLE PADDLEWHEEL BOAT CRUISES

2501 River Drive **Moline** 61265

    Phone: (309) 764-1952 or (800) 297-0034 **www.celebrationbelle.com**
    Admission: Sightseeing $10.00-$15.00. Double the rate for lunch cruises. The child's rate is for 3-10 year olds.
    Tours: Running mostly Thursday-Saturdays, lunch, afternoon and dinner tours. 100 mile all day cruise runs Tuesdays and Wednesdays.

Explore the majestic Mississippi River aboard a riverboat. Experience the power and mystique of the river that captivated the likes of Tom Sawyer and Huck Finn as it sweeps around the riverbend and flows east to west through the Quad cities for the only time in its great length. Cruise or dine aboard the huge 850 person capacity boat - the largest non-gaming luxury excursion vessel on the upper Mississippi River. Guests aboard can go topside and sit with the Captain of the Belle as he maneuvers the paddlewheel along the mighty river. Or, find a comfortable lounge chair and relax while a captain tells you about the history of the river, the Rock Island Arsenal, Lock & Dam 15, and other historic sites along the shore.

CHANNEL CAT WATER TAXI

2501 River Drive (Celebration Belle dock, riverfront) **Moline** 61265

    Phone: (309) 788-3360 **www.gogreenmetro.com**
    Hours: Weekdays 11:00am-8:00pm, Weekends 9:00am-8:00pm (Memorial Day-Labor Day). Weekends only in September and on East Moline Quarter route.
    Admission: $6.00 adult, $3.00 child (2-10). Tickets are for all-day unlimited use on day of purchase. Buy your tickets on board or at Centre Station Gifts.

Take a trip on the Water Taxi open-air boat stopping at different boat landings on both the Iowa and Illinois banks of the Mississippi River. The Channel Cat returns every hour to take passengers back and forth across the river. Bicyclists use the Cat to go to bike trails on both sides of the river. You even go through an old lock and see the unusual system they used to pour concrete.

JOHN DEERE PAVILION & COLLECTORS CENTER

1400 River Drive (riverfront @ John Deere Commons) **Moline** 61265

- Phone: (309) 765-1000 **www.johndeerepavilion.com**
- Hours: Monday-Friday 9:00am-5:00pm, Saturday 10:00am-5:00pm, Sunday Noon-4:00pm. Closed on Easter, Thanksgiving, Christmas and New Years.
- Admission: FREE
- Note: THE GREAT RIVER TRAIL bike path follows the river along the Commons. It makes a great place to start or end your bike ride.

Celebrate the American heartland from the first horse-drawn plow to the latest modern-day combines and tractors. In the early 1900s, Moline was the undisputed agricultural center of the Midwest (taking advantage of the water power and transportation offered by the Mississippi River). The whole family can enjoy interactive, hands-on computer displays that include virtual tours of the company's combine factory and a fun and educational journey through the generations of a family farm. Watch the very inspiring video that is an Anthem to farming families. Games and a Kids Corner have fun trivia games. Children and adults can climb on or sit in the driver's seat of Deere's agricultural and construction equipment. This is the best part - you'll feel like a giant! Some cabs are equipped with CD players and AC - why? (think about it as the farmer's office). Other exhibits show the challenges of farming in the future. Can you figure out how to feed the nations better? This is a really fun center for the whole family.

HOLIDAY POPS CONCERT

Moline - *The Mark on the Deere Commons. The concert features the Quad City Symphony Orchestra; the Quad City Arts Visiting Artist performer; skaters from the Figure Skating Club; The Sanctuary Choir and the Holiday Pops Children's Chorus. Come early and enjoy the "Lighting of the Commons". Take a horse-drawn wagon ride; meet Santa; listen to carolers; warm up with cider and cookies; and see the lights and fireworks brighten the sky. Admission for concert. (Saturday before Christmas)*

LAGOMARCINO'S

Moline - *1422 Fifth Avenue, downtown, just blocks from the John Deere Pavilion. 61265. (309) 764-1814 or www.lagomarcinos.com. In 1908, Angelo Lagomarcino, an immigrant from Northern Italy, founded this Confectionary and Ice Cream Parlor. Homemade candy remains a big part of the business. At Easter and Christmas, Lagomarino's continues the old European art of casting chocolate eggs or ornaments filled with individually wrapped chocolates or children's candies. Now also serving lunch, try ham salad or a tuna melt with a signature soda - a Green River (tastes like liquid lime Jell-O) or a fruity Lago. Top it off with a famous Hot Fudge Sundae. On your way out, purchase a box of some unique chocolate bark - peppermint, lemon, pretzel or almond.*

RADISSON ON JOHN DEERE COMMONS

Moline - *1415 River Drive. 61265. (309) 764-1000 or www.radisson.com/molineil. The scenic river front property, located right next door to the John Deere commons is within a walk or short drive of most attractions. Relax in this spotless, friendly hotel along the banks of the mighty Mississippi River with rooms featuring wi-fi, Sleep Number beds (dial your own comfort), and spacious. Try the indoor pool and jacuzzi after you eat a casual, fun-food meal or snack at the attached T.G.I. Fridays. Complimentary continental breakfast is included w/guest room. Most rooms around $109/night.*

RIVERWAY PARKS AND TRAILS
Start at CVB Welcome Centers Moline 61265

Phone: (800) 747-7800 **www.riveraction.org**
Admission: You can rent bikes by the hour or day.

Riverway - the Quad Cities' scenic stretch of the Mississippi River with 65 miles of riverside parks, trails and overlooks between the river bluffs. Enjoy America's most famous river by walking or biking along its riverfront trails. Even follow old train bridges over to small islands or along the river. Bike, roller blade, walk, or run with maps available online or at the Welcome Centers.

YA MAKA MY WEEKEND

Moline - *Take a trip to the Caribbean islands at this all ages event – Caribbean fare, reggae music, Jamaican food, children's village, pirate costume contest and a sand volleyball tournament. (third weekend in August)*

ERIN FEIS IRISH FAMILY FESTIVAL

Moline - *Great River Plaza. www.stpatqc.com. St. Patrick's Day in September? It features food, drink, memorabilia, culture displays, events for children and an array of continuous Irish entertainment on two stages. (second Sunday in September)*

CHRISTMAS AT HISTORIC DEERE-WIMAN HOUSE AND BUTTERWORTH CENTER

Moline - *www.butterworthcenter.com. John Deere legacy homes feature Christmas decorations typical of the Victorian era. The dining room is set for a formal Victorian Christmas dinner. Mrs. Butterworth was the granddaughter of John Deere. Dried flowers from the garden add a special touch to the house's many evergreen wreaths, garlands and trees. FREE, donations accepted. (first Sunday in December)*

BACKWATER GAMBLERS WATER SKI SHOWS

5000 44th Street (I-74, take the John Deere Road West Exit. Ben Williamson Park on the Rock River) Travel approximately 2 miles. Turn left at 44th Street) **Moline (Rock Island)** 61201

- Phone: (309) 788-7312 **www.backwatergamblers.com**
- Shows: Two shows each week at 6:30pm on Sunday and Wednesday (Memorial Day-Labor Day)
- Admission: FREE. Bleacher Seating with Concessions. Donations suggested.
- Note: Before or after the show, stop by Happy Joe's Pizza (www.happyjoes. com) for a bite to eat, (try veggie pizza with sauerkraut - it's really good), followed by yummy, thick Special Shakes (forget about using a straw) at Whitey's Ice Cream. Both are just minutes away on 16th Street.

The Backwater Gamblers Water Ski Show Club was founded as a non profit organization: To provide free, quality water ski entertainment to the Quad City area; and, to become one of the top rated ski clubs in show competition. The free, one hour, fun-filled family show is a themed performance combining skits, music, dance, and water-skiing. Dare-devil maneuvers occur with flips and spins over the jump ramp; boat speeds up to 40 miles per hour pull skiers on their bare feet; and costumed girls slalom ski in a ballet line and gracefully turn and twist. The highlight: 18+ skiers pull together to build a huge pyramid formation in the air while continuing to water-ski.

BLACK HAWK STATE HISTORIC SITE

1510 46th Avenue, SR 5 (I-280, take the Milan Exit (US 67)
Moline (Rock Island) 61201

Phone: (309) 788-0177 **www.blackhawkpark.org**
Hours: Black Hawk State Historic Site is open year-round from sunrise to 10:00pm. The Hauberg Museum is open Wednesday-Sunday 9:00am-5:00pm except for major holidays. Closes at 4:00pm winters.
Admission: FREE. Donations accepted.
Note: The area is a nature preserve with picnic sites and hiking trails.

This site is a wooded, steeply rolling 208-acre tract that borders the Rock River. Prehistoric Indians and 19th century settlers made their homes in the area. It was even once an amusement park. It is most closely identified with the Sauk nation and the warrior whose name it bears - Black Hawk. Visit one of the largest Native-American centers in North America. The Hauburg Indian Museum interprets the Indian cultures with full-size replicas of Sauk winter and summer houses, dioramas with life-size figures depict activities of the Sauk and Mesquakie people typical of the period 1750-1830. There's also many artifacts, including authentic trade goods, jewelry, and domestic items.

CIRCA 21 DINNER PLAYHOUSE

1828 Third Avenue **Moline (Rock Island)** 61201

Phone: (309) 786-7733 **www.circa21.com**
Shows: Wednesday Matinee @ Noon; Wednesday-Saturday Evenings @ 6:00pm; Sunday Evenings @ 4:00pm.
Admission: $50.00 adult, $30.00 student. Prices include a professional production, a six entree buffet and tax. For the matinee performances there is a plated lunch served at your table with your choice of three entree's. No cancellations or refunds.

Experience the excitement of live theater with such shows as *Fiddler on the Roof*, *Footloose* or *Winnie the Pooh*, all directed, designed and performed by artists from New York and other top theatrical centers. Every seat is a box seat. Not only does it offer an intimate and unobstructed view of the stage, but it also surrounds you with the beauty of a refurbished 1921 décor.

Before the performance, you'll enjoy a dinner buffet of snappy salads, sizzling beef, ham or seafood served by Roaring Twenties era wait staff. Friendly Bootleggers tend to your every need - even as they perform the rollicking pre-show musical review.

QUAD CITY BOTANICAL GARDEN

2525 4th Avenue (I-74 Moline River Drive, 7th Ave exit - head west. In Rock Island, cross the tracks and take the first right on 5th. It becomes 4th Ave.)

Moline (Rock Island) 61201

☐ Phone: (309) 794-0991 **www.qcgardens.com**
☐ Hours: Monday-Saturday 10:00am-5:00pm, Sunday 11am-5:00pm. Reduced winter hours. Closed major winter holidays.
☐ Admission. $2.00 $6.00 (age 7+).

Impressive with its 70-feet tall skylight peak, the Botanical Center's Sun Garden conservatory offers an indoor tropical paradise. Visitors enter the foggy hidden garden at the back spillway of a 14-foot waterfall. Spanish moss and orchids cling to rocks as curving brick pathways lead visitors to the islands and reflective pools that hold tropical plants and flowers changing each season. Kids will admire tropical trees holding bananas, coconuts and coffee beans. Special signs were made for all of the plants that show the importance of tropical forests, whether for food, medicine, beauty or fresh air. Japanese Koi fish swim in the reflective pools that hold a variety of unusual water plants. Doors lead outside to the Conifer and Perennial Garden. The Physically Challenged Garden features garden beds, a gazebo and water fountain maintained by physically challenged gardeners. Youngsters will enjoy the ABC Greenhouse Garden, which features plants and flowers from every letter in the alphabet. The unusual variety of flowers, whimsical art, a playhouse, garden tools, sand and soil boxes, and a fish-filled water garden encourage children to interact.

GARDEN HARVEST FESTIVAL

Moline (Rock Island) - *Quad City Botanical Center. Carding wool, panning for gold, petting a goat, tasting fresh apple cider, watching a broom maker in action. Kids can make a friendship bracelet; do laundry by hand like the pioneers did; shave like Pa; mill grain and roll dough into buns; or play with pioneer toys and puzzles. Food, entertainment and dance demonstrations. Scarecrow contest. Kettle Korn, petting zoo, hayrides, too. Admission (ages 13+). (October)*

ROCK ISLAND ARSENAL / MISSISSIPPI RIVER VISITOR CENTER

1 Rock Island Arsenal (I-74 exit 2, 7th Avenue (west)). Right on
14th, across ramp to Rodman Ave. Right on Gillespie to Bldg. 60)
Moline (Rock Island) 61299

  Phone: (309) 782-5021 http://riamwr.com or www.mvr.usace.army.
  mil/Missions/Recreation/MississippiRiverProject/Recreation/
  MississippiRiverVisitorCenter.aspx
  Hours: Museum: Tuesday-Sunday 10:00am-4:00pm. Closed winter major
  holidays. Mississippi River Visitor Center: Daily 9:00am-5:00pm.
  Admission: FREE
  Tours: Lock and Dam tours on summer weekends at 11:00am and 2:00pm by
  appointment.
  Note: Biking trails around the Island. Food Court open weekdays 6:00am-
  1:30pm. For security reasons all persons over age 16 must carry a photo ID
  to enter the island. Vehicles are subject to search.

ARSENAL MUSEUM - Arsenal Island was originally purchased by the
government in 1804 as a part of a treaty with Sauk and Fox Indians. In 1817,
a fort was built on the western end of the island. During the Civil War, over
12,000 prisoners were housed on the island. Factory buildings were built in
the 1900s to supply military equipment. No longer used to build equipment,
the original limestone buildings are now used for office space and defense
warehousing. The Museum features the whole history of the island in exhibits
and photos, a model of the first fort built, Fort Armstrong, and the world's
largest collection of small firearms. In the Discovery Room, kids can try on
all sorts of military costumes. Work puzzles or start a scavenger hunt.

MISSISSIPPI RIVER VISITOR CENTER - From early April through mid-
December, visitors come to the visitor's center to watch boats pass through
the lock. The main lock can hold nine barges at a time. The barges may be
carrying coal, grain or scrap metal. It takes about one and one half hours to
lock through here at #15. No turbines are used in locks, just water released or
drained using a unique tunneled water system. The locks form a "stairway of
water" and one barge carries more cargo than 15 jumbo railcars or 58 semi-
trailers - thus, the reason cargo is still transported this way. The roller dam
at Locks and Dam 15 is the largest in the world. Watch a working model of
the Lock or flood a reservoir (using a bathtub). Observation deck, movie and
exhibits are also at the Mississippi River Center (309-794-5338)

BALD EAGLE DAYS

Moline (Rock Island) - *Rock Island Expo Center. Environmental fair celebrating the annual southern migration from Canada. Includes live wolves, birds of prey and river otters, exhibits, live eagle presentations and outdoor eagle watching.* **www. destinationquadcities.com/eagledays.htm** *(weekend after New Years)*

WORLD'S LARGEST KART RACE

Moline (Rock Island) - *Rock Island District.* **www.rockislandgrandprix.com**. *Go-karts will rule the streets. This race brings over 250 drivers from 32 states and countries. The world's best drivers come to compete for one of karting's largest cash purses. Festival week includes a race to raise money for charity, nightly outdoor concerts, driver's parade, fan autograph session, and car shows with food sold. (Labor Day Weekend)*

SEASON OF LIGHT – STAR OF BETHLEHEM

Moline (Rock Island) - *Augustana College Planetarium. Daily evening or matinee shows portray just what the Wise Men may have seen when they looked to the skies some 2,000 years ago. Reservations are required for this star-gazing show. FREE.* **http://helios.augustana.edu/astronomy/** *(first Monday in December thru weekend before Christmas)*

WYATT EARP BIRTHPLACE

406 South 3rd Street (Routes 34 & 67, southeast of city square, fifteen minutes west of I-74) **Monmouth** 61462

☐ Phone: (309) 734-3181 or (309) 723-6419 (curator)
www.earpmorgan.com/wyattearpbirthplacewebsite.html
☐ Hours: Open by appointment.
☐ Admission: Donations.

Deputy U.S. Marshal Wyatt Earp, an American hero who helped tame the Old West, was born in Monmouth over 150 years ago. Wyatt attended the first free public school here. Wyatt's father, a constable, helped organize the Republican party in town. Wyatt became a lawman in 1869 and is world famous for the OK Corral gunfight in Tombstone, Arizona Territory in 1881. Relive the Old West at the OK Corral (replica next door). Earp's Birthplace Home and Museum is listed on the National Register of Historic Places. It contains 1848-1881 period rooms with many Earp displays and a gift shop area. TIP: Rent some old Western movies to get the kids familiar with this time period. Bring your cowboy garb to play pretend in the OK Corral next door (they sell Wyatt Earp sheriff badges in the house).

WYATT EARP'S BIRTHDAY WESTERN WEEKEND

Monmouth - *Wyatt Earp Birthplace. Deputy U.S. Marshal Wyatt Earp, an American hero who helped tame the Old West, will have his birthday celebrated at his birthplace. Wear your Western duds and relive the West. The public is invited to eat and meet Earp fans and columnists. The Birthplace home will be open, live "saw" music performed, and even an O.K. Corral reenactment. (last weekend in July or early August)*

NAUVOO STATE PARK

Durphy Street (IL 96, south edge of town) **Nauvoo** 62354

Phone: (217) 453-2512

http://dnr.state.il.us/lands/landmgt/parks/r4/nauvoo.htm

Its first name was Quashquema, a Fox Indian word meaning "peaceful place." Its current name is Nauvoo, a Hebrew word for "beautiful place" or "pleasant land." This historic town is the backdrop for Nauvoo State Park, on the banks of the Mississippi River. The 148-acre park includes a 13-acre lake with a mile-long shoreline. In addition to fishing, boating, camping and hiking, they offer a timbered nature trail and small prairie plot. The Rheinberger Museum within the park focuses on the grape industry started here…plus Nauvoo Blue Cheese and Nauvoo wine.

DELABAR STATE PARK

RR 2, Box 27 (on the Mississippi River, one mile north of town, near Hwy 164) **Oquawka** 61469

Phone: (309) 374-2496

http://dnr.state.il.us/lands/Landmgt/PARKS/R1/DELABAR.HTM

Forested areas serve as natural habitat for a variety of wildlife species, including squirrel, rabbit, raccoon, deer, groundhog and quail. More than 50 species of birds have been identified in the park, making Delabar State Park a natural haven for birders from throughout the state. Enjoy camping under shady oak trees, boating access, and a children's play area. Many visitors take advantage of the backwaters of the Mississippi River for ice fishing and ice skating.

PEORIA HISTORY TROLLEY

(depart from various eateries downtown) **Peoria** 61602

- Phone: (309) 674-1921 **www.peoriahistoricalsociety.org/trolleytours.html**
- Admission: $8.00-$12.00 per seat.
- Tours: Thursday-Saturday Memorial Day weekend thru late October. 2-hour tours in morning and Saturday afternoon.

From the grand history of this River City to the grand homes. Visit Peoria's scenic drive that winds its way above the valley passing homes of today's and yesterday's prosperous merchants, landowners and professionals. Enjoy a trip back in time down Peoria streets with narration provided by trained guides from the Historical Society.

SPIRIT OF PEORIA RIVERBOAT

100 Northeast Water Street (Riverfront Park) **Peoria** 61602

- Phone: (309) 636-6166 **www.spiritofpeoria.com**
- Admission: $10.00-$16.00 sightseeing (June-September)
- Note: The Riverfront District is graced with cultural, entertainment, dining, shopping, historical and recreational activities. How to many popular festivals, outdoor concerts, professional theater, parks, marinas, biking trails, and sport courts.

This authentic replica of a turn-of-the 20th-century paddle wheeler embarks on regularly scheduled cruises to various Illinois River destinations including Starved Rock State Park and Pere Marquette State Park. One-hour public sightseeing cruises are also scheduled on a regular basis, as are various theme cruises.

SPIRIT OF PEORIA HOLIDAY SHOWS

Peoria - *Spirit of Peoria, Intimate and Merry Holiday Revue aboard the historic paddlewheeler. Matinee or dinner features homemade buffet, riverboat cruise and entertainment. Admission. (Saturday after Thanksgiving thru mid-December)*

GLEN OAK PARK, ZOO & GARDEN

2218 North Prospect Road (Glendale Ave exit off I-74. Turn right on Hamilton Blvd, then right onto Knoxville Ave...which turns into Glen Oak. Stay left onto Prospect) **Peoria** 61603

- Phone: (309) 681-2902park or (309) 686-3365 zoo **www.glenoakzoo.org**

Hours: Daily 10:00am-5:00pm.

Admission: $6.00-$9.00 per person (age 3+).

Glen Oak Park hosts daily visitors to the Zoo and Garden and various special events. Visitors can take advantage of the hiking/biking trail, fishing lagoon, fitness trail, picnic shelters, amphitheatre, lighted tennis and shuffleboard courts and several playgrounds. The Zoo has a reptile and primate house, aquatic animals, numerous exhibits and offers daily sea lion programs and critter chats, tours and behind-the-scenes tours. They even have a giraffe feeding deck. The Botanical Garden contains theme gardens including a children's garden and wildlife garden, and a conservatory.

WHEELS O' TIME MUSEUM

11923 N. Knoxville Avenue (Rte 40) (2 miles north of Rte. 6 on Rte 40)
Peoria 61612

Phone: (309) 243-9020 www.wheelsotime.org

Hours: Wednesday-Sunday Noon-5:00pm (May-October).

Admission: 6.50 adult, 3.50 child (3-11).

With too many antique autos to store, a couple of guys erected a building to house the cars and display them as a museum. 55 collectors own the museum and share their collections with the public. Three buildings house displays of autos, farm equipment, trains, bicycles, toys, clothing, fire apparatus, tools, clocks, and music machines. Many displays are interactive. Listen to a Presidential barbershop quartet, toot a whistle, run a Lionel train and see a 1940s radio station.

LAKEVIEW MUSEUM OF ARTS AND SCIENCES

1125 West Lake Avenue (I-74 exit 91/University Street north to Lake Avenue, east to Lakeview Park) **Peoria** 61614

Phone: (309) 686-7000 www.lakeview-museum.org

Hours: Tuesday-Saturday 10:00am-5:00pm; Sunday Noon-5:00pm.

Admission: Gallery only $4.00-$6.00, Planetarium only $3.50-$4.00, Combo $6.00-$8.00.

Note: Their gift shop if full of unusual, new educational toys.

Lakeview's large museum features a renowned planetarium and the world's largest solar system model, according to the Guinness Book of World Records.

The driving 50 mile system begins at the Museum - the Sun. Every few months, the museum offers a constant stream of exhibits and programming. An affiliate of the Smithsonian Institute, this facility features both temporary and permanent art and science exhibits plus an Illinois Folk Art Gallery. They have a permanent outdoor sculpture exhibit with a self-guided tour brochure that allows visitors to leisurely stroll the artistic grounds.

The Discovery Center is all hands-on and contains many original, easy areas of learning play. "Make an impression" on the Pin Screen - hilarious!; look at Fluorescent minerals; create lightning; make a kidquake or even a magnetic bridge. Simple, easy to understand physics! Good job.

WILDLIFE PRAIRIE STATE PARK

3826 N. Taylor Road (I-74 exit 82 or I-474 exit 3, follow signs to SR 8)
Peoria 61615

  Phone: (309) 676-0998 www.wildlifeprairiestatepark.org
  Hours: Daily 9:00am-6:30pm (summer); 9:00am-4:30pm (rest of year). Closed mid-December through February except weekends.
  Admission: $9 adult, $6 child (3-12). Free parking. Discounted winter admission.
  Note: Playgrounds and picnic areas. Craving BBQ? Head north to the Shops of Grand Prairie for some Famous Dave's BBQ (309) 683-2663 or www.famousdaves.com.

West of the Illinois River bluffs, the land levels off into rolling grasslands, occasionally dissected by small rivers and streams. This park features native state animals such as bison, elk, wolves, black bear, cougar, river otter, waterfowl and raptors, as well as various songbirds, butterflies and other native birds. Stop by the Park's Visitor Center and see their Animal Nursery and Museum. Join the excellent Naturalists at various interpretive programs. Ride the Park's train through restored Prairie Habitat, visit the Pioneer Farmstead Area, or hike 10 miles of trail and wildlife habitats. Adventure Trek takes you on tour within the bison/elk pasture ($2.00-$3.00 extra)! At 1:00pm each day, you'll want to watch the elk and bison being fed at a special platform where they come real close!

WILDLIFE PRAIRIE STATE PARK LODGING

Peoria - *3826 N Taylor Rd. 61615. (309) 676-0998 or www.wildlifeprairiestatepark.org.*

Spend the night on the Prairie! Several unique lodging facilities, including the Cabin on the Hill (with an adorable mini-cabin "next door" for the kiddies - the cabin is fashioned just like the Little House on the Prairie), Cottages by the Lake, Prairie Stables and Santa Fe Train Cabooses (most cabins are under $100 per night). Accommodations overlook the bison range or lake. `All Facilities Include: Two days Park admission, Charcoal grills and picnic tables, Televisions, Linens, Bathroom with showers, Bank fishing, and use of the Recreation Room located near the Prairie Stables. The Prairie View Café awaits you with good food and a breathtaking view of the bison range. Lunch and Sunday brunch.

ERIN FEIS

Peoria - *Riverfront Park. Experience the ambience of a grand Irish festival featuring music, dance, food, heritage displays and merchants in a fun, family environment.* **www.erinfeispeoria.com** *(last weekend in August)*

SPLASHDOWN WATERPARK AT EASTSIDE CENTRE

One Eastside Drive (I-74 to the Camp Street Exit (95C). At the 2 stoplight take a right onto Meadow Avenue (Route 150). Follow that road for about 2 miles) Peoria (East Peoria) 61611

- Phone: (309) 694-1867 **www.fondulacpark.com/facilities/splashdown-water-park/**
- Hours: Daily 11:00am-6:30pm (Memorial Day weekend through mid-August). Open one-half hour later on weekends.
- Admission: $7.25 adult (13-61). Spectators $3.00. Toddlers 3 & under Free. After 3:00 admission prices are reduced $1.00. Prices include use of all attractions, lifejackets, and inner tubes.

Splashdown is a 3-acre water entertainment complex jam-packed with wet 'n wild activities. It's very affordable for families and it's 100% accessible to persons with disabilities. Use your imagination to discover the wacky, hands-on water effects found on Splashtower Island. Here, "drenching the unsuspecting", even Mom and Dad, won't get you in trouble. Plunge into summer head, or feet first on an inner tube that careens the crazy and unpredictable curves of the Wild Ride tube slide. Take a breather floating along the Lazy River. Or, sit back and watch as little tikes waddle through the Splash n' Play pool.

STONEY CREEK INN

Peoria (East Peoria) - *101 Mariners Way (Rte 116) (exit 95A off I-74, east side of Illinois River). 61611.　(309) 694-1300　www.stoneycreekinn.com. So cozy and comfortable – set in a nautical outback lodge, they've got a free continental breakfast and a large indoor/outdoor heated pool and spa. There's a casual eatery there, too. Great family value for under $100.00 per night.*

MORTON PUMPKIN FESTIVAL

Peoria (Morton) - *Downtown. Home of Nestle/Libby's pumpkin plant, Morton processes 85 percent of the world's canned pumpkin. The entire community celebrates the beginning of the canning season with a Pumpkin 'chunkin' contest, pumpkin picking, hayrack rides, corn maze, live entertainment, parade and plenty of pumpkin products. www.mortonpumpkinfestival.org (second or third long weekend of September)*

TOWER PARK

1222 E. Kingman (off 4900 N. Prospect & Grandview Drive)
Peoria Heights 61616

☐　Phone: (309) 682-8732
☐　**www.peoriaheights.org/about-us/our-village/211-tower-park**
☐　Hours: Wednesday-Sunday 11:00am-7:00pm. Summer Daily until 9:00pm.
　　(April-October, weather permitting).
☐　Admission: $1.25-$2.00 (ages 5+).

The tower is the only structure of its kind in the United States, and features a glass elevator that glides up to the top of the 170 foot tower. View the many miles of the Illinois River Valley. On top of 500,000 gallons of clear, pure well water, there are three separate observation decks designed to provide a spectacular panorama in all directions. There are three telescopes available for even closer viewing.

FESTIVAL OF LIGHTS

Peoria, East - *(Folepi's, I-74 to exit 96). Maps and info available at Riverfront Visitors Center. (800) 365-3743. The festival begins with the Parade of Lights (Saturday after Thanksgiving) as 40 lighted floats glide through the heart of East Peoria ending with a display of fireworks. Now, drive in the warmth of your vehicle through an electric park featuring two miles of parade floats and lighted animated displays. Folepi's Fireworks*

Spectacular features 37 lighted displays towering 40 feet in the air, simulating a fireworks grand finale. Now, take in the sights and sounds of a realistic nativity scene as you view the five detailed near life-size structures and tune into your car radio for a 2-minute narration that makes the scene come alive. Santa is in the Enchanted Forest as are decorated Christmas trees, animated displays and decorated buildings in Fon du Lac Farm Park. Like theatre? Annually, Eastlight Theatre presents Joseph and the Amazing Technicolor Dreamcoat on select days in December. Admission for drive-thru, enchanted forest and theatre production. (Thanksgiving weekend thru December evenings)

HISTORIC OWEN LOVEJOY HOMESTEAD AND COLTON SCHOOLHOUSE

East Peru Street (Rtes. 26 & 6, east of Main Street) **Princeton** 61356

Phone: (815) 879-9151 **www.lovejoyhomestead.com**

Hours: Friday, Saturday and Sunday 1:00-4:00pm (May-September). April and October by appointment only.

Admission: Small admission is charged.

Note: The Colton Schoolhouse is located on the Owen Lovejoy Homestead property. This one-room schoolhouse was moved from its original location 2.5 miles east of the homestead. The school was built in 1849, with sessions of school held in the building from 1850 until the school's official closing in 1945.

Owen Lovejoy came to Princeton in 1838 to assume the ministry of a local church. He was a fiery abolitionist who preached his views from the pulpit, causing dissension in a community already divided by the slavery issue. An acquaintance of Abraham Lincoln, Lovejoy was elected to the State Legislature in 1854 and to the House of Representatives in 1856, where he served 5 terms. His home was one of the most important stations on the Underground Railroad in Illinois. Runaway slaves were harbored by the Lovejoy family until arrangements could be made for them to travel to the next station on their way to Canada and freedom. Furnishings in the Lovejoy home reflect the Civil war era and include pieces that are original to the family. There is also a document room with photos and copies of Lovejoy's speeches and letters. Once an important stop on the Underground Railroad, the restored Lovejoy Homestead is now on the National Register of Historic Places and open for tours.

GREAT RIVER TUB FEST

Quad Cities - *Mississippi River between Port Bryon, IL & LaClaire, IA. This annual event is the only tug-of-war across the mighty Mississippi putting teams from Iowa and Illinois against each other in a huge tug-of-war. Eleven teams from each side are formed from different organizations to compete. On this day, barge traffic, pleasure boats, and paddleboats yield the right of way to a 2,400 foot, 680 pound rope that stretches across the river. There are live bands, fireworks, and children's games including a children's tug.* **www.tugfest.org***. Admission. (second weekend in August)*

AVENUE OF LIGHTS

Quincy - *Wavering/Moorman Park. Two-mile long animated light festival that has over one million lights and 40 displays. Admission per car.* **www.facebook.com/pages/Avenue-of-Lights-Inc/260893823977508** *(Thanksgiving through New Years)*

HENNEPIN CANAL STATE TRAIL

16006-875 East Street (I-80 & IL 40) **Sheffield** 61361

Phone: (815) 454-2328
http://dnr.state.il.us/lands/Landmgt/PARKS/R1/HENNPIN.HTM
Hours: Monday-Friday 8:00am-4:00pm (visitors center).

Originally a canal waterway, the parkway was closed in the 1950s and re-opened as a recreation park. In the Visitors Center there are several displays that help illustrate the canal's past - including tools used to build and operate it. At the time the canal was built workers often made their own tools by hand. There's also a model of a lock with a boat going through it and a model of an aqueduct. Get a peek at the plant and animal life at the park through other displays at the center. Now, go outside and explore the 104-mile waterway and 5,000 acres for canoeing, fishing, hiking, horseback riding, biking, cross-country skiing, snowmobiling and camping.

TANNERS ORCHARD

Speer - *740 IL 40, Junction 17.* **www.tannersorchard.com***. The Apple Express Barrel Train is happily chugging along in this orchard. It's just one of the great entertainment options for families visiting the orchard. And with fun things like the Climb and Clamber fun, the Billy Goat Bridge and Tree House, the Pony Rides, Wagon rides and farm animal zoo, and the family corn maze you might want to save room for apples, pumpkins and cider. Admission. (daily 8:00am-8:00pm September & October)*

SKI SNOWSTAR

9500 128th Street West (just off IL Rt. 92 in Andalusia)
Taylor Ridge (Andalusia) 61284

Phone: (309) 798-2666 **www.skisnowstar.com**
Hours: Daily 9:00am-9:00pm (Thanksgiving - mid March).
Admission: $20.00-$31.00 lift passes.

When the snow flies, it's time for winter fun with downhill ski runs of all levels, a tube hill and plenty of lifts. Snow tubing allows all ages to slide down one of the groomed chutes on giant inner-tubes and then a specially designed tow takes them and the tube back to the top. (tubers must be 4 years old). The Ski School teaches beginners from age 4 and up. The lounge area has fireplaces and an outside patio with firepit.

AVANTI FOODS

109 Depot Street (I80 to SR 40N to SR 92E about 5 miles. Right on Main, left on Depot) **Walnut** 61376

Phone: (815) 379-2155 or (800) 243-3739 **www.avantifoods.com**
Hours: Monday-Friday 8:00am-5:00pm and Saturday 8:00am-1:00pm. Viewing area open each day the shop is open.
Tours: Offered only in April and May. Self-guided tours anytime open - best weekday mornings.

In 1932, Walnut Cheese was founded as a market for the milk produced by surrounding dairy farmers. In 1964 Avanti Foods was formed to produce frozen pizzas under the "Gino's" and "Swiss Party" labels (they produce several thousand pizzas per day). Their own Mozzarella cheese is used for the topping. Using time-tested methods and modern equipment, Bruno, the master cheesemaker, oversees daily production of 50,000 lbs. of milk into cheese. Watch through the observation windows as milk is turned into curds and whey, drained, flavored and cut. Next, venture across the street to watch 10 or more ladies hover over the conveyor table layering pizzas that are then quickly led to the freezer and wrapped and shipped. Need pizza making supplies? This is the place. New facilities make it possible for visitors to view the pizza and cheese production or browse in the Cheese and Gourmet Shop. Try their blue-ribbon State Fair Longhorn cheese - yum.

ROCK ISLAND TRAIL STATE PARK

311 East Williams Street (I-74 west to SR 6 west exit. Turn north on Allen
Road & follow curve) Wyoming 61491

☐ Phone: (309) 695-2228
   http://dnr.state.il.us/lands/Landmgt/PARKS/R1/ROCKISLE.HTM
☐ Admission: FREE

Rock Island Railroad busily carried freight and passengers between Peoria and Rock Island for over 40 years. By 1915, however, rail volume declined and ceased altogether by the mid-twentieth century. One of the premier rails-to-trails facilities in Illinois, this trail has 27 miles for hiking, biking and cross-country skiing between the communities of Alta and Toulon. Running through regenerated forest and tallgrass prairie habitats, the trail offers improved access at its southern terminus in Alta, at the Kickapoo Creek Recreation Area, at the Williams Street Depot Museum in Wyoming, and at the trail head in Toulon.

Activity Index

HISTORY (cont.)

HISTORY (cont.)

MUSEUMS

Outdoor Exploring (cont.)

Outdoor Exploring (cont.)

Seasonal & Special Events

Seasonal & Special Events (cont.)

TOURS (cont.)

Travel Journal & Notes:

Travel Journal & Notes:

Made in the USA
Charleston, SC
01 April 2016